AUG   2002

THE

ANTHROPOLOGY

OF TURQUOISE

PANTHEON BOOKS
60 YEARS OF PUBLISHING

THE ANTHROPOLOGY OF TURQUOISE

Meditations on Landscape, Art, and Spirit

ELLEN MELOY

PANTHEON BOOKS   NEW YORK

Pantheon Books and colophon are registered trademarks of Random House, Inc.

"Brides of Place" was previously published in slightly different form in *Northern
Lights*. • "The Silk That Hurls Us Down Its Spine," copyright © 1998 by Ellen
Meloy, was previously published in *Water, Earth, and Sky* by Michael Collier,
published by the University of Utah Press, 1999.

Grateful acknowledgment is made to Lola Haskins and Story Line Press for
permission to reprint the poem "Love" by Lola Haskins, from *Desire Lines*.
Copyright © 2001 by Lola Haskins. Reprinted by permission of the author
and Story Line Press (www.storylinepress.com).

Library of Congress Cataloging-in-Publication Data
Meloy, Ellen.
The anthropology of turquoise / Ellen Meloy.
p.   cm.
ISBN 0-375-40885-1
1. West (U.S.)—Description and travel.   2. Natural history—West (U.S.)
3. Wilderness areas—West (U.S.)   4. Meloy, Ellen—Journeys—West (U.S.)
5. Meloy, Ellen.   6. Women artists—West (U.S.)—Biography.
7. Women authors, American—West (U.S.)—Biography.   8. Women
naturalists—West (U.S.)—Biography.   9. West (U.S.)—Biography.   I. Title.

F595.3.M45 2002   917.904'33—dc21   2001055167

www.pantheonbooks.com

Illustrations by Ellen Meloy
Book design by Cassandra J. Pappas

Printed in the United States of America
First Edition
2 4 6 8 9 7 5 3 1

For my parents

For my brothers

For Mark

I have always kept ducks, he said, even as a child, and the colours of the plumage, in particular the dark green and snow white, seemed to me the only possible answers to the questions that are on my mind.

W. G. SEBALD
The Rings of Saturn

Contents

THE

ANTHROPOLOGY

OF TURQUOISE

The Deeds and Sufferings of Light

> Words begin as description. They are prismatic, vehicles
> of hidden, deeper shades of thought. You can hold them
> up at different angles until the light bursts through in an
> unexpected color.
>
> Susan Brind Morrow
> *The Names of Things*

Winter on the Colorado Plateau has not been arduous, only a thin cold without storms, a lucid map of stillness. Caught in the abrupt instant of its rising, our faces take the tangerine sun, our backs dissolve to silhouette in the brilliant dazzle of its incandescent beam. The nights come less as a smooth pause than as a steep, enduring purity of eye-blind dark. The mesas creak and strain in the frigid air, audible only if I lay my ear to them. The colors in their flanks—terra cotta, blood-red, salmon, vermilion—bear the temperament of iron.

On these days of winter I climb to the top of a sky-raking spine of sandstone and sit beside a juniper tree.

The ridge runs from a crumpled mountain range in southern Utah to the Arizona desert, jumping a river along its way. It is an elongated, asymmetrical reef of Mesozoic sandstone with a face and a flank, two sides so different you think that you are somewhere else when you are in the same place. The face rises brick-red from a broad wash, nearly vertical but for a skirt of boulders along its talus. The flank is the crazy side: an abruptly sloped flexure of ancient rock beds tilted upward into a jagged crest. Most of the massive slab is Navajo Sandstone, the Colorado Plateau's famously voluptuous field of windblown sand dunes now consolidated into nearly pure quartz crystals. Against the steel-blue sky of a summer monsoon, the ridge bleaches to white. Moonlight blues it, and bright sun turns it pale cream or, if you are making love atop it, blush pink.

From afar the stone reef appears continuous, exfoliating here and there into flakes the size of small European countries. Look more closely and you will see that box canyons cut across its length, ending in deep alcoves. Smaller fissures run in unexpected directions, and narrow valleys hang high toward the crest, where faults have filled with sandy soil held stable by the living organism of a black cryptobiotic crust. Yucca, single-leaf ash, Mormon tea, blackbrush, and other shrubs find purchase in pockets and cracks. However, most of the ridge is bare-boned slickrock. When you hike it in midsummer, you are lightning bait. I climb it with my paints and crayons, breath hard, heart pounding, up the slope to the isolated juniper tree. It is the far edge of winter, no longer bone-cold, not yet spring's exhalation of green. The surface of the slickrock is neither icy nor warm, just touchable.

On my first winter days on the ridge, I bring watercolors and the hope that the hand of my brother, an artist who died outdoors with his paint box near him, will guide the tip of my brush across the paper, rendering effortlessly exquisite art on paper and a Zen-like serenity in my heart. Then I change my expectations and carry a box of crayons up the ridge to the juniper tree. I blunt their tips with irresponsible yellow and the demands of green. I rub bold, wild strokes. I shuck the Zen crap and try to obey Ezra Pound's advice to artists: "Make the world strange."

Finger paints will be next in the lineup of media and with their slurpy nonchalance a release from the weight of a cerebral life—

what remains of it, that is, for in recent years I have suffered what neurologists call "a reduction in mental acuity." So far, it feels like a kind of carbonated brain fog, with perforations in memory that threaten to become air ducts. Because there is the possibility of an abrupt slide into chronic befuddlement, I thought it might be useful to acquire some basic motor and tactile skills, like pushing around cool, gooey paint in mindless, repetitive motions, as preparation for that freshly vacated space, that airy void between the ears.

On watercolor days I carry a field kit that belonged to my brother, a faded olive-green canvas bag that he slung over his shoulder when he went out to sketch and paint on the northern California coast where he lived. Over the years since he died, I have kept its contents intact: a tin of paints and camel-hair brushes, colored pencils bunched together like chopsticks and bound with a rubber band. A prism. A miniature pencil sharpener made to look like a shark's mouth. A sumi inkstone in a slender box marked by a column of Japanese characters and a vial once filled with water from a stream in the Sierra Nevada, where he and I often joined company in the summers. A Swiss Army knife and three orange juggling balls. From wherever he is—a ghost in his favorite denim jacket, a vapor hovering above me cross-legged on a cloud like a cotton puff, a mere slip of memory and thought—I want him to teach me to juggle, but mostly I want him to teach me to paint, to inform the movement of my brush across the rough blank of paper. I end up thinking more about him than about art, which is, after all, what I am supposed to do.

On crayon days I try to explode my hand, my eye, my past. For a number of years, in a previous life, I made a living in technical illustration, churning out laboriously stippled pen-and-ink drawings of bones, feathers, fish, and wolves; the orchid's calyx and the ear's canals and vestibules, which are the organs of balance; profiles of geological strata; maps of rivers and mountains; maps of islands known and islands imagined; diagrams of subatomic structure; meticulous renderings of leaves and seedpods, pebbles and aetites, stones with small clay cores that emerge when you break open their ironstone shells. By drawing these things I learned that sand dunes and the bends of rivers migrate and that stones could give birth. For relief from detail I drew cartoons, but they were not relief enough, so I painted barns. The idea of paints now, and of barns back then, is to leave behind those black-on-white, uptight stabs of a pinpoint pen and open my hand to a looser muscle of expression. I hope to make pictures like I walk in the desert—under a spell, an instinct of motion, a kind of knowing that is essentially indirect and sideways.

On crayon days I remember that burnt sienna and magenta pleased my mother because she loved Italy. Reluctantly, she bought us coloring books to go with our crayons. She was convinced that staying between the lines of factory-issue images only went so far before her children should think up lines of their own, on the blank white tablets she provided, and draw what stormed out of our little heads with the innocence of trickster stories. Crayon days on the ridge bring back the waxy taste of these bright sticks of paraffin and pigment. My brothers and I ate them, even when we were old enough to know better—bit off a chunk of carmine or blue-violet or cadmium yellow, choosing gem colors over pastels.

"Orange is like a man, convinced of his own powers," wrote Russian painter Vasily Kandinsky in his 1912 meditation, *On the Spiritual in Art.* On crayon days I have trouble with orange for its highway-cone authority, its Cheez Whiz intrusion. I am nervous about yellow, the preferred color of mental patients who regress to infantile levels. Raw umber seems overly shadowy, dutiful verging on paranoia. As a child I never liked raw umber. One of my brothers said it was poop, but we needed it to color the underside of Daffy Duck's feet. In today's box there are still those vain pinks, hungry greens, and crayons as blue as devotion. The power of profound meaning is blue, said Kandinsky, blue is concentric motion. Of red he wrote, "Red rings inwardly with a determined and powerful intensity. It glows in itself, maturely, and does not distribute its vigor aimlessly." The red I choose is the closest in color to the eyes of a goshawk.

The slender crayons and the round pans of paint in the water-color tin scatter unlikely chips of pigment on the cream-colored sandstone. The ridge bears the palette of a numb moon. The winter sun's low arc casts ebony shadows of me and the juniper tree, whose shaggy silver bark holds up a rough-needled canopy of brassy green. I place a scarlet crayon on a patch of aquamarine lichen on the slickrock.

Not far from my post a large pothole cups a catchment of autumn rains. The pool of water is emerald in the shade, a lapis sky mirror in the sun. In it grow blond spears of dried cattails and, on its rim, a spiky cluster of prickly pear cactus—odd marsh and desert bedfellows in a miniature garden. Do not think of a cactus acting like a cactus, with its apple-green paddles and white spines. In winter the prickly pear hallucinates. Its spines glow red-gold in the angled sun, like an electrocuted aura. The paddles are nearly the color of burgundy wine.

You would think that these rich colors reside in the thing itself, that the cactus, the crayons, the lichen *have* their colors. But colors are not possessions; they are the intimate revelations of an energy field. "Colours are the deeds and sufferings of light," wrote German poet and dramatist Johann Wolfgang von Goethe. They are light waves with mathematically precise lengths, and they are deep, reso-nant mysteries with boundless subjectivity.

Colors challenge language to encompass them. (It cannot; there are more sensations than words for them. Our eyes are far ahead of our tongues.) Colors bear the metaphors of entire cultures. They convey every sensation from lust to distress. They glow fluorescent on the flanks of a fish out of the water, then flee at its death. They mark the land of a woman deity who controls the soft desert rain. Flowers use colors ruthlessly for sex. Moths steal them from their surroundings and disappear. An octopus communicates by color;

an octopus blush is language. Humans imbibe colors as antidotes to emotional monotony. Our lives, when we pay attention to light, compel us to empathy with color.

IMAGINE THAT you have no eyes and this is how you must organize your perceptual life: by physical contact. You sneak or crawl or ooze over objects in your path, perhaps crash into them or knock them over. You stick out an advance appendage to fondle your terrain, hoping to come across something edible or matable or both. You might slip your appendage up and over the face of a cold, flat, steel plain and only seconds after severing that limb with a bloody spurt think "razor blade."

If you and your kind survive bruised foreheads, amputation, and impalement, particular cells may grow somewhere on your body surface, cells that become sensitive to light. Rather than form an image, the cells merely discern brightness from dimness. If, where these cells gather, your skin cups slightly, in a sort of lenslike curve, and if the cells form layers of rudimentary pigments, the cells will capture some of the light. Your nerves may translate this trapped light into information, perhaps distinguishing between something bright versus a shadow, say the shadow of a giant killer hyena, and with your sensory awareness by remote rather than physical contact, you might have a few seconds to flee before the hyena eats you. At this point the pigments, photoreceptive cells, cups, and nerve impulses, already vastly complex millions of years before they become eyes, are moving along the dense evolutionary path toward vision—toward color vision—as we know it.

When someone says they *feel* color, the serene caress of jade or the acidic bite of yellow, do not accuse them of using illegal drugs. In primitive life forms the eye began as a light-sensitive depression in the skin; the sense of sight likely evolved from the sense of *touch*.

The complex human eye harvests light. It perceives seven to ten million colors through a synaptic flash: one-tenth of a second from retina to brain. *Homo sapiens* gangs up 70 percent of its sense receptors solely for vision, to anticipate danger and recognize reward, but also—more so—for beauty. We have eyes refined by the evolution of predation. We use a predator's eyes to marvel at the work of Titian or the Grand Canyon bathed in the copper light of a summer sunset.

The eye spreads light softly in the retina, across blood and long-stemmed nerves that resemble frilled balloons or leggy trees of bladder kelp. These nerves, called ganglion and bipolar cells, fled the cranium; they are actually parts of the brain that now live in the eyes. Toward the back of the retina, light reaches intricately sensitive photoreceptors that sort out, for example, a red sensation from a blue one. One set of receptors, the cones, functions for color and daylight, or *photopic* vision. The other set, the rods, operates in shades of gray for dim light, or *scotopic* vision. *Eye and Brain,* a classic by neuropsychologist Richard L. Gregory, notes an accidentally metaphorical middle world. "Between the brightness of sunlight and the dim light of the stars is the intermediate light from the moon, giving uneasy *mesopic* vision, which should not be trusted."

Throughout time, without words, nature and the artist have best explained the interactions of light, color, and mind. I can look at a canyon shadow or a Byzantine mosaic and understand blue better than I understand a dissertation on the comparatively stubby quantum of electromagnetic radiation measured as 4×10^{-7} meters (blue light).

How does vision, this tyrant of the senses, draw someone to a piece of earth? What do the eyes rest upon—mind disengaged, heart not—that combines senses and affection into a homeland? Do the eyes conspire with other senses in a kind of synesthetic faculty, an ability to respond to the colors of place as if they were taste and scent, sound and touch? On walks in my desert home a yellow cottonwood leaf stings my tongue like lemon, the indigo and copper margins of the river in shadow inflict the bruise of a frail wind on my skin. Somehow in the day's prismatic clarity, even in the untrustworthy moonlight, these orbs of blood and nerves understand that light is the language of the desert.

For astronomers in India color was the domain of the deity Surya, the sun and single ruler of light. Surya controlled eight celestial bodies, each emitting a pure color to the earth. With each color came a person's destiny. Over two thousand years ago the Greeks believed that rays of light shot out from our eyes to the object beheld; our inner fire, conspiring with daylight, illuminated an external world. Another Greek emanation theory sent the rays in the opposite direction—tiny husks, or replicas, of the object entered the eyes through a "visual spirit" that flowed back and forth between object and beholder. Proof of the husks, called *simulacra,* could be seen in someone else's dark, glassy pupil, an eye that reflected the images of a mountain or passing clouds or your own face.

In the late seventeenth century Isaac Newton set up his prism and bent a beam of light into a fan of colors, launching the earliest scientific studies of color optics. Three hundred years later, science still seeks a full understanding of light's dual properties as waves and particles in conversation with a brain that devotes so much of itself to them.

In 1810, Goethe published his *Theory of Colours,* an exhaustive observation of how we see light, how we process a chaotic influx of sensory stimuli into perception. Goethe was enamored of the illusions and anomalies of color. His disciplined inquiry did not diminish his belief that the world read by our senses was in itself a revelation. Absolute knowledge, an explanation of everything, was not vital for joy or contentment, he wrote. "The highest goal that man can achieve is amazement."

One of my great-uncles was colorblind. Eight percent of men have some deficiency in color vision, usually a difficulty in seeing red or green or both, compared to its rare occurrence in women. I worried about my great-uncle running traffic lights or confusing ketchup for jam. I wondered how he ate a gray banana or black tomatoes.

I wonder now at the luminous equatorial clouds, the ultramarine and turquoise sea, and the riotous colors of tropical flowers and greenery on the Micronesian island where few can see them, where true color is nearly missing from an entire culture. Oliver Sacks describes this concentration of congenital achromatopsia, a hereditary color blindness, in *The Island of the Colorblind.* The islander achromatopes live in a colorless but by no means impoverished world, Sacks tells us. They see variations in tones, textures, and brightness, a heightened sensation of what the rest of us call "gray." Lacking functional cones, they find bright daylight overwhelming. For them light is pain. They move gracefully in scotopic times (dawn and dusk), trust the uneasy mesopic (moonlight), and night-fish and navigate by the stars with the keen practice of Pacific natives.

One of Sacks's colorblind companions in Micronesia, a European, describes how other children teased him because he could not name the colors on scarves, hats, shirts, and other pieces of clothing. To avoid teasing he memorized the colors of his clothes. He learned the "most probable colours of various things."

Under normal vision the most probable colors of things do not necessarily match up with their names. Physically, eyes see the colors of the spectrum the same, but when we utter a term for a color, it is not the color's immutable property; it is the name of a *perception.* In the hands of language and culture, simple chromatic sensations acquire a kaleidoscope of reference and meaning. As writer Alexander Theroux suggests, color is fictive space.

When a name for a color is absent from a language, it is usually blue. When a name for a color is indefinite, it is usually green. Ancient Hebrew, Welsh, Vietnamese, and, until recently, Japanese, lack a word for blue. To name the color blue the Assyrians turned *uknu,* the noun for lapis lazuli, into an adjective. The Icelandic word for blue and black is the same, one word that fits sea, lava, and raven. Goethe's blue is the color of "enchanting nothingness."

It has been shown that the words for colors enter evolving languages in this order, nearly universally: black, white, and red, then yellow and green (in either order), with green covering blue until blue comes into itself. Once blue is acquired, it eclipses green. Once named, blue pushes green into a less definite version. Green confusion is manifest in turquoise, the is-it-blue-or-is-it-green color. Despite the complexities of color names even in the same language, we somehow make sense of another person's references. We know color as a perceptual "truth" that we imply and share without its direct experience, like feeling pain in a phantom limb or in another person's body.

Within every color lies a story, and stories are the binding agent of culture. The color name *ochre* comes from a word that Homer used with *chloros* (a greenish tinge) to express the pallor of men's faces in the fear of battle. Amethyst comes from the Greek *amethystos,* "not drunk," topaz from *topazein,* "to conjecture," because the Greeks believed the gem's source was an island hidden by clouds and fog. I dip my brush into a pan of lacustrine blue. Five centuries ago lapis lazuli came from the Sinai or across the sky-raking Hindu Kush to Europe, there to be ground into powder for painters of the Madonna's robes. The Maya mixed clay and indigo in a complex chemistry to find a blue that a person could take to the afterlife.

Until synthetic chemistry reproduced it, purple was among the rarest of dyes, a liqueur squeezed from the veins of a small mollusk. One mollusk yielded one drop; extracting a single ounce of the dye sacrificed 250,000 mollusks. In Mexico the shellfish dye was pressed onto the cloth of the Aztecs. Mediterranean species of the shellfish produced Tyrian purple, a color coveted by Roman nobility. In the first century, Roman naturalist Pliny the Elder noted that from the sea nature yielded its most precious resource in the form of the shellfish with purple in its veins; from land, the silkworm and the cochineal insect, whose scarlet fluids were extracted for dye and in later times for cosmetics that tinted the lips of women red, a color that quickens the hearts of men.

On a string of warm days I climb the sandstone ridge every afternoon. I am less in need of the crayons and more comfortable with the watercolors. I paint nonsense, but I paint. I dip my brush in water from a slickrock pothole and swirl it in a blue or purple cup of pigment in the watercolor tin. I think of my two living brothers, superbly talented artists who can teach me a thing or two about painting. One of them, once a juggler in a street circus, could show me how to send the orange balls into the air. I feel reckless and give the balls a toss, then foolishly chase two of them as they roll down the incline a quarter of a mile.

Atop the sandstone spine one afternoon the desert's calm is broken by a thick bass thud surging through the bedrock so abruptly that the juggling balls shake, the paint box clatters, the juniper tree shivers. An explosion of brown dust rises from a terrace about five miles distant, on the rim of the canyon that embraces the river. The dynamite calves a massive fragment from the terrace so that a gravel company can crush it into pieces, haul it off in trucks, and unload it on a low-level radioactive waste dump far to the north, the legacy of Cold War uranium milling in the region. The gravel operations have taken an enormous bite out of an ancient seabed. They are mining the oceanic memories of limestone, the calcified remains of millions of marine organisms, to cap the toxic heat of bomb-making detritus. At the gravel pit the silvery-blue limestone, when quarried, exposes a flesh-colored rawness that is unsettling.

The weather turns cold for a few days, and I walk without stopping to paint. One day it snows. The next day the snow melts quickly off the exposed slickrock, swells the pools and potholes, and lingers on the north side of every bush and juniper tree, leaving a patch of white lace in each shadow. The wine-red of the prickly pear cactus reaches such intensity that I wonder how the plants will ever find green again. Late winter's sharpness still wraps the ridge in vibrant, clear air. Any day spring will catch me off guard, not as a slow enfolding but borne atop the ebony carapace of a thawed-out beetle or riding a warm breeze, the gift from the depths of the Sonoran and Mojave Deserts to the southwest.

Some days, high on the ridge, with a seventy-mile view in all directions, I feel compelled to strike up an existential query and a lotus pose, forming profoundly spiritual questions and throwing them out into the ethos.

What do I know?

What is my place in the universe?

How little do I need to have everything?

What are the obligations of living a certain geography, of narrowing the distance between eye and beauty, of making the visible world an instinct?

Then—thank the river gods!—my feet fall asleep and I am wickedly distracted by potholes stair-stepping down the slope in pools of light, sometimes silver, sometimes turquoise or cerulean, like a necklace strung with luminous beads. One pool in the strand lies in a deep, cold fold of shade.

In this fold in the inert slickrock, water collects. Close up, too hidden to reflect the sky, the pool is emerald-green and as clear as a mirror, coated at its rims with a veil of hoary white, frozen solid in a sunless place. Encased in the emerald ice are the bodies of toads.

One toad squats in a clenched fist of dusky, mottled skin. The ice paralyzes the tension of its coiled muscles. Another toad is suspended mid-leap, a slender athlete of olive green and tenderly pale limbs and flanks that are so white they are blue. The leaper stretches its slim legs, it holds its toes with a ballerina's grace, casting behind it a wake of air bubbles stilled by the cold into bright diamonds. Eyefolds hide its black, glassy orbs. Somehow the ice does not seem like a prison. The toads are charged with an intensity of purpose, the too-late leap made without regard for time or the quickened, raw tongue of winter that caught them. If the toads died, I think, they died knowing something.

On some days my paintings are as small as postage stamps. Others grow hugely into the size of Persian miniatures—steady progress toward wall murals, I hope. I load up the sumi inkstone and write a story on a scroll of paper, making up my own characters: toads in ice, their colors then warmed and suffused with blood, finishing their leap when the spring thaw comes.

It seems as if the right words can come only out of the perfect space of a place you love. In canyon country they would begin with three colors: blue, terra-cotta, green. Sky, stone, life. Then some feather or pelt or lizard's back, the throat of a flower or ripple of sunlit river, would enter the script, and I would have to leap from three colors to uncountable thousands, all in some exquisite combination of Place, possessed by this one and no other. Between the senses and reason lies perception. At home or afield, that is where amazement resides, shunning explanation. Certain places, writes Jorge Luis Borges, "try to tell us something, or have said something we should not have missed, or are about to say something; this imminence of a revelation which does not occur is, perhaps, the aesthetic phenomenon."

I am not that presumptuous to think I could speak or paint or write the natural history of my home colors. I know only that they are to blame for intent and motion, for an asymmetrical journey of wonder and of trouble. Light can run a person's time and moods; it can explain everything. There is more to this bond than a cosmic flakiness, the experts say. The draw to certain kinds of landscapes is also biological. In *Consilience,* ecologist Edward O. Wilson writes: "People do not merely select roles suited to their native talents and personalities. They also gravitate to environments that reward their hereditary inclinations."

Neurobiologists suggest that a keen human sensitivity to color begins when we are infants. An aesthetic sense, an intuitive link between a chromatic band and emotion, can then grow as strong as a fingerprint, defying logic and inviting the helpless surrender of a love affair. Intoxication with color, sometimes subliminal, often fierce, may express itself as a profound attachment to landscape. It has been rightly said: Color is the first principle of Place.

On one trip to the ridge I stay until sunset. When the sun is low on the horizon, I set up my brother's prism on the rock and try to bend a beam of light. A precarious spectrum shivers on the pale quartz. I realize that I am looking at the universe backward. The rainbow must also pass back through the prism, recomposing itself as pure white light.

Beyond the ridge the river carves its profound canyon. My house sits a few miles upstream on a bench above the floodplain. I know a distant cliff to be the home of bighorn sheep that wear the color of the desert, making themselves nearly invisible against it. In the hundred square miles of wrinkles and folds of land around me, on mineral-varnished faces of sandstone, ancient farmers chiseled spirals and horned flute players, handprints, the tears of women in childbirth, and the figure of a man, three feet tall, whose giant penis hangs down to a body-width hole in a massive wall. If you crawl through the hole beneath that imposing phallus you swear you have had some sort of sexual experience.

In the sunset light mesas and buttes slip toward Arizona in painful crimson and faithless mauve. Colorado's brow lies on the eastern horizon, Prussian blue capped with lavender alpenglow. Aridity rules the air, weathering rules the rock, the shadows are as deep as time. This land was born at the center of old.

I put the prism in the faded canvas bag, slip the bag into the daypack with my water bottle and sweater, and hike downslope, off the spine.

For a homebody surrounded by the familiar or a traveler exploring the strange, there can be no better guide to a place than the weight of its air, the behavior of its light, the shape of its water, the textures of rock and feather, leaf and fur, and the ways that humans bless, mark, or obliterate them. Each of us possesses five fundamental, enthralling maps to the natural world: sight, touch, taste, hearing, smell. As we unravel the threads that bind us to nature, as denizens of data and artifice, amid crowds and clutter, we become miserly with these loyal and exquisite guides, we numb our sensory intelligence. This failure of attention will make orphans of us all.

When I am nearly off the ridge, I see what I must paint. I will beg for the guidance of my brothers' hands. If help does not come, I will brave it on my own. On the desert horizon at dusk, where red rock meets lapis sky, at the seam of the union, runs a band of turquoise, recumbent upon the land's great darkness. This color is transient. Before night falls, blue-green is the last quantum of visible light to pass through the atmosphere without scattering. It can draw a person right down to the skin of the world. The tidal pull of light can shape an entire life. Every heart-warmed pulse of blood and breath.

Swimming the Mojave

> I used to wonder why the sea was blue at a distance and green close up and colorless for that matter in your hands. A lot of life is like that. A lot of life is just a matter of learning to like blue.
>
> MIRIAM POLLARD
> *The Listening God*

When I was a little girl, I thought I was a boy. I thought I was stuck in a messy but minor anatomical complication that would eventually sort itself into a more certain gender. I did not think of specifics, like a penis, nor did I envy a male life. Rather, I wanted freedom from the horrifying prospect of Tupperware, voile, and a complexly wired bra with cone-shaped cups that made one's breasts "pert," a term I associated with cheerleaders' noses.

I thought I was a temporary girl until I was nearly fifteen, though more or less hypothetically toward the end. I thought about my three brothers. I thought about being one of them. I thought we should be like a fraternal clump of bananas, even and alike, oldest to youngest, no bump (me) in the middle. When I was a girl-boy, I preferred stuffed animals, maps, and geography books to dolls, and I thought my teddy bear and I would never get to places

18

like Arabia or the Seychelles fast enough. I thought I would never survive my own imagination. I thought about all of this, but here is what I spent a great deal of time thinking about: swimming pools.

Californians, of course, are born with swimming pools. When you are born, if your family does not already have a pool, one shalt be dug while the obstetrician snips thy umbilicus. The High Sierra and cooler north notwithstanding, in the popular mind a swimming pool is Golden State furniture. From a jetliner flying over the platter of human paella that is greater Los Angeles, if the glare bouncing off four hundred square miles of chrome and metal has not blinded you, you can see these birthrights behind nearly every house. The rectangles of bright turquoise swallow up backyard lawn space and send the palm trees to the front, along the avenues and boulevards. From the air the palms look like toothpicks with dreadlocks. All of it looks especially good if it is January and you are flying in from Bismarck, North Dakota. When the airplane banks a turn, the sun's radiant ball illuminates the glistening pools, changing them from Bulgari sapphires to opaque opals with a quickening surface of aquamarine moiré.

In neighborhoods built in the fifties and sixties, when pools were serious California totems, the lot-house-pool pattern follows the grid lines of street blocks, with everything squared at their corners. The newer suburbs are loopier, with curving streets, ovoid cul-de-sacs, and houses with pools shaped like L's or kidneys or Stealth bombers. From the air you do not see the pools of the filthy rich— too much greenery hides them, or (I'm guessing here) commercial air traffic penetrates only the airspace of the trailer parks and methadone clinics. In gated suburbs under construction in the outer L.A. Basin and Mojave hinterlands and in hot boom cities like Las Vegas and Phoenix, the new houses rise up, the pools are filled and chlorinated as the Sheetrock dust settles, and the desert is scraped away in a naked shriek until time and trees soften it. On the gray-beige scars sit pink fiberboard haciendas, ribbons of ebony asphalt, and small islands of turquoise.

My father was born and raised in Los Angeles, my mother in the San Joaquin Valley. Their first two of four children, my oldest brother and I, were born in Pasadena. My mother's family went back so many generations in California, I once believed that we descended from Aztecs—Aztecs cross-pollinated with Raymond Chandler, bloodletting Mesoamerican god-kings with manic socialites—for a Chandler novel was how I pictured my father's boyhood in the City of Angels in the twenties and thirties. Never mind that he grew up on a fruit farm in a predominantly Quaker neighborhood.

In our family were women adept with diamondback rattlesnakes. When the snakes endangered their children, they put down their bridge hands, rose from the porch, and sliced the rattlers in two with a shovel. They skinned them with embroidery scissors, freeing from the flesh a prayer-thin membrane marked from neck to tail with vivid brown diamonds. We had uncles in the family tree who, legend said, were captured by Indians but freed when they gave the Masonic sign. We had great-grandparents who, between world wars, visited California from England and brought their cook. Somewhere in the ancestral gaggle, among the flax-wearing, mead-swilling rabble on the mother isle, we had (I hoped) a forebear named Clovis the Riparian.

We had a branch in the family tree with a trait known as Vague About Details and an entire category that should have existed by default—or so I imagined because no one would speak about them. To myself I called them the Unsavories. From parents intent on holding up models of virtue, I could never learn anything about any Unsavories, largely because they may not have existed or because no one knew much, so selective was memory against closet skeletons in favor of an uninterrupted lineage of accomplished beings fed from the civilized shores of Scotland and England to California, where as soon as they disembarked from their first-class cabins on the HMS *Crouton,* they began goodly lives of impeccable behavior. However, a child's radar for rebelliousness may elbow past a less romantic truth. Too often the lives of my relatives seemed to come as résumés. Stories described what they did, not who they were, and in this record they did university, business, ranching, and unselfish deeds and mildly eccentric acts. Unless they were distant in the ancestral murk, they did not do divorce, alcohol, or mental illness, or, as I would learn later in life, own slaves on a sunlit island astride the Tropic of Cancer.

One side of the California family lost walnut and orange groves in the Great Depression. The other side lost their ranch to an Army Corps of Engineers dam and reservoir. Before the Depression, in prosperous times, the Los Angeles family partook in a local tradition of Iowa Picnics, outdoor meals held all over southern California by the hundreds of Iowans who had migrated there in the early decades of the century. Long Beach and Pasadena hosted the most famous Iowa Picnics, but my father's favorite was one in the suburb of Ontario, where, he said, tables laden with plump midwestern food ran from the foothills to the town's center, along the parkway in the middle of Euclid Avenue.

"Euclid was the main thoroughfare, a long, straight street with orange groves on either side," my father once recalled. "A lawn-covered parkway ran down the middle, shaded by pepper trees. The picnic tables ran single file down the parkway for a mile or more."

Imagine such a fête on this avenue today: skid marks across the lemon meringue, pot roast with a glaze of carbon monoxide, drive-by, lip-synching toasts, crosswalk suicides that simply cannot be avoided. And no one knowing the precise location of Iowa.

The yards of my relatives grew gardenias as thick as hedges and tomatoes as big as your face. We had china teacups melted by the heat of the fires of San Francisco's 1906 earthquake—survived by my maternal grandmother and her family—and a basket made by a Yokuts Indian woman before her tribe was diminished to near-extinction by what anthropologists called "factors of most unfortunate potency."

Although during temporary girlhood my grasp of history was imperfect, I sensed that somewhere in the smog with Chandler's *Big Sleep* and the defense industry boom—perhaps in the Governor Reagan, let-them-eat-cake years—lay California dreamland gone awry. Too many eager lungs had consumed the ether of promise but not the careening hunger. There was no oxygen left. Instead of the geographical distinctions of southern, northern, or central California, there were what writer and Fresno native Gerald Haslam called "personal Californias." Each generation, my parents' and my own, called its California the best California, and, according to the more cynical mantra of cultural decline, what has followed is "Place transformed into space," urban generica with warm winters and endemic gridlock.

My family knew freeways but not turnpikes, red ceramic roof tiles better than shingles, eucalyptus trees better than maples. We actually *saw* the Hollywood Hills, San Gabriel Mountains, and Catalina Island in the ultramarine ocean beyond the city, clear-sky views that reminded every presmog Californian why they lived there. Convertibles induced yawns rather than notice, and words like *palo verde* and *ciénaga* rolled off our lips. We ate artichokes back when everyone not from California thought of them as thistles.

Although we spent the preponderance of my childhood years living elsewhere, we always had a great deal of California about us. But there was one California thing we never had: a swimming pool.

As I drove out of Los Angeles on the Ventura and then the Foothill and San Bernardino freeways, I sought the appropriate metaphor of departure. The loud, separating, kissing suck of a cosmic suction cup. White noise at high treble, no bass, excruciatingly slow fade. The pinging trajectory of one humanoid subparticle turboaccelerating through 15 million other subparticles *and* their possessions. The bone-jarring *whumph* of the wimp flung out of the swinging saloon doors into the dust on his butt. None of these images was very flattering, but I was not, after all, at an Iowa Picnic or nibbling watercress stems in some nonchalantly blond bistro shaded by jacaranda trees. I was driving down a freeway.

Twice on this stretch a dense swell of moving vehicles pushed me right off the freeway onto an exit ramp not of my own choosing. I was trapped in one of the fourteen exit-only lanes, unable to move into any of the thirty-six through-traffic lanes because everyone was doing seventy with twenty-three centimeters between them, barely enough room for a well-oiled ferret to slip through without sliming the bumpers with grease marks.

Down unfamiliar streets I struggled back to the freeway, remembering the fellow who entered an exit ramp that he mistook for an on-ramp and ended up facing all fifty lanes of oncoming traffic that stops for nothing. He crashed. He died. He was from Montana. I live in a tiny southern Utah town in the middle of an enormous, empty desert. You can fly from L.A. to Phoenix in the time it takes me to drive from my house to the nearest chain hardware store. In land mass my county is one of the largest in the United States, larger than a few California counties combined, and just this year it had installed its first traffic light. Out here, staring at the nether parts of a UPS truck, I was unpracticed, I was vulnerable.

Heading out of Los Angeles for the Mojave Desert, lacking the locals' sizable volume of cool, I did my best to concentrate. I did not wish to arouse the ire of people who can drive, wave, jeer, shave, shoot whomever they perceive to be idiots, talk on their cell phones, check their teeth in the rearview mirror, groom their poodles, and smash Montanans, all at the same time. A sea-green, fur-lined, patent-leather sport utility Bentley, as sleek as wet kelp, passed me one lane over. The expression on the driver's face told me to add blow job to the list.

I spent several days in southern California, and now I was driving home to Utah with a mission. My route between the West

Coast and the Colorado Plateau would retrace family road trips in the early sixties. My trip would be a vindication, vindication of what I consider to have been a dire childhood deprivation.

We hurled down the highway in a station wagon as big as a cocktail lounge, my parents, my brothers, and I, propelled by the all-American notion that the pleasure of travel is a direct function of miles covered. The family was entirely willing and eager to camp every night—in a national park, in the backyard of a roadside reptile garden, in the middle of the desert with coyotes howling and the moon on our little faces—but we were overruled by my mother, who was not. A different edict came from my father: This family shall not stay at a motel with a swimming pool.

My father's Depression-era upbringing and economic sense made a motel with a swimming pool seem like an extravagance. No matter that rates for a motel with a pool differed little, if at all, from one without, or that frugality would never relegate us to the seediest dive. Instead, the Depression's ethos of fiscal restraint smashed head-on with the I-want-everything generation. Doing Without, especially anything considered frivolous, built character.

The full gamut of reasons—a tight budget, the hairshirt of Calvinism, a family story that has since been burnished to myth—is a declaration of memory, not fact. Day's end would come. We four kids unstuck our shorts from the seat vinyl and ricocheted off the windows, anticipating liberation from hours and hours of Balkans-style interaction inside the station wagon. We cruised past motels with happy children splashing in sunny blue pools until we found the only motel in town without one. And there we stopped.

The family budget and my status as a poolless Californian exacerbated my longing for those cool polygons of turquoise. I loved to swim. I loved swimming pools. Some four decades later, liberated from paternal principle and family dole, I plot my vindication. I will choose my stops like a road-trip version of John Cheever's story "The Swimmer," in which the main character swims home across the backyard pools of his suburban neighbors. I shall swim across the Mojave. I shall be a Californian with a pool all the way from Santa Monica to Monument Valley.

MY SOJOURN IN Los Angeles was not hell, as one might think it would be for a book-smart but street-dumb denizen of the outback, not at all a Tarzan Does Westminster sort of thing. My strategy was to adapt, to assume the laid-back L.A. pace. The L.A. pace made my laid-back home pace look like rigor mortis, so I had to speed things up a bit. I did not mind. In fact, I kind of got into just about every cool L.A. thing short of breast implants.

I went to a swank mall, where every thread-count-obsessed shopper in the place held me hostage to their cell-phone conversations. The mall's underground parking lot burrowed five levels into purgatory and I lost my truck in one of them. I roamed the cement catacombs for more than an hour trying to find it, convinced I would never again see the light of day. People who lose their cars here simply buy new ones, I thought. They have cell phones to keep in constant audio contact with their auto dealers.

In California, I found a hole in a chain-link fence and walked a piece of the Los Angeles River, a river sheathed in fifty-one miles of concrete, and the focus of "restoration" by a courageous citizens group that must convince people to love a river that looks nothing like a river. On a beach near Santa Barbara I swam in feisty surf and took walks on the beach. Treading water a hundred yards from shore, I stared back at the face of the continent, splendid and bold. On the sand, with my back to the continent, staring out to sea, I felt vastly content to watch the sun set over the Pacific, as if all my life, no matter where I was, this orb over this ocean was my Greenwich Meridian, everything set to its singular reliability.

With birthday money from my mother, who loves elegant things, I bought a set of blank books with handmade covers of a swirling cerulean peacock design and thick ivory pages that bore a watermark in the shape of an iris. *Papiro fiorentino,* paper from Florence, which I carry with me all over the desert and fill with notes, sketches, sand grains, cliffrose blossoms, smashed bugs, and salsa stains. I already had a shelf full of these Gospels of Wrath, their battered spines and corners reinforced with duct tape. The pages of each book were fat with scrawl about weather and personal anguish and quotes like this one from Ezra Pound: "At 70 I realized that instead of being a lunatic, I was a moron." I wonder how you say "duct tape" in Italian, I thought as I slipped into a freeway lane in front of a self-bailing Suburban stuffed with totally buffed rock stars. I was getting the hang of this.

During my California visit I enjoyed the company of fine friends whose grace and lack of complaint in their surroundings made me feel awkward and cynical and even envious. I envied their state's lack of an overbearing theocracy. I envied their libraries. They moved through life in eager states of spiritual delamination, not just happy, but kava-kava happy. I knew that the self-righteousness of my wilderness, escapist life set against the urban crush was actually quite thin. "I could live here," I said to my friends. "I could live in California again." No one believed me. At meals they spoke intelligently of early Burgundian oenological monographs. I explained drip irrigation. Sea air and the presence of many, many succulent green leaves beautifully hydrated their skin. I looked like a desert lizard. I ate my organic arugula with my fingers, dopey and slow like one of those Jurassic leaf-eaters with the pin head and body the size of a truck stop.

I dined in a restaurant perched on a rocky ledge of coast north of Malibu. Squeezed into the quarter-mile-wide sliver of available land between surf and the precipitous rise of the Coast Range were railroad tracks, a six-lane freeway, a convoy of RVs and campers parked nose-to-taillight along the *rincón,* their windows fogged with salty mist, and a surprisingly dense band of greenery. Palm trees waved their lacy fronds at offshore oil drilling rigs strung with looping scallops of bright lights. "Look at all those festive party boats," I remarked to my dinner companion, who, horrified at my stupidity, demanded that I surrender my California birth certificate.

I strolled through the lush gardens of the Huntington Library in San Marino and ate takeout sushi on a bench surrounded by crimson blooms so large, birds could live in them.

From the Huntington Library I walked across town to the quiet street where my aunt and uncle spent most of their lives. From the small California towns of their upbringing they came here after the war, like so many others, to make a home, work, and raise children in the sun-kissed, fruit-scented suburbs on L.A.'s fringe. After my uncle died, the house was sold. My aunt now lived under full-time care in the Bay Area. In her honor I wanted to stand at the front door of her old house and inhale gardenias.

Along the streets tall canopies of trees filtered the midday light into the eerie brightness of shredding ozone. Eucalyptus, magnolia, mimosa, jacaranda, orange, and lemon trees. Squat palms, skinny palms. Hedges of caragana and oleander. The wall of vegetation and elaborate security systems shielded backyard swimming pools. The houses were grand but, at this hour of the day, empty of life. In the past decade or so, San Marino had become populated by Asian-Americans, mostly Chinese—another generation drawn by the suburban dreams that still make southern California demographics so fluid within its own borders. Two Mexican gardeners and I provided diversity. They loaded shrub cuttings into the trailer behind their van.

I walked the final block to my aunt's house, remembering that she had a fine sense of humor and read more books than anyone I knew, and that she kept the wedding dress of her sister—my mother—in the closet of this house for nearly fifty years, a slim, Grecian-style dress the color of fresh cream. I remembered that my aunt grew a dense thicket of cream-colored gardenias and camellias at the house's front entry so that whenever I walked through the door I carried a head full of scent and, thus intoxicated, no one could get my attention, a disconnection that felt safe until my father began to tell people that he had three sons and a daughter who walked around in a coma. For the women of my family, gardenias and pearls were our California-ness. Nearly all of us were married in them.

Sprinklers hissed veils of mist over chive-green lawns. I passed jacaranda trees with more showy purple blooms than leaves, lemon trees with fruit that interested no one, ivy so large it bore branches rather than vines. Bark and leaves shed from the eucalyptus trees barely hit the pavement before the gardeners whisked them away and drove off. I was the sole human afoot on the streets of San Marino. The scent memory of gardenias pushed me toward a sad edge.

As I walked, a police cruiser pulled up beside me. A young, well-groomed officer in the passenger seat rolled down his window and asked, "Are you going somewhere special?"

I was, in my life, *nel mezzo del cammin,* a middle-aged woman who had, sometime in the past twenty-four hours, combed her hair. I never carried a purse. The sole weapon in my pocket was a pen, plus keys and a postcard reproduction of an illuminated manuscript in the Huntington collection. My body had no tattoos and a paltry three pierces doled out to two ears. I wore a sleeveless linen dress the color of the Chinle Formation. As far as I knew, I was wearing underwear. I was not a derelict. I was an Episcopalian. But I was neither Asian-American nor an employee of a landscaping service. I was out of place.

Special, I thought, moved to tears by this sensitive California man's uncanny perception of the wonders of family love, his empathy for this bittersweet pilgrimage on behalf of my beautiful, elegant aunt.

"Well, I have an aunt who now lives up north," I explained. "She and my uncle spent most of their lives on this very street. I haven't been here in years. I want to look at her house and, uh, try to remember things. I want to find her gardenias, make sure they're still there. You see, the locus of memory lies in the olfactory nerves. That's right, the human brain began as a primitive smell organ, ancient and limbic and emotionally intense. You simply inhale a scent and notalgia floods—"

Special!

"Where's your vehicle?" he snapped.

"I parked it at the Huntington Library," I answered.

He and his partner exchanged looks of incredulity. "That's a mile away. How did you get here?"

"I walked."

"You walked?"

"I walked."

Walking: propulsion by biology. A sensual engagement with terrain, weather, and one's own thoughts. In southern California walking had apparently jumped into the evolutionary compost with primal brains and the breasts you were born with. I began to feel indignant. I felt the rise of a scream in my throat. *I'm walking. And I just robbed the Bank of America.* I wondered if posh suburbs like San Marino had jails.

The officers changed their suspicion of criminal activity to suspicion of dim-wittedness. "How do you plan to get back to the Huntington?" one of the men asked, as if I were trying to make my way back to Ladakh.

"Where are you from?" his partner inquired.

The palms quietly absorbed car exhaust. The faces of the old, stately California homes remained blank against a constant hum: freeways, none of them ever out of earshot. I could see my aunt's house up the street. The trees that had once graced her front lawn were no longer there.

"I live near Monument Valley," I said. Both officers gave me blank looks. "You know, John Wayne movies and ads with Toyotas on top of spiky needles of red rock."

The Mexican gardeners had returned. So they could stay nearby and observe the unfolding drama, their lawn mower suddenly needed to be taken apart. They were attentive but with a wariness that bespoke a far different relationship with the law. Caught in the wrong place, one of them might end up in Juárez or Chihuahua. This white chick might end up at the precinct station with a take-out latte from Starbucks.

"Well, someone called in a stranger and we had to run a check," the officer said. His interest in the novelty of my existence afoot in an Asian-American suburb had waned. He eyed the Mexicans, who suddenly developed an intense interest in a rosebush. Then the policemen drove off.

I finished the sixty or so paces to my aunt's house—as before, on the sidewalk of zero pedestrians and sorely tempted to jump up and down on people's lawns, setting off security alarms. There stood the house, the old trees removed from the yard to reveal a pale gray stucco façade recognizable only by the upstairs windows, where I once stood in my cousin's room, planning to defect to a family with a swimming pool. A family with avocados and lime trees in their yard. A family that could handle a temporary girl.

The step-up porch entry had been remodeled into a flat, ground-level slab with a sort of druidic pyramid of lipstick-red brick that framed the front door. Mortar squished from the brick, hardened mid-ooze; the design motif required that it not be scraped away. Flanking the entry were two beds of hothouse petunias. There were no camellias, no gardenias. Which was fine with me, I thought, because I had not figured out how I would knock on the door of strangers and ask if I could stand at their entryway and breathe the thick perfume of creamy tropical flowers on an ever-green shrub, pulling deep into my heart all of my memories of my mother and her sister.

DIESEL AND JASMINE, the aromatic essence of southern California, roamed into my olfactory nerves and pricked the sting of reflection. As a baby, I had lived poolless in southern California. As an adult, I lived in the ancestral southern Sierra Nevada and fully surrendered heart and soul to its luminous beige granite and emerald rivers, place colors I thought would be home forever. Eventually, I had thinned out the social stimuli in my life and become a full-time desert ascetic. I admitted that I no longer knew my birthplace nor had the reflexes needed to survive it. I could not tell the difference between a cruise ship and an offshore oil rig. I had been away too long. A local journalist, whose name I can't recall, described Los Angeles as a place where you know beyond a reasonable doubt that a lot of people are awake all night long, a lot of people over the edge. Despite my determination to remain mellow, I felt the steady, low-grade sensation of being hunted.

Driving east, it seemed as if it was taking me four times longer to get out of Los Angeles than it had not too many years back. It was the traffic and the "infill" rather than the distance that deceived me. L.A.'s pattern of settlement—a collection of towns with truck gardens and citrus groves between them, merging into a single sprawling metropolis—repeats itself south to San Diego and all the way east to the San Bernardinos. Then it leaps over the mountains and takes up where it left off unless it butts up against military reserves and the remotest corners of the broiling Mojave.

The pattern catches up on itself in Las Vegas, Phoenix, Denver, Salt Lake City, and other western cities, whose outlying towns quickly evolve into traffic snarls, strip malls, fortified suburbs, and a populace that thwarts even the most modest growth controls, then swears up and down on their mothers' graves that they will never in a billion years let their town be anything remotely like that monster Los Angeles. Meanwhile, the monster itself softens the blatting engridment it inspired. The older neighborhoods enshroud themselves with Edenic vegetation. L.A.'s air has been cleaned up more progressively than Houston's. Truck gardens are on the comeback and a tiny banana farm pops up beside the freeway. Thick hedges obscure commercial zones, nasturtiums grow five feet tall, and local ordinances insist that the signs be more discreet than the nasturtiums.

By afternoon I had driven quite a distance from the breeze-swept beaches, last bastion of southern California's famed Mediterranean light. A scant mile or two inland, lacking the coastal air currents to blow them away, the plain's marine vapors, combined with a thick urban haze, erased the celebrated vistas and turned the opulent, blue-hued space flat and metallic, like tepid, airborne limeade. Close up, the smog was less visible, less likely to induce ravaging guilt over the squandering of paradise. This may be why Los Angelenos hold their gazes to the bougainvillea and verbena, to the mystically empathetic aqua of their surf trunks and the shocking green thatch of dew-tipped Tibetan grass atop their plates of piglet-lint tagliatelle. There, in the short and middle distance, may yet be room for the California dream.

The series of freeways along the L.A. Basin's northern edge skirted the San Gabriel Mountains. I knew the mountains were there because I remembered that they were there. Today, as on most days, they were lost behind the haze—the land seemed as flat as a midwestern prairie—and I would not likely see them until I crashed into them head-on, crashing being what everyone on the freeway was doing: I passed another rollover, the fourth wreck I had seen since leaving the coastline.

You could induce an urbanwide yawn among Los Angelenos if you broached the subject of their water. No one is clamoring to rent videos of *Chinatown*, the drama of how L.A. sucked the distant Owens Valley dry and flumed nearly the entire eastern Sierra runoff into the city to feed the deities of growth. Yet it was all here, the pipes and pumps, the aqueducts and reservoirs, that mass-plumbed the otherwise sere L.A. Basin.

Southern California specializes in the art and irony of municipal works designed to store water amid municipal works designed to deflect it. Along the canyons and drainages that carved the San

Gabriels ran the engineering that attempts to housebreak these rugged mountains: dikes, conduits, crib structures, and pit-dug basins that catch the debris shed by one of the continent's steepest, most geologically tense ranges, debris that would otherwise fill swimming pools, bury houses, and overlay with mud and boulders the dense real estate that has covered the bajadas between peaks and city. Along the stream channels, gabions—heaps of stone cobble riprap enclosed in wire cages—stabilized the banks. The dry stream bottoms were lined with concrete and tombstone-shaped uprights to slow and deflect the erosive velocity of runoff. The entire south flank of the San Gabriel mountain range was being held back by pits, wire, and tombstones.

West of San Bernardino, I stopped for gas. Mormon emigrants from Utah settled the San Bernardino Valley in the early 1850s, attracted by the agreeable climate and soils made fertile by the delta of the Santa Ana River. (The navel orange was born in nearby Riverside.) Brigham Young, social engineer, theologian, the powerful and abundantly wived leader of the Church of Jesus Christ of the Latter-day Saints, intended San Bernardino to be the southwestern outpost of the Mormon empire known as Deseret—over six hundred miles from headquarters in Salt Lake City. Although the empire later shrank to its present borders of statehood, San Bernardino is still home to Saints. I knew this because they were right here, in this service station, working hard.

I waited in line to pay for my gas, intrigued by the thickness of the bulletproof glass between customers and attendant. The glass was so thick everyone had to yell at him so he could hear, although it hardly mattered since he did not speak English. Behind me in line stood two youths in LDS missionary attire: neat ties, dark slacks, impeccable white shirts, obedient haircuts. Their name tags identified them as Elder So-and-so, but they were as young as puppies. In line they read aloud to one another from a church publication. I could hear them, but they thought I could not so they were not the least bit self-conscious. These young men led disciplined lives, with rules to govern their necktie styles and their bedtime. Today's text offered instructions on how to cool their temptation to masturbate.

" 'Tie your hand to the bedframe,' " one of the missionaries read.

"I pumped! I pumped!" someone ahead of us screamed to the attendant. "PUMP TWO!"

The book did not embarrass the young men. Instead, they were intent and they were worried. " 'Get out of bed and go fix yourself a snack.' "

Back on the freeway I pushed the truck through the limeade air, climbed over a pass, and dropped into an urbanized desert: overflow strip malls and endless pods of pastel housing within commuting distance of San Bernardino and Riverside—suburbs of suburbs, bedrooms of bedroom communities, absorbing the quality-of-life refugees until the refuge itself grew into an epicenter. Nothing remained undeveloped except the cemeteries. Only the dead had open space.

In ancient times, circa A.D. 1979, this stretch of the western Mojave Desert still held joshua trees, chollas, and chuckwallas. It had creosote forests, desert tortoises, blistering heat, and everything named for Satan or the private parts of recalcitrant mules. All but the heat has been swept aside, and you don't have to mess with it if you simply slip your air-conditioned suburban assault vehicle into the garage of your chablis four-bedroom in Château Fox Run Estancia Estates and shut the door against the tortoise ghosts and irksome dust behind you.

On my road map the nuevo-Mojave did not exist. On my map there were still wacky-armed joshua trees and the emblem of nothingness: a white blank with a single two-lane highway on the two hundred miles between Los Angeles and the Arizona border. The map that guided my Vindication Tour was printed in 1940. Despite the map's antiquity, I was not lost. How could I be? Three lanes of traffic were pushing me down the asphalt river like a stone in a flash flood. One lane was filled solid with semitrailer trucks so uniform in size and so close together, they looked like railroad cars on a ten-mile-long train. Sooner or later, they would have to exit and go home. Sooner or later, I would have the dry mauve dusk to myself, the open desert everywhere at the edge of my gaze. The perfume of night blossoms would find its way into windows finally opened to a caress of warm air. The indigo horizon would erase all anxiety until the darkness thickened and my headlights caught the dazzled eyes of jackrabbits, paralyzing them on the already bloodied tarmac.

JUST BEFORE MIDNIGHT I pulled into a McMojave motel, then settled into my assigned cubicle of flimsy Sheetrock, trying not to gag on the suffocating bomb of air freshener. The sealed-shut windows, the streaks of vacuum-cleaner wheels on the plum-colored carpet, the Lupe or Graciela on the "This room was cleaned by" card could plunge a person into existential despair. To wind down from road nerves I grabbed the remote control and turned on the television. The VCR accidentally kicked in with an involuntary click and whir.

A grainy picture showed a swimming pool in someone's back-yard. The someone was a doughy woman in a ruby-red bikini lounging poolside in a cheap plastic lawn chair. The video was jerky. I thought I saw the cameraman's foot. Across the patio a man appeared. He was the pool maintenance man, but he looked like an amphetamine junkie. A company or employee name was stitched in red across the front pocket of his blue chambray workshirt—something like Aqua Sluts or Johnnie Shotcrete. He messed with garden hoses, but a lot longer with one of those white plastic, encased-coil hoses that are as flexible as a Slinky. It snaked around his groin area or slithered into the pool. I could not believe I was watching this. My fingers were Super Glued to the remote.

Pool Man made eye contact with the woman, whose eyes were slits and whose breasts were heaving like berserk Wonder bread.

There was a lot of masturbatory behavior and not much pool maintenance. The red bikini landed on top of a patch of lurid green
Astroturf. Pool Man landed on top of the woman. I had never seen
cheap porno flicks, but I had heard enough about them to know
that this is what happens: Repair people and housewives copulate.
Perhaps, for variety, the FedEx man and an attorney home from
work with a headache.

The soundtrack pulsated very awful rock and roll. No more
pool in the camera's frame, just tongues and skin in a CPR-
practice-dummy pink and the woman's head thrown back with a
kind of *Bad Girls' Dormitory* expression of ecstasy. She had stripes
on the back of her thighs from sitting in the lawn chair. They did it
for a long time, time being a monument to male endurance. I
sipped icy Jack Daniel's and read from a geography textbook published in 1935. "Taming the pecan: In the American forests are more
kinds of wild nuts than grow in the forests of Europe and Asia,"
said the geography book. Pool Man thrusted. I flipped a page.
"Find some fruit-wrapping papers with the word *California* on
them." They were coupling on the Astroturf, on all fours. "Write a
story beginning, 'I am a fine large cantaloupe_____.' "

The lust on the porno flick was lust imagined by an adolescent,
perhaps someone who was bored out of his skull with vo-tech
plumbing classes. A guy with a future in pools. The sex seemed
extraordinarily dumb. I turned the television off and removed the
videocassette, too tired to care if someone had left it deliberately
or not.

THE WATER LOOKED LIKE Xiuhtecuhli, the Aztec prince of
turquoise, a name for the sun's male color and for the jade skirt of
the goddess of eternal renewal. The water was utterly turquoise
across distance and utterly colorless in the cup of my hands. Bright
sun transformed the pool's surface into a liquid mirror. Small
movements of my body scattered the mirror into a glossy, trem-

bling web, which in turn cast complex acts of light on the pool floor. This moment in the water overwhelmed me with desolation and desire, all in one extraordinary pull on my heart. To avoid the seduction I turned and floated on my back. My shadow on the bottom of the pool was deep violet, boneless.

There is an industrial paint color called Pacific Pool Supplies Blue. For the most basic of backyard swimming pools, the standard scheme has been a blinding, cool white on sides and bottom with a band of turquoise tiles or heavy latex around the rim, just above the water's surface. The chosen blue evokes serenity and escape. Too dark, the blue becomes edgy, like a lake with no bottom whatsoever, just infinity.

Clear water made blue-green in a pool is a fairly simple optical event. The white surface absorbs yellow, red, and other low-energy waves; the more energetic blue waves scatter and remain visible. Blue has enough energy to escape complete absorption by water, snow, and glacial ice. Its short wavelengths undergo the most scattering by atmospheric motes. It fills the sky with itself. In the family of light, blue is the fugitive. We are in full chase, writes Goethe in his *Theory of Colours:* "[A]s we readily follow an agreeable object that flies from us, so we love to contemplate blue, not because it advances to us, but because it draws us after it."

It was late morning, ninety-five degrees and climbing. I was plunked down in a rectangle of lagoon-blue plunked down in the white-hot Mojave. Hands on the edge of the pool, I hoisted myself out of the water and dove back in comet-style: arms straight in front of me, body svelte, a light lift from the balls of the feet perched on the pool's scorching concrete lip. The splash behind me was as silent, I hoped, as a black hole, all the dive's force confined underwater in a rush of silver bubbles. When I surfaced, I had nearly reached the other side of the pool. This reminded me how tall I am. Or how short I was when I loved swimming pools. There is nothing like a swimming pool to incite nostalgia, to emphasize the differences between the girl-boy you were and the woman you are. As I rose to the water's surface in a fluid arc, droplets made prisms on my eyelashes and turned the Mojave Desert into shimmering rainbows.

I had the pool to myself. It was the wrong time of day for the all-families-but-my-family families to conquer the motel pool after another four-hundred-mile day under their belts. I was grateful for pool space that would otherwise churn with excited children and their grazing kicks, while their parents sat poolside and tossed back diet sodas. Morning, I thought with no twinge of immunity, is motel pool time for old people. As strong as it blazed, the heat did not sterilize the smell of chlorine, the gallons and gallons of chlorine in the swimming pool meant to sterilize the guests.

Indigo tiles rimmed the pool. Patio tables with pine-green canvas umbrellas and a wooden-beamed ramada sat on the smooth concrete apron around the deck. Behind the wrought-iron fence that enclosed the pool area grew thick stands of oleander and palm trees with shaggy trunks and fanned topknots. From one of the trees a mourning dove sang its hollow coo.

By now the other guests had checked out and were pushing their survival modules over the bunny carnage left in the wake of a night's rolling armada of semitrailers, down the interstate to Los Angeles or Las Vegas and a car wash that would rinse the Mesozoic off their vehicles. Few travelers ever left the asphalt, and everything in sight was asphalted. Nevertheless, the pale dust coated the surfaces of all things. Behind the sliding glass doors of a room facing the pool, a curtain shifted slightly, blocking out the explosion of daylight.

The higher the sun climbed, the more the bright light bleached the air. If I was fully in that harsh glare, I would need to adjust my equilibrium, soften a gaze that tends to shatter in so much brilliance. Here, breast-deep in the water, the colors remained vivid and deep. The sun on my wet skin contoured my shoulders, arms, and collarbone, reminding me that I had muscles and shape. I floated on my stomach, jackknifed at the waist, and raised my legs to the air, slipping them into the water like the blade of a sword. I emerged with eyes closed and head thrown back, the water pressing my hair in a heavy weight against my shoulder blades.

In ancient Rome women were inclined to wear nothing but pearls when they swam in the sea. *Non recte recipit haec nos rerum natura nisi nudos,* wrote Pliny, the Roman naturalist. The sea receives us in a proper way only when we are naked. Water on the skin, surrounding unclad limbs, urges forth some forgotten impulse toward bliss. If this were not the Vindication Tour, I would be where I have been accustomed to *nuda* and to swimming since leaving childhood behind: in river, lake, or sea.

The swim across the Mojave began here, in surroundings alien to an inveterate camper like me, who by habit would much prefer to leave the highway and seek a dirt tributary to nowhere. On a starry desert flat or on a bajada, I liked to throw down a sleeping bag among the spiky yucca and the cynical grins of night lizards and there sleep like a rock until dawn arrived or a band of bighorn sheep hitchhiked across my hair. Here in the concrete lagoon of a corporate master plan, I tried to make the best of things.

For Californians without a pool—and for years without California actually under our feet—my brothers and I spent a great deal of time in swimming pools. My mother, who was deathly afraid of the water and not a good swimmer, insisted that we learn how to swim when we were very young, and swim well. She arranged for lessons and lifesaving classes and frequent occasions to play in neighbors' or community pools.

I swam like an otter, in deep end and shallow, a hundred aquamammal moves and endless, dripping loops from ladder to diving board to water to ladder, practicing and practicing what I envisioned as the quintessential dolphin leap—legs together and toes pointed, a perfect arc with a sense of slow motion at its apex, and a mere kiss of a splash behind my feet. After repeated tries and exploding lungs, I made my first underwater swim across the width of a backyard pool. Then I swam the length, and it seemed as if I were swimming underwater from Australia to Borneo.

My father was a superb swimmer; he grew up on Pacific surf. He rather than my mother escorted us on weekend swims at the public pool. Under my mother's supervision, despite the presence of other adults, there was an undercurrent of anxiety. She sat in the shade to protect her fair redhead's skin from blistering in the sun, her frown riveted to her slicked down, honey-brown wild things. She did not get into the water with us. She called for frequent rest periods. We played hard and, when I think of it now, surely she needed a respite from what must have been an awful tension, her fear that her children might come to harm in the water. During rest time we lay facedown on the hot concrete with towels thrown over us, molding our wet biscuit butts, counting the minutes before we could return to the water.

We children thought of pool time as exuberant, anarchic play that could go on, if only our parents would allow it, from dawn to dusk. The grown-ups thought of "going for a swim" as just that: a few methodical laps up and down the pool, then retirement to lawn chairs to argue about school integration and fallout shelters.

The fathers turned the pool into a hippo pond, sending the kids screaming to the edges. The mothers donned tight rubber caps with chin straps and rosettes of floppy rubber flowers on one ear. Like an enraged bobcat, I resisted the bathing caps and, when they were required, always "lost" mine so my hair could feel the water and my brain wouldn't be compressed into inert putty. The mothers slipped through the water with ladylike, Esther Williams strokes, furious about the ruination of their hairdos. The women with penciled eyebrows kept their egg-shaped heads well above the water. Seldom did a woman look or act anything like us, the sleek, blithe otters, and if she did she was usually the swimming teacher or a "college girl" whose days were numbered before she joined the rubber-helmet, coconut-oil, eyebrow crowd smoking Viceroys around the patio table, retouching their lips with creamy sticks of Revlon. *Wah Wah Sulk. Suddenly Fig.*

On pool days I stayed in the water until my fingertips were pruny and I was exhausted, then I wrapped myself in a beach towel and stood dripping, with chlorine-stung eyes, bony knees, and wet hair slicked back like the pintail of a duckling. All summer long, it seemed, I reeked of chlorine. My hair turned green. I had ear infections. I could not get enough of the water. Although I am certain I swam with my brothers or with friends, I recall instead a solitary, private world of sun and turquoise, leaving behind the sultry summer air, the lulling chorus of cicadas, and an interminable girl-boy geekiness to slip beneath the surface and stroke along the silent bottom of the pool—agile and fearless in water honeycombed with light.

THE POOL-TO-POOL pilgrimage of Neddy Merrill, Cheever's character in "The Swimmer," is motivated by the delight of a whim and Merrill's certainty that a long swim would "enlarge and celebrate" the beauty of a summer day. To him "the day was lovely, and that he lived in a world so generously supplied with water seemed like a clemency, a beneficence."

Cheever's character made his cross-country swim in suburban Connecticut. In Connecticut you could wring out a few lawns and supply the entire city of Los Angeles with enough water for a year. In a basin not far from the motel swimming pool, no precipitation fell between 1909 and 1912. Larger towns in the Mojave now overcome this formidable aridity by pumping groundwater and water from the reservoirs along the lower Colorado River. The driving forces of monoculture—population, technology, speed, convenience—abbreviate the land's true character—difficult, prickly, monumentally "empty"—into oases of predictable amenities and little incentive to venture far off the beaten track or suffer a land not meant to be venal but simply a desert.

I wanted to ask someone how much water evaporated from this pool on a summer day, in hundred-degree heat. As a maintenance man in a blue chambray shirt sauntered across the pool deck, some instinct snuffed this quest for knowledge and, in fact, compelled me to pinch my nose, blow out my cheeks, and visit the bottom of the pool for as long as I could hold my breath.

Everything about my swimming pool fascination may come down to this: blue. In the West there is so much blue you can fall right into it head first, something I tried often as a child. Blue was a good place to go, a country unto itself, transcendent and calm, and I would not have to talk to anyone. I spent hours thinking of ways to design camouflage, a little suit I could wear that would make me invisible to others when I stood against that vast, hallucinatory sky. My favorite swimsuit was one with thin stripes of aqua, emerald, and blue-glass blue. Wearing it was like wearing water. I was a very young girl-boy, with a mother who chose my clothes, but I believe I picked out this swimsuit myself, even though it is said that a young child's attraction to color begins with yellow and arrives at blue last, passing through green to reach it.

Perhaps when you are small and dependent, with parents who are not nudists, with a cautious, caring mother who cannot swim well, your blue water must come in these concrete rectangles of safe quarter. Perhaps my father could not imagine paddling around his beloved Pacific surf with children who weighed less than the undertow. He had to keep his fishlets in the nursery.

Young native fish in the canyon rivers of my Utah home grow their fins and gills in the still pools of backwater nurseries left by high-water floods. By the time the backwaters evaporate, the young fish are ready to swim off into the swift current of the mainstem. As I grew, the backyard pools shrank as small as bathtubs and I seemed destined for the eyebrow crowd around the patio table. Instead, I headed for ocean and river. I could swim well enough to manage wild places. I learned that wearing your skin was the only way to wear water.

So far the Vindication Tour did not feel like a celebration. It felt mundane and ridiculous. As usual, I aimed my imagination too far away from this world. I felt the snug fit of a metaphorical strait-jacket of my own stitching. In the pool's deep end, near the drain, lay a videocassette weighted down with pebbles and complimentary shampoo bottles stuffed into the take-up reel. The cluttered highway strip beyond the motel obliterated the real desert, where I knew how to move about and how to be brave. Two maids pushed a housekeeping cart along the shaded bank of rooms. They talked quietly in Spanish. *Come swim,* I wanted to cry out. *Bring your pearls.*

IN NEEDLES, CALIFORNIA, a dozen languorous sidestrokes took me across the next piece of Mojave Desert. Several armed seven-year-olds blocked my return swim down the pool's length. Their water pistols were bigger than they were. There was no parent in sight, so I presumed that I had involuntarily become their life-guard.

Behind the iron railing that enclosed the pool, a nervous woman paced and chain-smoked Marlboro Lights and cast apprehensive glances toward the motel parking lot—probably waiting for some incredibly huge drug heist from L.A., I thought, and it's her first job and she is so out of control, she will blow the deal, and I will be too busy saving the seven-year-olds from drowning because they cracked their heads open with their plastic water weapons, so I am stuck here dragging them to the deck one by one while she stands beneath a motel marquee that says GOD IS KING. HBO AND COMPLIMENTARY BREAKFAST and rings herself with crushed cigarette butts, and her cohorts, three skinny guys with black mustaches and purple suede Tony Lamas, storm in and grab one another by the neck with furious choking motions because someone forgot the keys to the bulging trunk of the rental Buick, and when they open it with a screwdriver and kicks from their purple boots, about sixty semiautomatic weapons and hand grenades clatter to the tarmac, then the police come and I am put in a witness protection program and sent far from the desert to a place I absolutely do not want to live, like Ohio.

I wanted to leave the pool, yet I could not live with myself if the children drowned. This was precisely what their parents counted on when they abandoned their kids to go up to their room to watch the Discovery Channel, a far more comfortable way to see a desert than braving the rattler-infested, dead-star landscape just outside of town. As soon as someone who remotely resembled a parent approached the pool, I was out of there with a trail of drip marks behind me.

The nervous, chain-smoking woman was in the room next to mine. She threw back the curtain and furiously washed the inside of the window, which was the last thing I would ever think of doing when you go to a motel, not to mention stay in a motel in the first place when I would rather be out there with the creosote and the scrabbly noises of the chuckwallas, a thought that made me so homesick I started to cry. I had an earache. My hair was turning green. I was looking pathetic.

I checked out of the motel and walked to the parking lot. Under the windshield wiper of my truck I found a note penciled on the back of a sales receipt. I had left my book, *Their Heads Are Green and Their Hands Are Blue* by Paul Bowles, on the truck seat. The note read: "Paul Bowles stands head and shoulders above almost any other 20th-century writer. May I recommend *The Sheltering Sky* or for short stories *Delicate Prey.*" This message bolstered my faith in humanity. Hallelujah, the world may be wallowing in greed, hatred, and nukes in suitcases, but literary exchanges, I rejoiced, are still possible in parking lots. Then I read on: "I have a thing for women with long legs. Come on up to Room 242." Signed "Another Lost Soul from Utah."

Man-oh-man, I was too old for this, and since when did I think I would be anything but restless when I was nowhere near where I knew how to be? I found the only other vehicle besides mine with Utah plates, scribbled a note, and impaled it on the wiper blade. "Get out of bed and go fix yourself a snack."

In downtown Needles the hot sun chased everyone away from the public square near the old railroad station—El Garcés, a Harvey House built in 1906 but now boarded up and doing its best not to disintegrate. Two stragglers braved the heat. One wore a shiny green sport coat the color of an Amazonian tree frog, canary-yellow slacks, and a headset whose ear covers looked like two orange turtles. The other, a bag-lady guy, pushed a shopping cart loaded with wads of cloth toward the shade of the pepper trees and gangly Washingtonia palms that still enclosed the two-story building. With its palm-frond boa, red-brick platform skirt, elegant iron rails, a full sweep of verandas held up by slender columns, and a full sweep of razor wire held up by a chain-link fence, the deserted depot looked like an impoverished dowager turned dominatrix.

"In this torrid square," said a WPA guide to California, published in 1939, when the El Garcés scene was alive and snooty, "where temperatures often are 112 degrees at midnight . . . swarthy Mojaves [*sic*], garbed in gaudy scarlets, blues, and yellows loiter about." Actually, the Mohave Indians were trying to make a living, as railroad workers and as vendors of clay toys and vessels, baskets, and strands of white and blue beads, which they presented to the railway passengers during the meal stop at Needles.

As I drove past the depot and down the old Route 66 through Needles, I was certain that we passed through here on family trips. I did not remember the railroad station; only one stretch of street and a few southern-California–style stucco bungalows appeared familiar. What I did recall was the pale rose blush of the Mojave Desert evening, the buff-colored sand, a ribbon of muddy Colorado River, a poolless motel, and the demise of a family named Quigley. Near Needles, on the old bridge that crossed the river from California to Arizona, my brother and I rid ourselves of them.

My mother remembers the Quigleys as my invention. "The

Quigleys lived inside your tummy," she recalled for me. "They usually appeared at moments of excitement or anxiety. I never questioned it. It was a very private group."

Children with imaginary friends were once considered gifted or deranged, minisociopaths or loners, depending on how deeply one succumbed to the wobbly wisdom of folklore. From a child's point of view it probably wasn't a bad idea to have some giant bunny or urchin around to take the blame for your wretched behavior. A small contingent of adults claimed there was nothing imaginary at all: The fall guys were, in fact, *ghosts*. A father in Texas, for example, noticed that chairs moved and doors opened by themselves whenever his young son said his imaginary friend was around. In his own house, the fellow asserted, books were being flung across the room by someone called Baby Michael. He then "found evidence" that a stimulated pineal gland could tune a person into paranormal phenomena. Since children's brains were bathed in oxygen-rich blood, he concluded, they could see frequencies not visible to grown-ups, whose pineal glands were less active.

By the time the World War II generation was raising kids, child psychologists had debunked the flaming-pineal theory and soothed parental fears. As a parent who never failed to encourage her children's creativity, my mother did not need Dr. Spock to assure her that imaginary friends were a normal and healthy element of childhood, a means to experiment safely with emotions and control the circumstances of play. The experts would have told her not to worry about an inability to distinguish fantasy from reality unless I was, say, fifty.

In contrast to my mother's recollection that I invented the Quigleys, I believe that my older brother and I created and embellished the fantasy together. At first he saw the Quigleys as I did, helping me make tiny library cards for them, building little pretend forts, taking them for swims. Then, almost overnight, he entered the fantasy only to sabotage it, to ratchet up the perils or steal the story out from under me and manipulate the Quigleys into his own control.

I would have the Quigleys packing for a trip to Yemen. He would have them get on the wrong airplane and end up tied to a cactus with Apache arrows in their chests. I would lead the Quigleys on a crawl around the perimeter of the living room, behind the furniture. The bare hardwood floor between the edge of the carpet and the wall formed a trail. The carpet was a dire swamp or hopeless quicksand. My brother changed the quicksand to snake vomit and shoved the Quigleys into it, where we watched them disappear slowly, their little arms waving in terror until the carpet closed over their heads with a murderous quiver.

The Quigleys were more affluent than the scavenging, slightly ragged troupe of minimidgets in Mary Norton's children's story *The Borrowers.* The Quigleys stood about four inches tall. They had no first names and an uncertain number of family members, but absolutely for certain one beagle and a car. They did not fling books, but they were mildly disobedient.

On family trips we rode in the station wagon while the Quigleys followed, and I had to do a lot of neck craning to make sure they were behind us whenever my father made fancy turns. This was difficult because one of my younger brother's imaginary friends was a full-size horse that had to be hauled in an imaginary, full-size trailer, which obscured the view of the Quigleys in their miniature vehicle. Always they would make it to the motel with us. Actually, the motel *next* to us, the one with the swimming pool. The Quigleys swam. We did not. I am not sure what we did between checking in to the motel and dinner and bedtime because, not understanding the caution that parents must take when traveling with four children, I remember only a list of things we could not do, like swim, take a walk alone near the motel, talk to strangers, or leave home and get our own apartment at the age of ten.

Beyond Needles loomed the Chemehuevi and Dead Mountains

and other island ranges that wear down as they rise, shedding themselves into the basins that separate them. The creosote forests—
they cover three-quarters of the Mojave, the coldest desert they can
tolerate—gave way to cliffrose along the interstate median strip and
pinyon and juniper on the rises. I drove past wash after dry wash.
Devil's Wash. Walnut Wash. Frog Wash. Good places to wash one's
devils, walnuts, and frogs. I pulled over to a rest area to stretch my
legs. Two other travelers parked and staggered out of their vehicle.
Their pants were unzipped. A number of signs told us what not to
do, including a warning: UNLOADING LIVESTOCK IN REST AREA PRO-
HIBITED. I opened the tailgate of my pickup and let out about fifty
head of bawling Herefords. A few ocotillos grew in the pet exercise
area. Their thin arms shot out from the ground like green wire,
each branch tipped with flame-red blossoms.

At a picnic table beneath a ramada I leafed through my antique
geography book. The scanty Southwest chapter (the authors devoted most of their ink to Iowa) described the region as "virtually
damless. No one lived in this land." Sixty years later, of course, the
Southwest is no longer virtually damless but virtually riverless, its
waterways dammed, reservoired and rerouted not to flow to the sea
but to cities and industrial farms.

The book offered an inexhaustible supply of photogenic peasants. Like the later versions that fed my childhood reveries, this
text, too, managed to piece the world together in a timelessly exotic
variety. On a page about sub-Saharan Africa was a photograph of a
man and his camel sitting side by side on a featureless plain. In
robes and turban the man held a pipe to his lips. "Why does he
wear so many clothes in a temperature which may reach 140°?" the
caption asks. "He is smoking hashish. Look up hashish."

To protect the Quigleys, more and more I kept their adventures
to myself. Secrets give courage. My imaginary friends matched a
physical world but thwarted a social one. I organized a Quigley
episode in my head, then modified it if situations like quicksand or
decapitation crept in without bidding. The plots were minimal.

Instead, I wove their stories against intricate and elaborate settings fed by images from encyclopedias and geography books.

The Quigleys had a miniature rambling California beach house with a sparkling turquoise pool the shape of the Caspian Sea. They visited my uncles, aunts, and cousins in England, sipping tea from Ceylon, then they went to Ceylon, before it became Sri Lanka, to see the tea itself. Wherever the Quigleys and I ventured, the Gobi or the Amazon, Tahiti or Corfu, it was by entering an animated, mind's-eye version of pictures in books, pictures overwhelmingly devoted to oxen pulling carts. In their jet-black burkas the women of Islam stood like tall laundry, giving no idea which was front or back unless you looked at the direction of their toes. The nomads of North Africa, Arabia, and the Asian steppes guaranteed hours of fascination. *Monsoon* and *oasis,* words I loved, entered the stories frequently.

In Australia upside-down Quigleys kept pet upside-down kangaroos with no sign of protest from the beagle. The favored scenes were cliff dwellings in the American Southwest or a desert caravan, in which we crossed the Sahara in flowing robes with silver bells on their hems and slept on richly colored rugs in an indigo tent. Our noisy but loyal camels wore bands of blue-glazed ceramic beads across their foreheads, as I had seen in *National Geographic.* They carried silk and fragrant spices. Around small cooking fires we held bowls with food and slices of lemon. Because I so loved them, I was the one who carried the maps. My caravan journeys muddled cultures and places, but each included a sea of wind-carved sand dunes, heat that was both refreshing and turbulent, and an oasis at the end of the day with date palms, houses of sun-dried brick, a swimming pool, and violet light on the horizon at dusk, from which emanated forces unknown and immensely pleasurable.

When my brother joined the play, the adventures went domestic, usually western, with tiny boots and spurs, chaps, and thimble-sized Stetsons for the Quigleys. Westerns shaped baby-boomer games; other themes felt intangible or boring. As for the rest of

America, our geography books showed a politically laden counterpoint to the oxcart: hyperactive tractors, mills, factories, hydroelectric dams and power stations, industrial cotton fields the size of Iraq, and charts that listed the "Rank of the World's Leading Countries in Zinc Production."

The Quigleys dove completely underground when my brother went from dominating the fantasy to saying it was plain dumb. The Quigleys, he said, were *stupid*, implying, of course, that I was stupid and a baby and a girl if I continued to hang around with invisible dwarfs. This attitude hinted at a common childhood schism, when playmates once too young for gender baggage begin to segregate into girl and boy groups. I did not want to lose my brother. I wanted to keep up with him and his older-by-two-years world, in which he and his buddies hid in a dry irrigation ditch smoking Kents from somebody's parents' complimentary four-pack, an inflight gift from the airlines back when the airlines accommodated more vices. In this world there was no room for the stupid Quigleys. The way the boys smoked—coughing, choking, holding the snow-white filters against lips too pursed—looked dumb too, but far less dumb than dolls and fairies, and in possession of secrets that seductively upped the stakes. The worst fate was to be left behind, so I spent a lot of time crashing my bike and flinging myself out of trees in the best spirit of their play. Then, with a sudden jerk, my brother weaned us from our imaginary friends.

The rest-area crowd thinned out, leaving me with the ocotillos and an RV with a pair of stuffed mammals on the dashboard. A sign next to them said ASK ME ABOUT MY WEASELS. The eastbound traffic roared off the Mojave and geared up for the climb onto the Arizona plateaus, there to visit or bypass the Grand Canyon.

Years ago a trip brought the family across the Mojave to that astounding chasm in a night so dark it erased all but the immense shape of emptiness that abruptly split northern Arizona in two. On the way to our lodging we stopped. My brother and I escaped from the car before anyone could hold us back, leaving my mother paralyzed with fright as two of her children raced, Keds smoking, toward an edge without a guardrail. Two children on the brink of the Grand Canyon in the pitch dark, held fast by the plenty of family love. This brother would not live past the age of thirty-seven. I cannot ask him for his version of the Quigleys and how we sent them packing. The details remain vague, but I think it happened in a somewhat simple way.

Time passed. We outgrew our seersucker sunsuits. The Quigleys had lain dormant for some time. Then, driving over a bridge across the mighty Colorado River en route to the Grand Canyon, we turned around in our seats and peered intently out the back window of the station wagon. My brother "detached" the invisible horse trailer from the hitch and hooked it to the Quigleys' car, an act he described to our younger brother, who began to cry. The Quigley vehicle wobbled with the new weight.

At an intersection we turned in different directions. We were headed for Arizona, my father told us, and a restaurant that served ground beef patties in the shape of steers. The Quigleys clicked on their turn signal and headed for Nevada. Unlike their snake-vomit swamp mishap, this time they would not return. Their departure was the least dramatic of all their adventures.

I did not know much about Nevada, but I was quite certain it had swimming pools. I asked my father if we could stay at a motel with a swimming pool in the town with the steer-shaped hamburgers. He said, "We'll see." This is what he always said, *We'll see,* with its beguiling morsel of hope. Then we would cruise down the main drag past every last pool in town until we found a motel without one.

HINDU, MUSLIM, CHRISTIAN, JEW. Pantheistic Greeks, Romans, and Egyptians. All, in the earliest of times, believed in the ritual purification of bathing. Amid marble statuary and mosaic floors, Pompeiians of the second century B.C. moved from *calidar-*

ium and *laconicum* to *tepidarium* and *frigidarium,* rooms of hot, steaming, lukewarm, and cold water. Ancient Greeks sat in tubs and stood under primitive showers. In the manner of Scythian nomads of the Eurasian steppes, Finns and Russians enclosed themselves in wooden huts with heated rocks and steam. The Japanese, Turks, and the Moors of Spain bathed often. Early Christians, medieval northern Europeans, and colonial American Puritans did not. Between the first and fourth centuries A.D. the Romans built five imperial *thermae,* leaving behind the remnants of three—the Baths of Caracalla, Titus, and Diocletian—and a mythic stereotype of excess and debauchery.

Some carnivorous globule of technotopia has re-created an Italianesque *thermae* fantasy in the cusp of a Las Vegas high-rise known as the Bellagio Hotel. Here lay William Randolph Hearst's San Simeon for the masses, here Caracalla met Pebble Tec. I had come where no baby-boomer family, not my family, not even an avant-garde Quigley, would have dared to go. I was in territory that was exotic to my own feral nature, to a congenital allergy to Industrialized Fun.

What could be found in such a place? There was not just one dinky turquoise rectangle with a chrome ladder. There were six courtyards of pools, ranging from Olympian rectangles to intimate polygons and circles. There were trimmed hedges and lawns, walkways arched with ivy, beds of roses, lantana, ornamental rosemary, and petunias, and scattered stands of Aleppo pines and Lombardy-style cedars shaped like suppositories. There were elaborate fountains and overhead traffic helicopters, a man in a tiny orange Speedo, and a grand staircase in shell pink with a statue of Bacchus at its foot, genitals understated. There were canvas-walled rental cabanas with overhead spray misters, cable TV, and a personal host in a crisp polo shirt. The soundtrack was backhoes, the temperature was 102 degrees.

Now this, I thought as I slipped into one of the turquoise pools below the Bellagio's towering pastel wings, *this is a Motel with a Pool.*

For this stop on my Mojave swim my husband joined me. I arrived with a raging ear infection, the pressure of tidal waves roaring in my head. Because it was Sunday we had to go to an emergency room at one of the hospitals. Every seat was taken by mothers flushed with worry sitting beside kids flushed with fever. I could not bear to take up a doctor's time while these children waited. So we drove to a different clinic, where a nurse relieved my ear's impacted cerumen.

"How have you managed so much blockage?" he asked as he swabbed and cleaned my ear.

"Maybe it's because I've been sleeping in the wind and sand for so many years," I replied.

I forgot to mention that Mark and I live outdoors for much of the year, camping for pleasure and because of his job as a backcountry river ranger. The nurse started talking about soup kitchens and beds indoors, out of the elements. He thought I was a homeless person. While the nurse treated my ear, Mark disappeared, then returned with a plastic bucket filled with silver dollars and offered to pay the bill.

After a handful of visits over the years we now discovered that Las Vegas no longer amused us. We once forced it upon ourselves as a ritualistic counterpoint to our "wilderness" lives, an alarm bell to the outbacker's tendency to deny the Spectacle, an oblique means to understand water in the desert West and the telling juxtaposition of neighborhoods: "Father Knows Best" Utah and "Father Goes to Brothels" Nevada. Sin City and the Nevada Test Site, ground zero for decades of atomic testing. An hour's drive north of Las Vegas, the bombing range lay dormant under a test moratorium but never failed to inspire a lurking creepiness. It had left an ongoing dump-it-here legacy, making lab rats out of the citizens of Nevada and Utah.

All of Vegas's revelry, the ephemeral shelf life of hotels that once struck a high note of absurdity, was now reduced to a pain in the butt. Crowds. Waiting lines. Spaces so choked with entertainment they were bone- and brain-dead. Noise. Pollution. Traffic. Gluttony. We were wracked with guilt about contributing to the gluttony.

"Everyone has too much money," Mark groaned as we skirted the Bellagio's eight-acre replica of Lake Como.

"Everyone thinks this is Lake Como," I moaned.

Pool by pool I swam across a piece of the Mojave Desert dressed up like a Mediterranean villa. I ended up at an octagonal pool with a royal blue and yellow design on its bottom and a fountain in the center. On each side of the fountain was a sculpted head with a stern visage, beard, and wild hair, a sort of lion-human spewing an arc of water from his mouth. The head looked like Charlton Heston as Moses after the Burning Bush scene. Not far away stood caryatids, fauns, urns on pedestals, and a statue of a turtle ridden by a satyr with a bambino satyr on his shoulders. Everything appeared a bit off-ripe, not quite northern Italy or Hearst Castle, more like a depraved shopping mall.

In the deck chair next to mine sat a fortyish, heavyset man with the scars of knife wounds in his belly. He listened intently to the wiry fellow in the orange Speedo, who was taking him into his confidence about a sinister event. The Speedo was smaller than his Elvis sunglasses. He spoke in a heavy southern European accent with, strangely, Elmer Fudd *R*'s. "I wun. I wun like hell. I see bwoken glass all over," he exclaimed with a stay-with-me-on-this-one-babe gesture. "Now. Tell me. What I do?"

Back when the family bypassed swimming pools, they most definitely bypassed Las Vegas. Las Vegas was, to my parents, expensive and vulgar. It was the very place my brothers and I wanted to see. In those days no one but Caesar's Palace had gone berserk over campy statuary. Swimming was secondary to slot machines and game rooms, the pool was where you parked your mistress while you lost your shorts at blackjack. Now the sin of the city was its profoundly casual consumption of water to feed voracious growth. Pools were an industry that filled eight Yellow Pages in the city phone book.

Curious, I had looked up pools under "P" and found "Pools— see Swimming Pools" listed after "Political Parties" (the Campaign for Scientific Government, the Libertarian Answerman). The phone book's voluminous "Escort Girls" pages had been ripped out. Under the correct listing I found pool contractors, suppliers, repair and maintenance services, and the assertion that shoppers do not want a swimming pool for their home, they want an *aquascape,* a springs-pool-spa with options for waterfalls, streams, pregrown palm trees, lagoons with a choice between "rock" or "real rock," beachfront entries, designer barbecues, scum pumps, robo-sweepers, and Pebble Tec decks or interior pool finishes, made from a slurry of cement and small, uniformly round stones. To cool us down in the blistering Mojave air, the pools of Nevada require tons of landscaping rock and the industrial luxury of water pumped from the Colorado River and its reservoirs east of the city.

I thought about my fifteen-dollar turquoise plastic kiddie wading pool at home, set up on a sandy plot amid rabbitbrush and greasewood. On hot days I sat in the pool and read a book, trying my best to ignore the annoying static of its decoration: a few cartoons and repeated warnings, plastered over the bottom and sides in three languages, about the dangers of leaving children unattended in its six inches of water. It was such a paranoid pool. I shut my eyes and ears to Speedo Man and stuck my head under one of the fountains. I imagined a miniature Bellagio spa at my house, muscular but mute surfers to porter my gin and tonics, a statuary nook with naked satyrs, a small beachfront, a few lagoons slurping into the rabbitbrush, the tranquil immutability of dyed Pebble Tec. Would I choose Caribbean Aquamarine or Sedona Skyline? The inky dark of a midnight lagoon or the pearl white of a sandy beach?

Around the Charlton Heston pool there seemed to be many amorous couples who were married but not actually to one another.

The skimpy bathing attire of most women was not meant to be wet; it was made from strawberry fruit rolls instead of fabric. My body was the only unreconstructed body on the premises. Like our predecessors of ancient times, all of us at the Bellagio *thermae* performed the spa ritual, the taking of the waters. I had a motel with a pool not because I wanted to but because I could.

The family ghosts give this place wide berth but not without vapor trails of guilt and parental admonition against excess. Before my thoughts hopped on the Deprived Innocents track, I suddenly saw this vast public bath as my mother and father might have seen it so many years ago, when frugality, principle, and other antipool strictures dissolved against another possibility. With shameful horror I recalled what parents like mine had to face.

Shortly before my brothers and I took to the water, children between the ages of five and ten were the primary victims of polio, a debilitating disease also known as infantile paralysis. For fear the virus might spread further, officials throughout the country shut down public swimming pools. By 1954, mass inoculation curbed the polio epidemic; we swam through our childhood with the immunity of the Salk vaccine. Yet, as witnesses of the polio epidemic, many parents must have held residual fears every time their children strained to jump into the turquoise waters.

This place had enough chlorine to bleach a sperm whale. It felt like Pompeii with Vesuvius erupting and everyone urgently on cell phones to their stockbrokers. Among the hedonistic loungers in the deck chairs around me, aquascape had inspired expressions of utter boredom. As the crowd grew, hundreds of bodies obliterated the turquoise. Blue, the fugitive light, had a diminishing surface of entry. But the children, the splashing, wet-shiny children, remained oblivious to all but the glory of water and sun.

Our stay at the Bellagio made Mark and me feel as if we were here on vacation from some place we did not live, like Indianapolis. We were bored. Mark wanted to return to Utah. I wanted to get back on the road. In Vegas's endless vending of the fantasy de jour,

Mark thought that the trend in upscale, *très sushi* hotels like the Bellagio, MGM, and Mirage had peaked. What's next, I wondered. A "we are not alone," *X-Files, Road Warrior* sort of thing, he speculated. Rural Nevadans, who tend to be more obsessed with aliens than most people, might welcome this at last legitimized marriage, gambling and the nuclear legacy finally in synch. In casino decor this would likely mean great walls of exposed ductwork, crash-test dummies, giant protean blobs, a lot of heavily lacquered rooms, a lot of black pointy things, buffets full of cognitive enhancement drugs, and wherever you looked, endless morphing.

Our room on the twenty-fifth floor of a disposable hotel on the Vegas Strip overlooked a spectacular view of Mt. Charleston and the craggy slate and mauve ridge that held it. Subdivisions spread to the northwest, nearly to the lip of the Nevada Test Site. The window was thick and tightly sealed, which was a good thing because if I opened it I might have jumped out of it in a crazed paroxysm of claustrophobia. The late afternoon sun played on the mountains, taut and glowing. Mark and I put on our matching terrycloth courtesy bathrobes and posted our chairs in front of the glass.

ASKED TO DESCRIBE the character of his state, a Nevadan paused and said, "Well, it's all out-of-doors." The trouble is, except for the center and north, Nevada has gone indoors. At the century's turn, the holding capacity of Las Vegas approached over 127,000 hotel rooms. Give up trying to tally the space of a nontransient population that increased by several thousand each month. Seen from a voyeur's point of view, the numbers bulge up the crowd cover.

As Las Vegas's ectoplasmic haciendas spread southward into Nevada's wedge-shaped tip, the boonies are shrinking and decompression from the overstimulation takes longer. Not many years ago the boys could bring the dead bodies to the open desert in the trunk of the Cadillac, dump them in a sandy wash, wipe the dust off their wingtips, and be back in town with the first blush of dawn. The new, gangster-Disney Las Vegas pushes back the line between city and wilderness, forcing the boys to steer through malls, gated neighborhoods, controlled intersections, forests of injury-lawyer billboards, construction detours, and speed bumps. They will be lucky to be back in time for their massage at the Venetian. When the bubbleheads screw up and you have to rub them out, you may end up driving halfway across California. "Bwuno," the boss says, "take 'em out."

The road I take leads from depravity to desolation. I welcomed desolation, it felt like home. I had returned to the empty-quartered spaces of my 1940 road map. I had slowly dislodged the neon shrapnel from my fantasy-pelted hide and readjusted to the desert's muted, powdery light. In the high sun the land distinguished itself by form rather than color: crimped mountains, sweeping bajadas, broad basins that still bear an affinity with a vanished sea. The last quarter of the Mojave rendered a final asceticism before the land rose, rippled, cracked, and reddened into the Colorado Plateau.

On an empty stretch of back road I pulled over to walk around and imbibe the humbling silence that resided in so much heat and space, a silence broken by a passing flock of songbirds with the sound of dry, rustling grass in their wings. I rubbed creosote leaves between my fingers for their sharp scent and stretched out on the ground to observe whatever sauntered through the first two inches immediately above Earth. Ants and a darkling beetle. A chuckwalla, *Sauromalus obesus* or "fat bad lizard," which I liked to think of as a fat and bad fat-bad lizard. Faint tail bands marked this one as a female or juvenile. In mating season, an erotic time in chuckwalla life, she belongs to a harem lorded over by a tyrant male. Researchers who spend time on the sex lives of lizards say she arouses the male by rubbing and licking him. Bad! She also can wedge herself into a rock crevice, gulp in air, and inflate her loose folds of skin so that no predator can remove her puffed-up body from the crack. Fat! Mateless and svelte at the moment, this chuck-walla scrambled up a creosote bush and shook it as I got up to leave. Williams, Arizona, is surrounded by the Kaibab National Forest, high enough in elevation to grow the first trees of size that I had seen since San Bernardino and the master-planned nursery palms of Las Vegas. Stands of ponderosa pine skirted open meadows. The air filled with the crystalline spice of streams and lakes.

Williams began as a lumber and railroad town, then found itself in the cross traffic of Route 66, the highway John Steinbeck called "the path of people in flight." It straddled the junction of decision for Route 66 travelers: On to California or a quickie to the Grand Canyon? The main street still devoted itself to both the canyon and the cult, evident by a dense underbrush of Route 66 memorabilia, plus a massage therapist and an espresso bar with a Harley-Davidson motif. Otherwise little had changed architecturally since the fifties.

Jumbled storefronts wore bright new coats of paint and enough care to preserve their vintage neon signs. Their goods venerated America's Mother Road and portrayed Grand Canyon National Park as the home of a rather kitschy tribe of Sioux. Here could be found the same curios I gazed upon when I was wrangling Quigleys: beaded belts, sheriff badges, toy drums with dyed chicken feathers, spears, tomahawks, fringed Naugahyde vests, scorpion paperweights, whips, fake rattlesnake eggs, cedar jewelry boxes, stamped leather wallets with edges braided in rawhide. Back then I would not have seen the current inventory of dream catchers, wind chimes, Kokopelli everything, red-chile-pepper everything. In an antique store I noticed an old framed photo of a family camping in a national park. A sign painted on the side of their car declared NOBODY FROM NOWHERE, GOING BACK.

Years ago in Williams, Arizona, the strife of a poolless California girl-boy with pitiable hope for a motel pool must have been great. None of the vintage fifties motels on Williams's main drag had a pool. Cruising down Main in the mobile cocktail lounge, the clunky steel and chrome station wagon with its huge steering wheel, my father might have changed *We'll see* to *Too bad*. Today the motels, street, and stores appeared squeezed and shrunken to miniatures. Was it because I held images of a smaller self against a larger physical world? Or had I lived in Utah too long, accustomed to streets so wide you could run them in M1 tanks, six abreast?

On the family trip we checked into a motel—and we lived it up. We broke from routine and ate at a steakhouse. As usual, the adults in charge of our lives qualified the extravagance. We can stay in motels, they implied, but no pools. We can eat in lusher surroundings, but no steak. The parental injunction came down: Order hamburger.

The human body needs the embrace of water. The fifties boom in California swimming pools, and the attachment of pools to the culture of a mobilized America, announced affluence, comfort, and good climate, and it made the embrace available in controlled circumstances: big recreational bathtubs gone outdoors, with no worry about what might lurk in their depths. For everyone but children, for whom it is a baptism of sheer joy, a pool holds more chlorine than wonder.

I floated around the last swimming pool of the tour, exiled to a chain motel on the strip off the interstate, a travelers' ghetto removed from the distraction of a real town and anything unsightly that might spill out of the Canyon Club bar. I felt like Neddy Merrill at the end of "The Swimmer," shivering and dripping in front of his empty house in his vicious little suburb. I was weary of rooms with sparkles on their ceiling plaster, and I wanted to return to my own planet. I wanted to swim in the silty canyon river. I wanted to sleep on the ground on some godforsaken mesa top where I belonged.

I once vowed that when I was grown and on my own I would always stay at a motel with a pool when I traveled. I would be able to do this because I would no longer be subject to another's principles. I would have my own, although at the time I had no clue what they would be, and surely they should have been loftier than a self-indulgent, spoiled-rotten fixation on cement and water, when there was a world full of underfed, disheartened people, people in my own country who could not read or write or who were beaten daily, children who were not having any fun in their entire lives.

I once imagined living in southern California, where I could walk out the back door and slide into my own private piece of blue water with liquid nets of sun wavering in its depths. I imagined teaching children of my own to swim, with me in the water along-side them from the start or holding out my bare, wet arms and a big fluffy towel to grab them, while they ran away shrieking with mis-chief. I imagined driving down long, empty desert roads with a rectangle of turquoise at the end of each day. I imagined a brother who would grow old with the rest of his siblings.

Life's trajectory shed all but the desert part of that itinerary, not as broken dreams but as the husks of fate and fiercer desires. Like the Quigleys, I flipped on my turn signal. Meanwhile, a child stuck in a station wagon for three hundred miles simply wants some time to play.

It is said that some people retain a vivid memory of the passage from earliest childhood and its magical, fluid world to an awareness of the discrete and ordered adult world. Visual, tactile, and other sensory impressions mark such children so profoundly, they forever seek to reexperience or re-create them, to keep life sensuous, myste-rious, and whole, perhaps to the point of changing appearances and meaning. Perception rides on watery ripples, "real" life refuses to stay within the lines. Storytellers and artists mine these veins. Real-ity masks a different language, beauty its antecedent and far, far closer to instinct.

An infant's heightened perception of yellow moves to green then to red and blue, the home colors of mature vision. What if you are lost on your way to blue, stranded in Goethe's "enchanting nothingness," the blue we so love to ponder not because it presses in on us but because it pulls us after it? In the dazzling Arizona sun I slipped underwater, willing my skin to take on the liquid stillness, the shimmering turquoise light. I was wearing my little sky suit I so longed for, the camouflage that could dream me out of one existence into another, invisible and floating and edgeless.

THE SIGN'S BROWN AND WHITE neon-lit Hereford, anatomically incorrect but squat in the legs and horned like a bull, stood in a stocky, livestock-sale profile atop the steakhouse roof. The Big Meat motif hurled through the interior as well, scattering cattle, fences, brands, broncs, saddles, spurs, and wagon wheels onto every plate, cup, napkin, and water pitcher in sight. A sign by the cashier's desk implored PLEASE CONTROL YOUR CHILDREN.

From a table in a nearly empty dining room, I wished I could see more clearly four children in clean clothes and combed hair, their not quite perfect manners straining to cover the tremors of energy and restlessness, their young lives held safely within the aura of love from two adults who were about to give them the gift of the Grand Canyon. But when I tried, I saw a self so surprising I could not believe it was me. I wished I saw a mind as restful as a pond, but I saw longing and fury. I wished I liked hamburger, but I do not. With little other choice in this monument to beef, I ordered a small portion anyway. The inside of the restaurant was dim and redolent of singed meat. Outside, the desert sun fired up to a white, flattening blaze.

Remember yourself simply, I thought, a child caught in the safe ecstasy of imagination and an inconstant external world. The server placed my plate before me. Ground beef, cut and cooked in the shape of a little steer.

Waiting Its Occasions

She is not afraid of the snow for her household: for all her
household are clothed in scarlet.

Proverbs 31:21

Ihave a basket made over 150 years ago by a Yokuts Indian
woman. She wove bracken fern, saw grass, redbud, and deer
grass into the diamond backs of rattlesnakes and the wing patterns
of geese in flight. Instead of a plain rim, as in Yokuts custom, she
ticked it with alternating dark and light stitches, a design common
to the basketry of the Panamints of Death Valley, with whom she
may have had blood ties. The Yokuts wintered in California's San
Joaquin Valley and migrated into the nearby Sierra Nevada during
the summer, taking advantage of seasonal climate and food sources.
They divided all of nature into two halves, with animals on each
side—ravens, coyotes, eagles, bears—that gave a person an identity.
They called the years "worlds."

In the 1850s a Yokuts, perhaps the weaver herself, gave the basket to my maternal great-great-grandmother Sarah, whose ranch
straddled a river that meandered through southern Sierra foothills
the color of washed gold. Above the ranch rose John Muir's Range
of Light, a cloud-raking spine of granite and ice with Mt. Whitney
at its crest, the Kings, Kern, and Kaweah Rivers in its belly, and the

largest living trees on earth on its flanks. The basket survives, passed down five generations, woman to woman, from Sarah to me. The ranch and river did not. Both lie beneath a reservoir behind a dam, one of many dams that tap the Sierra's runoff along its entire four-hundred-mile reach, from Mt. Lassen to the Mojave Desert.

The ancestors made their way to the San Joaquin's promise early, just behind the frenzy of the Gold Rush. Old photographs show the women buttoned up tight from waist to neck. They are the mothers and grandmothers of single-minded women who knew what to do with a ranch, a pie, a rattlesnake, or three months alone at a backcountry fire lookout. They tucked their families against the Sierra and, like the native people they and their neighbors displaced, they used the valley and mountains seasonally. Each summer, from the late 1850s until the turn of the century, my great-great-grandparents and their descendents moved livestock from the foothill ranch to pastures below Mt. Whitney. A nearby peak and meadow bear my great-grandfather's name. The family backyard became Sequoia National Park and the national forest that bordered it.

My grandfather, Scots-born and unaccustomed to the blistering heat at valley elevations, summered his family in the high country as well, in a cabin on a private inholding in the national forest. Wild ginger grew at the foot of a *Sequoiadendron giganteum* in the yard, and out the front door lay broad slabs of gray rock pecked with smooth, deep holes. In these fixed mortars Yokuts women ground acorns into flour.

A ponderosa pine grew up through an opening in the cabin's porch. Each year someone had to enlarge the hole with a handsaw so the porch floor would not strangle the trunk of the pine—over three feet across at maturity—or so the pine would not rip up the floor planks like some hormone-crazed beanstalk. No one ever considered cutting down the tree. For at least three generations the tree grew and the porch shrank.

The Yokuts women who had worn down granite with their arm muscles and grinding tools were likely from bands of Yaudanchi or Bokninuwad, *bok* from the word for "find" and a reputation for not returning lost items to their owners. The Spaniards called them *tulareños* after the tule marshes that grew in the San Joaquin Valley's once vast wetlands, where the Yokuts people wintered. Their best clothes were crowns of magpie and crow feathers and skirts made from strings of eagle down. They placed toxins from buckeye, soap plant, and *calabacilla loca* (also known as squirting cucumber) into small pools in streams, bringing the fish belly-up for dinner.

The Yokuts cremated their dead and gave the funerary goods of the deceased to the *tunosim*, transvestites awarded the privilege of preparing the body. According to anthropologist Alfred Kroeber, the transvestites were "called by their nature to be so" and thus were tolerated and awarded function. Also acceptable, as a hereditary and lifetime position, was the *hiauta*, a clown whose duty was to mock ceremonies, speak in contradictions, and "be indecent and act nonsensically." Weather doctors tended to rain. Rattlesnake doctors cured actual bites and by clairvoyance identified future victims and cured their future bites. The Yokuts traded deerskins, baskets, and acorns for pinyon nuts, obsidian, red paint, and bows made by neighboring Paiutes, bows that were desirable for their strong sinews.

In the Yokuts' time a meadow likely surrounded the grinding stones in the cabin yard. In my grandparents' time incense cedars sprouted at the meadow's edges. My grandmother draped her laundry over these small trees to dry. In my time, under a canopy of mature cedars, I found the fixed mortars eroded to an aged roughness and lined with lichen in the deeper holes. It seemed a fine place for work and gossip.

I once gathered acorns, removed their little turban caps, and ground them in one of my predecessors' mortars. With the meal I made flat cakes, baked them on a fire, and served them with the spinachlike leaves of miner's lettuce picked beside a nearby stream:

Yokuts pitas. Although it seemed noble to be eating an oak, the acorn cakes were bitter and needed a throat wash of cold Dos Equis. I had not known to leach the tannin from the ground meal. In the night a masked raccoon picked up the leftover cakes in its tiny child's hands and carried them off.

Incense cedar, sugar pine, ponderosa, sequoia—these trees gave me explanations that no one else was asking for. The sugar pine in particular held me in thrall. It grows by itself or in twos or threes amid mixed conifers, seldom in pure stands. Straight and un-branched for much of its span, a mature sugar pine can rise over 150 feet from a carpet of mariposa lilies and a dreamy whirl of California sister butterflies. The branches sweep down, then curve upward in graceful gestures, tipped by slender cones. The blue-green nee-dles are as long as whisk brooms and quiver in a river of wind. The cones are among the largest in the genus *Pinus,* a few inches short of a foot long, with thick brown and russet scales.

Although I eagerly studied the homeland flora and fauna, I stopped short of learning too much about the sugar pine, for this tree bore a beauty that preceded fact. It stood apart from any rela-tionship of possession. John Fowles, the English novelist, wrote, "The deepest thing we can learn about nature is not how it works, but that it is the *poetry of survival*." On the flanks of the peak near-est the cabin, when the light was right, I could pick out the sugar pines in the thick forest for a radiance all their own. Each day I tried to note the same two trees, as if their tranquil persistence would fix the wild Sierra, and me, more securely to California's bedrock.

Like those before me, as a young adult I made forays from the cabin into nearby Sequoia National Park on foot and horseback, hardly aware of the border I crossed. Our trails were miles from the busy highway that fed tourists into Giant Forest Village and the drive-by sequoias. The family geography lay in the park's wilder fringes, which remained unroaded not by intent but by virtue of formidable topography and the Park Service's chronic administrative poverty. To reach most places I followed verbal directions from relatives or neighbors, with generous and, I thought, deliciously wicked possibilities for getting lost. I came to know the country from experience and from descriptions such as "Cross the meadow past the lake where so-and-so nearly drowned his sister, who never again went into the water as long as she lived."

Sometimes I drove to a place on the eastern Sierra, where a trail took me to a camp with a high view of the Owens Valley, a deep trough of alluvial fill that lay between the massifs of the Sierra and the Inyo and White Mountains to the east. I pretended I could see all the way into Nevada and probably did. Beneath the Sierra's abrupt escarpment lay an austere desert. I was a pine-cedar dweller, denizen of the mountains' gentler, more temperate west flank. But I knew that I could defect to this desert valley in a heartbeat. From camp at sunset the Sierra cast its shadow over the valley to the Inyos. The shadow was twenty miles across.

I often hiked to a fire lookout tower south of the Whitney crest, where my grandmother's sister spent her summers during World War II. Since both of my grandparents died before the war, before I was born, my great-aunt was one of the few of this generation that I would know. The men of her neighborhood went off to war and, as a single woman and a schoolteacher with free time during the fire season, she went off to her job of keeping a large chunk of the southern Sierra from burning. The tower perched atop an exposed needle of granite. The steel stairs that led to the one-room lookout were narrow, open to abrupt vertical drops on both sides, and always frightening. My great-aunt went up and down these stairs as if they led to a home attic. When summer lightning storms—and her vigilance for fires—were at their fiercest, she sat on a stool whose legs were encased in glass insulators.

In 1929, when she was nine, my mother bellied up to the edge of a sheer cliff on a 14,495-foot Sierra peak and, while someone held her feet, stared down into empty blue-white space. Local newspapers reported her as the youngest child thus far to climb Mt. Whitney. When her family reached the top of the peak, they signed the climbers' book and her mother promptly lay down and took a nap. Ignoring their arduous, rock-scrambling uphill route, my mother and her brother and sister came quickly off the mountain down gravel chutes, wearing the leather off their boots and the seats off their pants. "On that three-week Mt. Whitney trip we saw one other pack train from a distance," she recalled, "and we said the mountains were getting crowded."

Years later I followed her route in the same manner—horse and pack stock from the cabin up the Little Kern River and over Siberian Pass to Whitney's base; final ascent on foot, along the same trails through thick forests of ponderosa, sugar pine, lodgepole, and fir, forests that held the skin on the western Sierra. I saw three parties, advance troops for the coming tsunami of backpackers, and I said the mountains were getting crowded. I camped along the creeks where my mother and her family had fished for native trout with flanks the color of the orange-gold tiger lilies that grew in the Sierra's high meadows. In the years between her trek and mine, golden trout had become rare, but the streams still ran clear and cool between boulders of polished beige granite, where rattlers sunned themselves in graceful coils of diamonds like the red and black patterns on my Yokuts basket.

No other places in Sequoia or its environs drew me like those waters. Their beauty was of a magnitude that touched a threshold of pain. I spent all my summers beside them, not in the alpine or foothill country but at mid-elevations, amid blankets of mustang clover and bracken fern, manzanita, oak, and the first stands of incense cedar and ponderosa. For hours, sometimes days if I had backpacked to a remote place, I would stretch my limbs across a smooth beige boulder beside an emerald river and listen to the water find its way down the mountain. I took from the river a calm primed by something explosive, which, in those days, was precisely the kind of person I wanted to be. *Breathing,* it seemed to me, was a proper attribute for the mountains that knifed through California's heart, mountains that quietly functioned as a single thing with a rhythmic inhale-exhale I could feel whenever I lay facedown on the warm granite, arms outstretched and heart pounding, surrounded by Muir's "glorious array of white peaks deep in the sky, every feature glowing, radiating beauty that pours into the flesh and bones like heat rays from fire."

THE SIERRA DAYS WERE MARKED with long sojourns at the cabin and biweekly trips down the mountain to the valley for supplies. I descended from conifers to chaparral, through mixed oak and grassland, past the reservoir that covered the family ranch, then through citrus groves and into the flats of town and the San Joaquin Valley proper. On the return trip I lingered at only one place: the lemon groves.

Off the highway a dirt road led through endless rows of citrus trees to an unmarked cantina for the Mexicans who worked the fruit. In a shady clearing a woman cooked at a sawhorse-plywood table and a barbecue made from half of a steel drum set on wrought-iron legs. On the coals of orange and lemon wood she simmered pots of frijoles and rice and sold her fare to the workers and pickers. She shaped balls of *masa* dough into tortillas by slapping them back and forth between her hands. She slathered my burrito with the hottest salsa so that everyone could watch what they considered a most amusing phenomenon: a *gringa* rendered speechless by sheer hellfire on her tongue.

The fruit workers convinced me that slapping tortillas eventually wore off your fingerprints so that you could then quit your life as a tortilla maker and lead a life of crime without being caught. I left for the mountains with my fingerprints intact and scar tissue on my chile-seared throat and my pockets full of fragrant, bitter lemons, gifts from the workers.

One summer I rode in the mountains with a Paiute Indian cowboy who, according to local lore, bit the heads off rattlesnakes, but only if they came too close to him. Because he was a large, heavyset man, he needed a strong horse. His pinto grunted when he mounted it, and on searches for stray cattle in the meadows named for my great-grandfather, he teasingly warned me that if he butchered a calf in the field I would have to carry it across my saddle. The idea was preposterous and I knew it. Nevertheless, I was grateful for the times we rode deep inside the national park—no cattle there—so I didn't have to suffer florid chunks of beef in my lap and blood dripping down my kneecaps. All I ever brought home from those sojourns was a head full of high country and the spicy fragrance of bear clover. Warmed by the sun, these groundcover plants, also known as kit-kit-dizze, transferred their spicy fragrance from their thick, resinous leaves to my clothes and skin.

My friend sang strange songs when he ran his hand over the boulders by the river, and the beauty of the land was a cold, hard pain in his chest. So that he could be the only Paiute in the world to smoke like a KGB agent, I taught him to hold a cigarette in the Russian manner, between index finger and thumb, palm toward the face. On our rides at higher altitudes we often lingered at a west-facing outcrop or a clearing between aspen groves. There we dismounted and rested and on sunny days gazed clear across California's girth to the Coast Range a hundred miles away.

To the east lay the Whitney crest and a precipitous plunge to Death Valley and other lowlands of the Great Basin, places of salt and irrational immensity and heat so fierce you stop noticing things. In that rain shadow the Panamint Indians occupied a formidable desert between the Argus, Coso, Funeral, and Panamint Mountains. They traded with the Yokuts and, according to some claims, made finer baskets than any of their neighbors.

One group of Panamints in particular, the Tübatulabal on the Kern River, carried culture and craft between the Yokuts and the desert tribes by virtue of their geographical position between the two groups. The maker of my basket may have seen the baskets of Panamint women, with signature ticking on their rims, and borrowed the design for hers. Perhaps she was of Panamint blood herself and brought the variation with her to the other side of the Sierra. For both groups basketry bound the land to artistry and desire. In contrast, their ceramics were as awkward as homesickness; they did not seem to fit any place that was familiar. Of Yokuts pottery Kroeber wrote, "A row of the vessels looks as if produced by children or experiments."

From a flat bottom of coils my Yokuts basket flares to eighteen inches across, a fit under the full circle of my arm, held on the pelvic bone. Against a field of amber-colored stitches, bands of red diamondbacks edged in black ring the flare, ending in a black chevron border and the unusual and delicate rim ticking. There is a pinpoint hole where the coil begins at the base. Otherwise the dense weave is watertight and meticulously even. Such baskets held acorns, acorn meal, or hot stones for cooking. In larger baskets mothers ferried their babies across rivers. A newborn would fit inside mine.

When I look at this basket, I do not know how it was made, but I know that the soul of the Sierra Nevada went into the weave.

In late summer or early fall the weaver harvested long stalks of deer grass (*Muhlenbergia rigens*) from meadows or sandy places along streams. She cleaned the chaff from the stalks and arranged them in bundles by size. Deer grass was her basket's foundation. For the amber coils in her weft she used saw grass (*Cladium mariscus*). Deer grass and saw grass flourished in an abundance too difficult to conjure now, for they succumbed early to the imperative of whites' agriculture, including my own family's livestock in the 1800s, and all the damming and draining of wetlands that followed.

For the diamondback pattern she found redbud in the brushy chaparral of the foothills and gathered its bark after fall's first frost. Redbud trees (*Cercis occidentalis*) grew amid buckeyes and oaks at an old camp arrayed with grinding mortars, a favored site of Yokuts women. In Anglo time, pack trains assembled at the camp, then headed up the mountain. From this camp my mother, at age six months, made her first trip to the family cabin on horseback, in a sling rigged to the shoulders of a cowboy. A road replaced the pack trail soon thereafter and, in my years at the cabin, the old camp was a roadside picnic area. Today it is the favored venue of unemployed men, who drink beer until they pass out beneath redbud trees covered (if it is springtime) in rose-pink flowers and headdresses of delirious bees.

With the root of the bracken fern (*Pteridium aquilinum*), the basketmaker bordered the red diamonds in black and sent the V's of geese flying around the rim. She collected the roots in spring or fall and split them into two parts, keeping one and discarding the other. (As neighboring basketmakers of the Western Mono group advised, "Throw the belly away.") By burying the roots in mud, the black might be intensified.

At cabin elevations bracken fern grew under the sequoia, ponderosa, and cedar that filled the yard. The lacy ferns greened up in June around the time the rivers dropped after spring runoff and trout could be pulled from calmer waters. In this sun-dappled "lawn" of green feathers I sat with my sketchbook, drawing the ferns and miner's lettuce, wild ginger, ponderosa pine cones, kit-kit-dizze, anything that might impart knowledge of the Sierra by re-creating its shapes and forms through my awkward hand. The results looked as if made by children or experiments.

Many times I have tried to imagine the Yokuts woman selling her basket to my great-great-grandmother Sarah, in a foothill ranch cut through by an eager river. Family stories and old photographs help me to envision their surroundings and Sarah herself in long skirts and buttons up to the neck, maybe wearing the gold cufflinks that I have since inherited, her eyes large and round, her hair pulled back to a trim knot. The Yokuts woman cannot be easily conjured. Is she from the winter camp east of the ranch known to her people as Shawahtau? Is she Sarah's age? How deep has she ground her mortars into the Sierra's silver granite? Like the Paiute basketmaker in Mary Austin's *Land of Little Rain,* did she make her basket for love and sell it for money, in a generation that desired cast-iron pots?

Around the women are rosebushes and behind them is a porch with rocking chairs. The Indians who work on the ranch often ask to take turns sitting in them, and Sarah and her successors never refuse. Across the arc of blue air that separates bodies of common womanliness lies a chasm of social difference. On Sundays, Sarah bakes a cake for her children, a yellow slab cake with a glaze of sweet white icing. The Yokuts woman feeds her children the seed meal of California black oaks and the tongues of meadowlarks to make their speech agile. The basketmaker has no rights, no welcome to the land her people know better than anyone, its bracken fern and redbud and the seasons that mark the time to cut deer grass and pull the strands through her teeth to make them supple. The story keepers are assembling the details of Sarah's family tenure in this place—the cake, the rosebushes, the rocking chairs—but the Indian woman's stories are displaced and unraveling. She and her family are lower in status than the ranch's Mexican shearers. Here against the silken layers of the Sierra, she hands over this work of great beauty, while others rest and rock in creaky chairs.

Sarah and her family witnessed the removal of most of the Indians to reservations and missions, where they traded their eagle-down skirts for cloth and buttons up to the neck. By the time Sarah's granddaughter inherited the basket—in barely two generations—the Yokuts had been reduced to a fraction of their original numbers, less than 5 percent in Kroeber's estimate of the 1910 census. Eventually, fewer and fewer knew how to weave baskets, dig tule roots, turn fish belly-up in a river, and be mothers to *hiauta,* the clowns of contrary actions, whom I envy for the perfect clarity of not getting along with the world so that you must live it backward, finding humor and edges in all that is ordinary and all that is sacred.

VERY SELDOM, only on a scattering of clear days, can you see what the Paiute cowboy and I saw on our rides: the breadth of

California from the Sierra to the Coast Range. Haze now reduces the view to five miles or less, and more than 30 million people live within a day's drive of Sequoia and Kings Canyon National Parks. Space atop Mt. Whitney is rationed; you need a reservation to climb it from the east. The granite pinnacles beneath the once remote fire lookout tower manned by my great-aunt during the war are now wrapped in rock climbers, ropes, pitons, and passive nuts. The family ranch lies under a reservoir. Yokuts basketmaking has few practitioners. The cantina is gone, and so are the lemon groves, replaced by houses and convenience stores. Several women hikers have been assaulted along river reaches easily accessible to roads. At least in the front country, solitude no longer comes without fear, a fear that severs Sierra women from the emerald river and pale curves of watersmooth granite that hold us to the breath of the mountains.

It has come quickly, this crushing, industrial love of paradise. The pervert-free, less-trammeled, hundred-mile-view days were little more than two decades past, not so very long ago. Yet already my own history sounds like another country.

The true heart of a place does not come in a week's vacation. To know it well, as Mary Austin wrote, one must "wait its occasions"—follow full seasons and cycles, a retreating snowpack, a six-year drought, a ponderosa pine eating up a porch. Wild mountains offer a promise of undomesticated life, even in so overdomesticated a place as California, and by necessity and sheer numbers of nature-starved pilgrims, visits there must be brief. I was fortunate to be a transient with a longer tenure and a family imprint. Memory, however, can still ignite a consuming longing for those Sierra days of witless youth and enflamed senses. I still carry the land so deep in my bones that I cannot bear to go back.

In times of drought, when food was scarce, Paiute women cut their long hair to make snares for trapping quail. California quail were not on my wild-food diet because I did not like the idea of roasting their frail chests. I kept to miner's lettuce, elderberries, manzanita-berry tea, and survival rations from raids on distant supermarkets. My Scots grandfather hunted birds with a shotgun, in knickers, necktie, and argyle socks. His daughters and grand-daughters took from him his height and from the mountains their own stories.

Today no one in the family, nuclear or extended, lives in the Sierra homelands. The sole member of the Paiute KGB died. When I breathe the scent from an old sprig of kit-kit-dizze stuck in one of my books, the fragrance grounds me to my years—my "worlds"—in the Sierra Nevada. In a Yokuts basket dancing with geese and rat-tlesnakes, I see my ancestral landscape. Perhaps to know so familiar a place better it must become strange again.

AhaMakav Walkabout

Always remember that the value of any given stone is
strictly dependent upon how much someone wants it—
that is, a stone's value is by no measure absolute.

R. V. Dietrich
Stones

The Pediment

S tand in the parched and wide-open Mojave.
        To your back a twisted escarpment of rock rises abruptly
from the floodplain, its peaks as jagged as shark's teeth. These
mountains are utterly bare and nearly waterless, announcing what
you can expect from them: a tension that is precise and useful.

Stone by stone, down clefts and canyons etched with vigorous
erosion, the mountains cast themselves off and bury their flanks in
a broad apron of their own debris. The apron forms a bajada, a gently sloped terrace carved with dry washes. A scattered veneer of alluvial gravel overlays the terrace's surface, or pediment, turning the
landscape the color of moths. Wind, weather, and desert varnish
have given each piece of gravel a lustrous patina. Most of the chocolate-brown stones are so darkly patinated they cast blue-violet hues
where they fracture or their edges keel. This darkness is startling
because the stones lie against a surface as pale as candles.

The light and dark are seen as random scatter unless you stoop down and set aside the stones to reveal larger areas of pallid ground. Let's say you do this in long parallel rows about three feet apart, a natural spacing if you walk along and work the rock at arm's length. You pick up or brush aside the surface materials until they pile in eight-inch-high ridges lined across the desert. You rearrange the pediment: dark stones in rows, paths of pale bared ground between them.

You run your rows straight, sometimes curved. Sometimes you widen or detour the path around a stone with particular meaning. Along the peripheries of the terrace you end your rows abruptly at a place that makes no sense—not at the precipice of a deep-cut wash where erosion would otherwise erase them, but in the middle of nowhere. In places you run a series of rows into another series of rows. Thus your bared paths dead-end when they intersect other paths. You can easily step over the berms of stone into the next path, but you don't. Although you are working the terrace entirely by hand, from a hawk's view the pattern looks as if a giant raked tool is scraping contoured grooves into the pediment, from the foot of the mountains to the lip of the terrace.

Farthest from the seam where the mountains meet the terrace, you open the rows to another junction: terrace and river. The river flows across an enormous expanse of desert that is flat but for another saw-toothed island of rock on the opposite bank, mountains turned watery blue by distance. You have seen the river swell and edge against the toe of the terrace. Downstream from your rows of stone the river tongues into a sharp, narrow gorge—this, too, a kind of seam or portal.

The floodplain speaks of life, with the river's power at the edge of memory like a nervous tic. In the whiteness of the sun you drop off the terrace and go to the river to rest and eat. The gorge splices the mountains, a deep gash between the shark's teeth. There you must move differently, as if ghosts are trying to tip you over.

The summer air crackles with dry lightning. Far into the distance monsoons roll northward, clouds with bellies full of moist air pulled from the distant ocean. Time passes. You move rock. The autumn stars are bright enough to bore holes in your head. The mountains finger their winter cold across your back. The spring sun rises to full and vibrant mornings, then sets as a ball of orange against violet.

Perhaps you build the rows alone, but others likely help you. Someone may know the design that will emerge, the sum of the parts, and why it must be so. Perhaps they dreamed it and try to make it true to what they dreamed. Your dreams reveal themselves while you sleep by the big river: a shimmer of copper-colored water that pools below the dark mountains, a platter of songbirds laid before you, damp, delicate gray fox noses nuzzling your ears. Soon you have moved so many stones the pattern itself becomes part of your dreams.

You work for many days, many years, moving cobbles and pebbles by hand. By day the sun-heated stones scald your fingertips. At night the moon silvers the rows into luminous stitches against the gnarled mountains above them, the mother of each stone. From the wear on the stones' surfaces you can decipher the direction of the prevailing winds.

You know where to start the rows and where to turn them. The turns are sinuous. All of the rows are perfectly even. You move millions of pieces of cast-off mountain into the bermed paths. The paths cover one full sweep of the depositional fan in front of the mountains. There is one path bigger than what you have made: the river. When the sun gathers warmth and the days grow long, the river runs below your marked terrace in a widening swath, as if spreading was more important than flowing, as if gravity was a nuisance.

The Dreamer

You are a fish eater and grower of beans. No, not a bean grower, a sleeper so laden with dreams that all during the day you carry them into waking as thick stones, as stories that leave the flavors of fog in your head until the stones of the next night's sleep replace them. On some nights your rest is as deep as blood. On other nights it is the fragile sleep in which something remains alert, like a night lit by the full moon. No matter the depth of sleep, you dream. You dreamed before birth, you dream all your life, you will dream in the afterlife, while you are the ghost in a deep rocky gorge, the ghost you are before you become charcoal strewn on the desert floor.

You speak your dreams aloud. The people around you pronounce them ordinary or great—just another mental image of the cattail trail, the one that leads to the beanfield, or a dream with enough power to alter everyone's behavior, to march them off to the Pacific for shells with pink pearled cusps or to launch the omen of death before a person dies, singing the not-yet-dead person's mourning song, upsetting everyone with all your wailing and shrieking.

The reason that you can dream or walk to the Pacific or go to war: You are well fed. What feeds you is the big river in an enormous desert. Distant mountains, a cordillera of snowy rock that straddles the continent, gather the river in their crowns and in spring unloose it in a swollen torrent that overflows the banks and covers the sandy bottomlands. Behind the flood the receding waters deposit the rich silt that grows your crops.

Beyond the river, above the floodplain, lie bone-dry aprons of land where ragged ribs of mountains shed and bury themselves up to their shoulders in broken stone. A worn trail leads to a terrace near the mouth of the gorge that splits the mountain range in two. On this terrace lies a maze of paths made by lifting and scraping aside dark stones from a pale desert. The maze of rows is vast. It has been there longer than anyone can remember. It holds its makers' truth and the compulsion of others to lie about it. Nevertheless, you and your people have explanations for it.

When stones are moved and rearranged, they speak to other worlds. You remember the evil giant that terrorized the river people until they shaped a god of stone, flat on the desert floor, to intimidate the giant. When you relate these stories to the white people who move into the river valley, the white people say, *You are dreaming.*

IN NEVADA WITH PLINY

Four panting breaths short of heatstroke I have come to the conclusion that Pliny the Elder and a road map from 1940 are inadequate guides to the Mojave Desert.

The antiquated map marks Death Valley, the lower Colorado River, the joining borders of California, Nevada, and Arizona, and so few roads that they look like a two-legged spider smashed on a white sheet. I fell off the landmarks into the map's blank spaces, seeking the sites of old turquoise mines. I am so close to a border, I could be in California or in Nevada. This ambiguity allows me to take the land for itself: a 360-degree sweep of the infernal Mojave. If you are asked for its color you will have to say that this desert is the color of creosote bushes, a vegetable green with an odd cast of rust.

Most of the dirt roads and railroad spurs that once fed the mining settlements have faded into faint scrapes on the desert floor, enfolded in creosote, cholla, and other scrub. I cannot define the actual sites of the turn-of-the-century mines and, because the temperature is approaching a hundred degrees, I want to stop looking for them.

From the gneiss, schist, and granite porphyry the miners extracted blue stone of marketable grade. They worked near caves and saucerlike pits filled with debris, remnants left by turquoise seekers who preceded them by at least a thousand years. Stone hammers, adzes, and small bits of turquoise were found amid the prehistoric workings, which stretched for fifteen miles across the desert. The nearby cliffs and boulders in jumbled rockfalls bore an abundance of ancient rock art, including what archaeologists of the time were calling "Aztec water signs"—petroglyphs, they said, that pointed the way to springs.

Although the mines that I cannot find were exhausted by the early 1900s, in Nevada other turquoise mines in other locales would eventually become among the most productive in the country. In sun that burns white-hot I say aloud the names of Nevada mines for a coolness that a word might bring. The Blue Fern Mine. The Blue Goose Claim. The Blue Jay, Blue Matrix, Blue Friday, Blue Silver, Easter Blue Mines. Mines that come in shades—New, Royal, and Sky Blue—and in certainty: the Right Blue Claim. Turquoise from the Nevada mines bore a notable amount of matrix, stone with thin veinlets of other minerals. Without the matrix, it was said to be the purest sky-blue in color.

I drink another quart of water and pull out my copy of *Natural History*, an encyclopedia of science and art by Pliny the Elder, a Roman naturalist in the first century A.D. "The nature of stones remains to be considered—a particular source of irresponsible behaviour in men," he wrote toward the end of his text. He lambasted underground mining as criminal, an act that unearthed greed, self-indulgence, and cheating along with the ore. He wondered why humans sought minerals from "the bowels of the earth where the spirits of the dead have their abode, as though the part we walk upon is not sufficiently bountiful and productive." The earth's outer skin—like this jumbled surface of rock and sand scattered across the backside of California (or is it Nevada?)—held for Pliny more than adequate riches and fascination.

Even without wresting it from earth disemboweled and turned upside down, humans *move* rock. We simply use stones as they might be picked up. Stones make paperweights and counter-weights, doorstops and surfaces on which to flail laundry. They weigh down pearl divers, suicides by drowning, and the core of the Great Wall of China. They anchor heavy boats and thin filaments of fishing line. They fill a gaucho's bola and miles of riprap. Hansel,

Gretel, and thousands of hikers use them to mark trails. Sea otters break shells with them, and male Adélie penguins present stones to their mates during the building of nests.

In situ or hauled from afar, stones were moved by ancient people and arranged on the earth's surface in cryptic shapes. I am traveling in a region with an extraordinary concentration of stones moved for ritual, not mined or quarried but simply used as they might be picked up, used to connect earth life to a mythical one.

While Pliny considered gold to be a crime against humanity, in the realm of gemstones he succumbed to the seduction of color. For their color, luster, hardness, and scarcity, gems arouse human desire. Gems are useful as well as ornamental, Pliny said. Emeralds soothe weary eyes, amethysts cure drunkenness, beryls imitate the green of the sea. In precious stones, he wrote, "Nature reaches its utmost concentration and in no department does she arouse more wonder."

Turquoise was among the precious stones known to the ancients, but in the minds of later scholars and gemologists Pliny did not clearly differentiate it from chrysolite and other blue-green stones. Some argue that what Pliny called *callaina* was peridot, also known as olivine, rather than turquoise. Pliny's *callaina* was coveted by people so accustomed to riding horseback, or so fearful of climbing to its protrusions among the "frozen and inaccessible rocks," they would instead "attack the stones with slings from a distance and so bring them down, moss and all."

It is argued that what Pliny called *callais* was more analogous to turquoise than was *callaina*. Sitting in the shade of a boulder, I imbibe his description. "The *callais* is like *sapphiros* [lapis lazuli] in color, only that it is paler and more closely resembles the tint of water near the seashore in appearance." This phrase plunges me into such vibrant hallucinations of the luscious turquoise coasts of the Gulf Stream, Caribbean, and South Pacific, I feel as if cactus spines are penetrating my cranium. I am not walking, I am cowering.

The horizon ripples. The midday Mojave sun pounds out a

hard chalky light. It seems impossible that the bleached desert air, the tawny rock and sand, could have held in its skin a stone the color of a parrot's wing. Today only a large body of water would carry the intense colors of cooling depth, and the nearest body of water lies southeast of these unfound mines. I pack up Pliny and leave the shade of the boulder. In the truck I sit with my face pressed to the air-conditioning vents. Then I head off the blank spaces toward the spider legs of marked territory on the old road map.

Tethered to the Hellish

Before the railroad and the modern highways, crossing the Mojave Desert was a terrifying prospect—an obstacle to life itself—or, at best, a tedious bore across a boundless "sandscape." Even today, with preparation and comforts, there lingers at the edge of travel the knowledge that the heat and aridity can kill you, and if they do not, you might die from the intimidating despair evoked by a vast emptiness that is wholly indifferent to your existence.

Then and now, much of life in the Mojave is spent as a crossing. Culture along the old Route 66 and the interstate highway that replaced it is a transient culture with a self-contained civilization to supply it with fuel, food, lodging, and jackalope postcards. In the days of rough and often impassable roads, a few migrants took up residence in the desert towns where their cars broke down. However, the preponderance of travelers had new, California lives in their future and Arizona and previous lives in their rearview mirrors. Before the advent of motorized leisure—four-wheel drive, dirt bikes, recreational vehicles with generators powerful enough to air-condition small Middle Eastern countries—the Mojave was not a place to travel for the hell of it. That is, unless you were born to a people who were tethered to the hellish by blood, culture, and curiosity.

Although the Mohave Indians traded goods with groups on

the Pacific coast, there is evidence that trade, and raids or war on their enemies, were frequently secondary reasons for their treks. Mohaves simply liked to walk over two hundred miles to the ocean, east to the Hopi mesas, or to other places beyond their homelands along the lower Colorado River. Notorious aggressors, notorious travelers, the Mohave routinely slaughtered their neighbors and routinely crisscrossed the desert to take in the sights. "They liked to see lands," wrote anthropologist Alfred Kroeber, "timidity did not discourage them; and they were as eager to know the manners of other people as they were careful to hold aloof from adopting them."

Mohave magnanimity allowed the Chemehuevi, a seminomadic group, to remain along the river south of them in peace (sometimes). Mohave ferocity led them to join the neighboring Quechan in campaigns against the Cocopa, a group on the Colorado River delta known for their elaborate mourning ceremonies, held today in the reservation's Cry Houses. After attacks on the Maricopa the Mohave warriors trotted home from the Maricopa settlements on the Gila River. According to Kroeber's informants, a group would sleep one night on Maricopa soil, five nights in Yavapai territory, and one night in Walapai territory, then arrive home on the eighth— eight days to cover more than 150 miles as the crow flies, an arduous journey on the rugged, nearly waterless ground. For a pack a warrior attached his gear to his bow with pieces of twine. In this way he might carry hide sandals, arrows, a wooden club, a gourd water bottle in a fiber net bag, a small sack of mesquite seeds for food, and a hair ornament of flicker feathers.

The Mohave defined their desert with the most fundamental poetry of human experience: the naming of places. A river slough might be a river slough, but the name *fear slough* gave it a past, a story, a meaning, and a guarantee against dislocation on a Mohave walk. From the Mohave language Kroeber translated compound place names of "unwieldy length": fear slough, whispering place, cut earth, fat earth; three mountains, sharp mountain, blue mountain; owls regarding each other, mosquito cannot, dove's breast; willow water, duck water, no water.

Mohave rituals were simple to the point of insignificance, Kroeber noted, except for funerals and a storytelling that was largely based on the images of the subconscious. Whatever a Mohave knew, he or she knew it from their dreams. The clear or tangled images of sleep became a body of knowledge. Distant groups had sweathouses and kivas, but the Mohave stood up anywhere and sang their dreams in repeated cycles. Alfred Kroeber heard their songs. He describes them as

a style of literature which is as . . . decorative as a patterned textile. The pattern is far from random; but it is its color and intricacy, its fineness or splendor, that have meaning, not the action told by its figures; and as a simple but religious people don the same garment for festivity or worship, for dress or interment, provided only it is gorgeously pleasing enough, so the Mohave weave their many myths in one ornamental style and sing them on every occasion that calls for music.

Kroeber, to whom a captive Yahi Indian named Ishi once taught a thing or two, devoted time and ink to the Mohave in his 1925 Bureau of Ethnology opus, *Handbook of the Indians of California*. He liked the Mohave. Against them, even with his thick Eurocentric filter, he considered other California natives "sluggish" and "unresponsive." He wrote of the Mohave, "Altogether it is a nation, half child, half warrior, likeable in its simple spontaneity, and commanding respect with its inherent manliness."

Mohaves were imposingly tall (many of them over six feet), copiously tattooed (women as well as men), and destined to go to a rat's hole instead of a pleasant after-death place if they went through life without tattoos. Kroeber describes them as good swimmers, voracious eaters and jokers, obstinate and never shy, and disdainful of excess material goods, which were burned with their bodies at their funerals.

They called themselves *hamakhav* and their valley the Aha-Makav (*aha* is the word for water). Their melons, beans, corn, and pumpkins grew with the tempo of a flooding and receding Colorado River. For food they favored fish more than wild game. Their pottery often bore the design of a fish bone or the leaf of a cottonwood, the totem tree of the lower Colorado before dams and reservoirs drowned the once considerable galleries that grew along the riverbanks. In historic times the Mohave took to glass trade beads with extraordinary eagerness and wore them against their mahogany skin as neck and wrist strands and carefully beaded shoulder capes. Almost exclusively they chose beads of bright white and cobalt blue, the blue of deep, deep time.

An hour's drive from the turquoise mines, I am still reluctant to leave my mobile air-conditioning unit to head across the desert on foot. I bear no delusions that I could survive a Mohave walk. I know how to move my limbs in a desert, but I do not *know* anything—where to find water, how to pace a journey, what kind of snare would trick a rabbit, how to cook a yucca, how to make use of hallucinations, where to cross the serrated mountain ranges that rise up from the low-lying basins like the backs of a fleet of stegosauruses. If, here on a patch of desert south of Needles, California, I had native guides, perhaps I might go along as a topophiliac and a heavy dreamer, endearing myself to people for whom geography and dreams were nearly an obsession. The most difficult premise of this fantasy: how to envision the terrain of the pre-Columbian river people, how to make any progress once we trekkers took our very first step. The challenges to a twenty-first-century Mohave walk are formidable.

In the past hundred years the river has been massively reengineered to feed the thirsts of California agribusiness and the urban Southwest. The river makes the joining borders of California, Arizona, and Nevada curvy and wobbly compared to the other survey-straight lines that define them. In flow and velocity, however, the river no longer resembles its description in the 1939 Works Progress Administration guidebook to California, "a lazy-looking stream that periodically goes on a bridge-smashing rampage." From Glen Canyon Dam on the Arizona-Utah border, minus a brief hiccup of wild water through the Grand Canyon, downstream to Hoover Dam and on to what was once its delta at Mexico's Sea of Cortez, the red-brown, silt-laden Colorado River is now greenish, sometimes blue, but no longer *colorado* nor river. It is a series of reservoirs pinched by a string of dams. One of these reservoirs will cool me off.

Pipelines, pumps, canals, trailer parks, and marinas penetrate the banks, but no invader can match the tamarisk, a Eurasian shrub that dominates the riparian Southwest. Thick jungles of these gauzy-leafed exotics block anyone foolish enough to want to take a quiet walk along the reservoir known as Lake Mohave. To find an easier approach I pull into a small park, a patch of manicured nature devoted to getting motorboats into the water and day-users down paved paths to picnic tables.

Lake Mohave couture is baggy shorts and string bikinis and a chilled long-neck in every fist. At the sight of public beer I glance around furtively, expecting a raid of arrests, if not collective scorn, then I think to myself, My God, I've been in Utah too long. Around me are sixteen-year-old girls in Wonderbras who could dismantle and reassemble twin 75-horse Mercs in sixty seconds. In age everyone seems to postdate the bridge-smashing Colorado by at least two generations. For them the river has never been a river except in name and in old photographs of dust-blown flats, sluggish, silty water, and gaunt, hollow-cheeked families out of *The Grapes of Wrath*.

The lake pulsates with jet boats, Jet Skis, jet everything. The interstate parallels its shore; streams of traffic flow through the desert, one on asphalt, one on water. I park a mile or two down the road from the busy marina and bushwhack through the tamarisk in search of a quieter beach. Edged against pale, goldish sand, the water is blue enough to cool me down—that is, if I can find enough of it for a swim. The shoreline is solid with boats and Jet Skis, some parked, others moving, leaving very little space between them. The entire state of California is here, boating. I can continue to die of heatstroke or I can swim and be pulverized by a dozen boat propellers. I feel like a cheap raisin in a giant compacter.

On the riverbank I find a patch of shallow water jammed with mothers and their toddlers. I slip into the lake. To wet more than my kneecaps I must lie down, trying not to knock over any toddlers. The water is lukewarm and murky, but I feel refreshed and emerge with all limbs intact. Then I head off for a Mohave walk on a bluff above the river.

The Maze

The bluff holds a monument so ancient and enigmatic, surely it must be holy. But it most definitely is not a park or museum. It is a battered piece of industrial frontage. I am hemmed in by the buzzing marina, the interstate highway's broad corridor, railroad tracks, a swarming mesh of pipelines carrying natural gas, a rock quarry, and a gas compressor station, an enormous power plant that hums loudly and vibrates the ground beneath my feet.

When I face the river, at my back lies a razorback of gray-brown rock so abrupt and craggy it looks like shark's teeth. Predating the industrial clutter, my 1940 map shows these mountains as the Chemehuevis and a cluster of spiky pinnacles as the Needles. The map also marks a few scattered towns and the reservations that are now home to the indigenous river peoples. But it was a descriptive notation on the map that sucked me away from the crowded river. "Rock Maze," it reads. "According to legend, built so the spirits of the dead could shake off the evil ones pursuing them in these tangled paths."

I was with my husband when I first saw this place, which is also known as the Mystic Maze or the Topock Maze, named for a nearby town on the Arizona side of the river. Neither of us knew what to expect. Denizens of canyon country, we pictured a deep sandstone labyrinth with elbow-grazing walls and a slot of sky above our heads—a "mule twister," as they call such canyons at home in southern Utah, perhaps a crack in the flank of the shark-teeth mountains.

We searched a desert bluff stitched with vehicle tracks, gas line access roads, and piles of discarded motor-oil bottles. The Mystic Maze, I told Mark in my most mystic voice, where the spirits of the living come to shake off their evil oil filters. It seemed an oil-changing, bottle-smashing, flung-condoms sort of place until we looked harder and arrived at the site. Today I know where to find it.

On this treeless, tawny bluff above the Colorado River, row after row of sun-polished stones parallel one another in curving swaths. The furrows between the stone berms are as wide as a foot-path and slightly depressed into the desert floor. The rows run in concentric as well as intersecting patterns, giving the impression that someone has contour-plowed the entire crunching pediment. Imagine a rugged desert surface blanketed by a mosaic of stones, the detritus of the eroding mountains above it. Then imagine this surface rearranged by hand, stone by stone, to outline paths side by side in curving swathes that lead nowhere.

I set off into the maze with a bottle of water and no intentions. The fierce afternoon sun slowly descends toward the western hori-zon, where layers of mountains recede in ripples of silken blue-violet. The paths beneath my sandals are pale Mojave buff, the color of earth exposed when the stones were removed. The piled stones bear a lustrous coating of weathered minerals, the deep brown patina of weather and desert varnish. Their darkness has absorbed the day's solar fire. They are scorching to the touch. They leave the scent of stone heat on my hands.

◆ ◆ ◆

THE MAZE FALLS into the archaeologist's category of geoglyph (some use the term *intaglio*), earth art created by clearing stones and gravel from the desert pediment in a purposeful design. The Pleistocene pavements of the lower Colorado and Gila Rivers made a perfect medium for geoglyphs: gravel mounds, rock alignments, and cleared circles; paths trodden in repeated patterns, over and over, by slow-dancing feet; anthropomorphic and animal figures and geometric designs so large they are best seen from the vantage of a raptor circling above them on a thermal.

In a feature common to several geoglyphs, dance paths splice the kneecaps of human figures, as if that was the right place of contact. On other geoglyphs, bulldozer or Jeep trails cross dance circles, figures—kneecaps and all—and paths that according to ethnographic accounts may represent the Milky Way. There are over two hundred known geoglyphs in the lower Colorado region, a few in the Panamint Valley to the west, and more in the volcanic *pedregal* of Sonora, Mexico, to the southeast. It is as if this desert inspired an enigmatic picture mapping, *a directing of attention* in space so open and soaring, both your body and your vision need grounding.

Although the maze likely predates European contact, its age is unclear, given variously as five hundred to a thousand years or more. It has been open to vandalism for at least a century. It covers about ten acres, the remains of an estimated eighteen-acre, more extensive and complex geoglyph at the site. Railroad construction in the late nineteenth century obliterated much of its northern portion, including what would have been its intriguing junction with the river. A highway took away more of the maze in the 1970s. Off-road vehicles, the most common instrument of damage to the region's intaglios, gnawed at the remnant until a fence was built to protect it.

A labyrinth has rhythmic paths to its center. A maze is a labyrinth with tangled paths, dead ends, and confusion. Physical mazes, but more often their images, in parallel lines or circular form, are found throughout the world. The geoglyph at Topock is not a true maze in the sense of a walked puzzle. The term "maze" is the imposition of an Anglo culture. Collectively, the rows do not add up to a discernible shape nor do they ask you to find a way in or out. They sweep across the terrace like the contour lines of a topographical map writ large. If oral history is accurate, they once framed the more organic, recognizable figure of a human being.

Railroad tracks laid in 1891 ran through what might have been the maze's heart, stranding two small islands off the main section. According to observers at the time, the disturbed area erased an intaglio of an anthropomorphic figure with a distinct left hand and a right arm holding a wavy, serpentlike line that ran down along the body and wrapped the figure's foot. Made the same way the maze was made—moving rock by hand and tamping down the bared pediment—the figure was allegedly 150 feet long and 60 feet wide, with its head on the river end and its feet toward the craggy escarpment.

Descriptions of the anthropomorph were verbal, the recollections of old-timers who saw it before the railroad construction, but they were not far-fetched. In form the figure would have resembled petroglyphs elsewhere in the Mojave. In scale it resembled other desert intaglios, including a male figure far downriver that held a serpent (or whip or lightning bolt) in his hand ("male" because of a penis nearly as long as his legs).

In historic times Anglos in the Needles area believed the Mohave Indians built the maze for ceremonial purposes. Postcards sold by the Fred Harvey Company at the railroad station in Needles showed a drawing of "the Mystic Maze of the Mojave Indians" as a cross between a true maze-puzzle and a too-green farm field with windrows, plus a few fantasy saguaro cacti and a rather Siouxlooking warrior on horseback. The Mohave claimed the maze as theirs, albeit the work of the "old ones," referring to cultures that predated their arrival in the lower Colorado River country in the tenth century. Either way, very few people disputed its aboriginal origin unless it was expedient to do so. In order to alter the site without public backlash, there had to be a logic of "no harm": If the intaglio was not a monument of antiquity, its destruction would not matter.

In 1883, the Atlantic & Pacific Railroad of Topeka, Kansas, built a cantilever bridge across the river at Topock, just below the terrace. In 1891, the year track was to be laid to the bridge, a report by the American Society of Civil Engineers stated that Mohave laborers had raked the terrace rows during bridge construction, collecting tons of gravel to support the piers. Others suggested that teams of horses pulling a fresno scraper had carved the windrows. In other words, the "maze" was a modern rock quarry, not a treasure of antiquity. The track building proceeded, with the railroad engineers assuring the public that nothing was being demolished but the remnants of earlier commercial construction.

Extensive research by Arda M. Haenszel of the San Bernardino County Museum, published in 1978, provided careful and strong evidence for the maze's prehistoric rather than commercial origin. There is little doubt that laborers hauled gravel for the bridge piers, Haenszel said. However, the gravel likely came from a different source, one closer to the river or on the Arizona side. Some Mohave informants remembered the raking of gravel, others stated that the maze had long been used for sacred rites. Nevertheless, when the tracks to the bridge were laid in 1891, the human-snake intaglio and the northern portion of the maze disappeared.

The people of Needles and San Bernardino County not only knew about the Mystic Maze, they defended it in what were unenlightened times. According to Haenszel, there was citizen resistance to the railroad route over the site in 1891. Route 66 and some of the natural gas lines were later rerouted south of the maze, "just in case the Maze was really prehistoric," Haenszel wrote. However, the engineers of Interstate 40 in the 1970s were rabid disciples of the straight line, and the swath needed for the four-lane that sped people between Los Angeles and Arizona was a broad one. It nibbled away another corner of the maze. In 1976, a motorcycle club proposed a hundred-mile course for a cross-country race, with a concession stand and restrooms atop the terrace and a race section directly through part of the maze. The San Bernardino County Museum Association and its Needles chapter persuaded the responsible authorities to deny approval of the race course. Volunteers then partially fenced the site.

You will still find people who are convinced that the maze was a prehistoric farm, sown to grow corn and beans in neat rows and to direct irrigation water from the river. Never mind a few pesky contradictions to this theory: The rugged apron of pediment along the foot of the mountains hardly seems arable; tidy, contoured, Missouri-style rows were not the way of early farmers, who used digging sticks and plots. If you peel off the highways, reservoirs, compression plant, railroad tracks, and a number of centuries, the paths seem to honor a different miracle.

The "maze" is a detailed form made giant in scale. In *Overlay*, art writer Lucy R. Lippard speculates that prehistoric geoglyphs in North and South America were "so large, and almost incomprehensible from the ground, they are assumed to have been intended for the hovering spirits alone." For cultures that did not fly (unless by astral projection), an "aerial" view was possible simply through the fundamental concept of mapping, the fusion of the real and the abstract. You could, in your head, imagine the maze. You could, on the ground, translate that image onto eighteen acres.

The Mohave Indians, heirs of the maze, shed faint light on its history and purpose. Their lore may be the origin of the "Rock Maze" annotation on my 1940 map—bad spirits losing their way in a stone puzzle so that good spirits could safely reach the afterlife. Like the map, the 1939 WPA guidebook to California associates the geoglyph with the supernatural: "Resembling at a distance a plowed field, this work of prehistoric aborigines is believed to have been a place for funeral rites. . . . A local legend relates that the spirits of the dead, floating down the Colorado, entered the maze and shook off the evil spirits chasing them by losing them in the tangled pathways."

Like maps, geographical focal points pull together land, sky, and human experience. They are stills of a journey. What if the maze was a journey? What if, after death, your soul had to travel across the desert, much like the treks of your lifetime, and you had to know the way or be lost and forever thirsty?

The soul of a Mohave was sung off the cremation pyre by the mourners. The soul rode the songs and high-pitched wails down-river to the land of the dead, where there were other souls and plenty of food. The land of the dead was not distant. It was neither subterranean nor celestial. It was close by, near the Needles, the slab of metamorphic rock that spikes out the desert to comb the dry air with its sharky peaks. After a second death and cremation by other ghosts, your soul would end up not in eternity but as charcoal strewn across the desert.

The makers of the sign presently at the site—more recent than my antique map and guidebook, and likely made with Mohave assistance—believe that walkers with bodies used the maze; the maze was built for the living. "To this site the AhaMakav warriors returning from battle first paused for purification before continuing home," the sign reads. Because the stone berms are barely a foot high, and I can see across the bluff from here to wide-open eternity, this is not a place of blind alleys and physical confusion. Instead, the paths can be compared to the *ceques,* ancient processional ways incised into the plains of Nazca in Peru. Followed long enough, the paths might reveal a route. The route might lead to nothing else but a necessary faith in time.

THE TOASTER

The maze's silence begs for narrative. Legends ease their way across its strangeness, shaped by quirk and desire. Humans long for connection and continuity, for insight into the past endeavors of their species that ultimately affirm their own lives, whether by empathy or by contrast. For postmodern empiricists, foggy indeterminacy won't do. Knowledge must be tidy with meaning, the mysteries solved, the experiences beneath the dust carefully measured. When we forage for stories, we may end up telling our own. When we cannot possess the thoughts of past cultures, we possess their *things*.

This is what I love best about museums in small towns: the marvelous shuffle of *things* and the indomitable women who tend them. By accident or by intent, the museum in Needles, California, housed in a storefront near the old railroad station, specializes in the ordinary. It is both a collection and a hoard. Its proprietors are desert women of retirement age, who keep the shelves and aisles crammed and interesting.

Needles is a railroad town, with more railroadness in its past than in its present. The museum holds paraphernalia from the golden age of rails, when the transcontinental trains stopped in the heart of the Mojave Desert as they traveled to and from the green promise of southern California. Like so many others, I, too, passed through this place on a train, in utero, when my pregnant mother and toddler brother returned home to California from Texas. Old photographs in the museum show El Garcés, the railway hotel that refreshed the passengers beneath an oasis of palms. Fenced off and boarded up, a grand palace of pigeon habitat, the station now awaits restoration.

Beneath a panoramic photograph of El Garcés in its prime, its employees lined up to pose on its lawn, lies a jumble of manos and metates, prehistoric stone tools for grinding cornmeal. On a shelf of manos a handwritten tag reads, "C—— found in his garage. May have more items." There are Navajo rugs, "Mojave Dolls made of Topock clay," and *ollas* in pale yellow clay painted with red leaf fronds and bighorn sheep—"maybe Mohave, maybe Chemehuevi," says a tag with an honest confusion about the pottery's origins from local river tribes. Baskets have come from the Pomo and Mono in California and the Pima and Papago of Arizona. An exquisite Pueblo-style bowl has come from a donor who insists that it always stay in Needles. It seems that whatever pours across the transom, the museum ladies accept, catalogue, and display it with the curatorial care of a polymath.

There are military uniforms, train tickets, Mohave beadwork collars with the favored cobalt-blue beads, a chunk of adobe "from a frozen food locker," a bracelet from Rhodesia (tag unchanged to Zimbabwe), and a department of local natural history: a notebook with faded color photos and pressed sprigs of California fan palm, Mexican fan palm, date palm, Canary Island palm, Australian bottle tree, California pepper tree—trees that do not grow well in the open desert but bless the town with their shade. There are prom dresses and there is a toaster. On a low shelf lies a chunk of sandstone the size of a yeti's footprint, chipped with a petroglyph of dotted circles. "Found in mine south of Needles," the tag says of this ancient fragment hacked from a rock face by some reprehensible vandal.

A high school yearbook, dated 1928 and called "The Mystic Maze," sprouts Hollywood's concept of Indian heaven and the opportunity for a morality tale. The brief foreword subscribes to the dead-spirit legend, calling the maze a place where, if the deceased "had lived true to the Indian tradition his spirit would find the way from this maze and proceed up the path to the Happy Hunting Grounds." If he failed to live a moral life, he was doomed to roam through the labyrinth forever. On the chance that the graduating students missed it, the allegory is drawn clear: "[T]here are many bright and seemingly lovely paths that only wander aimlessly on—that lead to nothing but dissipation, idleness, and disgrace. Do not be deceived by these bright artificial ways—seek diligently the paths that lead to success and happiness."

The museum is oddment verging on chaos. I like the proximity of lacy prom dresses and work-worn metates. I like the toaster. I like the casual array, the muddled arrival of artifacts from garages, the sincerity of donations made out of hope that they might have some value or fear they might be lost. Most of all I find here a deliciously misinformed but creative explanation for the maze above the river. Next to a prehistoric hammer and pounder stone is this tag: "Stone Hammer and Chopper found in the area of the Topock Mystic Maze 1975. Both are of quartzite material. They are believed to be artifacts left by an ancient pebble culture."

A NIGHT WITH THE PEBBLE PEOPLE

Cut off by the interstate and railroad tracks, two faded remnants of the maze lie close to the Pacific Gas & Electric Company's compression plant. I feel polite enough to ask permission to see the remnants, so I walk the half-mile across the bluff to a road marked NO TRESPASSING: AUTHORIZED VEHICLES ONLY and stroll right in (I was, after all, once a PG&E stockholder). The place is deserted. The place is loud. Everyone must be wearing earplugs and cannot hear the approach of a stranger.

I trudge back to the main maze and cool my baking brain inside the truck, the only shade on the terrace. With both doors flung open for air, my feet stick out of the passenger door. Ravens fly by with french fries and Rice Krispies bars in their beaks, booty from the picnic grounds and marina. Below the maze, cars, trucks, boats, trains, and natural gas lunge through space, never pausing for antiquity. The Mystic Maze is definitely not museumified with ropes and interpretive stops and solemn tenor history voices over loudspeakers. This makes it all my own for the afternoon. Waves of heat rise from the stone paths, with no fool but me to witness them.

How can ten acres of sacred stone under the sky of eternity look so forlorn?

When the sun drops lower, I set off into the maze again. Amid a scattering of creosote bushes I find what has been called the "eye" figure. Along with the missing snake-gripping anthropomorph and several dotted circles, the "eye" is one of the few shapes that is not a windrow. In photographs taken when it was more distinct, the figure resembles a phallus, an elongated omega with balls for feet, or the eye half of an old-fashioned hook-and-eye fastener on a garment. It was a long loop of piled stones ending in two circles: ♎ A rock cairn stood at its base, and windrows outlined it on either side in a V-shape that pointed toward the river and Boundary Cone in the Black Mountains, a conspicuous landmark. Some time between 1940 and 1963 a vehicle with a caterpillar tread ran over the "eye," scattering the cairn and disturbing one side of the figure. Nevertheless, I can make out its faint shape in the pediment.

With so few clues to its function and so many associations of our own, it is difficult to start from scratch, to shed the notion of the maze as a maze, a place that ritually or otherwise defined a path or procession. The lower Colorado River desert is full of circles and paths worn by repeated dances; it is marked with *avenidas*—long cleared areas with no evidence of their use as trails or dancing grounds. Quite simply, the ancients held great reverence for the mystic powers of stones. I think of the Fir Bolg, post–Roman-era occupants of the British Isles who carried soil in bags, who never stopped moving dirt and so became known as "men of the bags." Here on the Mojave, people remapped the desert pediment, they picked up weathered bits of the exfoliating Chemehuevi Mountains—pieces of granite, biotite schist, and milk quartz—and formed them into knowledge. They leaned down and moved rock. The pebble people.

In the maze I feel as if I am walking along someone's fingerprint whorls or the ripple marks left in mud by the river, then petrified into loose, crumbling pieces. Sometimes one swath of ripples ends abruptly against ripples going in a different direction. What if the intaglio had nothing to do with land or heaven and everything to do with water—water in one of the continent's most waterless places?

My path ends. I can step over the row of stones, but should I? The notion of "solving" the maze, of finding a set internal form, throws me off balance for a moment. I must come up with my own maze rules. I take a path that leads to the edge of the terrace, the lip of cliff closest to the river. For me the river is the magnet of all movement.

The maze ends in thin air. Below the lip of the bluff the land has been rearranged for a railroad corridor, a snarl of natural gas lines, the extraordinary amount of room required for an interstate highway, and a river that is no longer a river but a tri-state drip irrigation system. Earth movers shredded the array of chocolate-colored stones set in careful rows by hand. It is impossible to guess how the huge intaglio met the old river, what sort of relationship river and stone had in this space.

In the angled light of sunset the reservoir turns deep indigo, unzipped to white by the wakes of dozens of motorboats moving in two traffic lanes, upstream and down, mirroring the flow of road traffic, the numbing rush of people going somewhere else from wherever. I hike back through the maze, following the sinuous paths. I am the slowest thing for miles and the only thing that is not moving in a straight line wired to the gods of speed.

The gas compression plant throbs and hums. I feel its vibration through my soles as I walk. The desert's fundamental stillness does not live here. I think it is way out there somewhere, across the blue vault of air. I see it over a bajada taking on the mauve shadow of dusk. Silence is the place that makes your comfort shift uneasily. Then you move forward into it, to paraphrase Thomas Merton's words about the desert, to swim for your life into an apparently irrational void.

THE MOHAVE AND other Colorado River people put great stock in dreams. Any skill or power, any knowledge of love, war, or gambling, for instance, came through dreaming. Dreams shaped a life, and all dreams retold would unfurl as journeys. The journeys described when the dreamers traveled, what they ate, where they slept, the creatures and landmarks they saw—the equivalent, in a stretch, of a travelogue of a great Mohave trek.

Dreams remembered over time became oral myths, or "dreamed

singings." In these song-stories, the telling varied. The plot and tune remained fluid, and few events occurred other than the journey itself. To tell your story you recited the names of things, the springs, rocks, plants, animals, stars, mountains, rivers. To tell your story you sang a map. You set geography to voice.

fear slough
fat earth
duck water
no water

For modern, often sleep-deprived humans there is less communication between dreams and waking life. We have lost the ancestral enchantment with mystery. We have severed ourselves from what were once the wellsprings of myth. When we do dream, we dismiss it as static, conjure up some Freudian dreck, or bore others to death with the telling. Friedrich Nietzsche wrote, "In the old days people knew how to dream. They did not have to go to sleep first." There must have been nothing quite like a trek to the Pacific with a Nietzschean Mohave.

Far into the valley below the terrace, islands of light appear in the creeping dusk. I unpack a pad, pillow, and cotton Mexican blanket—it is too hot for a sleeping bag—and make a bed at the edge of the maze, near a creosote bush with the memory of rain scent in its sticky, bright green leaves. Tonight I will sleep here.

Surrounding me is a desert West as true as the secret, sacred, sunset-kissed place in a remote canyon, the cosmic navel, stripped-down-to-God, buffed spirituality West, where the coyotes howl and the desolate emptiness is stuffed to the mesa tops with meaning. I make a bed in the West of junked cars, interstate-delirious cars, cars that cost more than a house, a place of crumbling mines, factory outlet malls, replumbed watersheds, vandalized rock art, and gut-shot appliances strewn about dry washes, a desert slashed by off-road vehicles or enveloped into protected national monuments that some people want to deprotect and dedesignate. The two Wests squeeze against one another like neurotic tectonic plates. In a bed on the terrace below the spiky peaks of the Chemehuevi Mountains I recite the place names:

electrified campground
pipeline hydrocarbons
the boulder where the raven poops and drops her french fry
stars visible, ghost gorge not
designer water
motorhead water
no water
and oh dear God my river

And smack in the heart of it all, this maze, this ten-acre riddle of immutable pebbles. You have to believe it to see it.

I HAVE ALWAYS BEEN a heavy dreamer, blooming thick nocturnal epics like the one about ice-skating on a frozen emerald river while pulling a grand piano camouflaged with whale-gray boulders, imps helping me slip it along without hindrance, the piano, boulders, imps, and I flying down the ice, everyone speaking Mayan and I understand it perfectly. I sleep in a forest of mental forms that I cannot penetrate but remember and hold like stones in my head when I awaken.

Here, by the ancient intaglio, I will dream a dream of great significance. This dream will offer a clear and subtle illumination. It will forever direct my life.

Desert dark is velvet dark. The night is moonless. The ground hums beneath my hipbones, the vibrations of the highway and the compression plant. For the first time in a long, long time my sleep is total blackness. I do not dream a single dream.

A Wilderness of Monkeys

The Mexicans were accustomed to say that at one time all men have been stones; and acting literally upon this conviction, they interred with the bones of the dead a small green stone, which was called the principal of life.

D. G. BRINTON
Myths of the New World

Turquoise helps a person feel intuitively the difference between good and evil.

Traditional saying from ancient Persia

A story of turquoise: Although the density of buildings, traffic, and other city clutter may distract you from its contours, the heart of El Paso is a pass that cuts through the Franklin Mountains. In the morning light the jagged Franklins rose in flat gray, bristling with radio towers. On foot I headed across the pass from downtown El Paso to downtown Juárez, from Texas to Mexico. The bridge across the border straddled a muddy and languid Rio Grande.

In Juárez there were discos and petite Indian women at the bottom of the street-vending pecking order and a man who asked me if I wanted a taxi. To where? I asked. To Mexico City, he shrugged.

Two middle-aged *gringos* emblazoned from head to toe in sport logos passed me on the sidewalk. One of them told his friend, "I'd like to find something to buy, maybe a switchblade." The taxi driver offered them prescription drugs. "Viagra?" he said with his eyebrows raised.

In a shop that sold religious objects I bought a blue Plexiglas paperweight molded in the shape of a pyramid. Inside the pyramid was a miniature shrine made of sequins, beads, *milagros,* a flat plastic elephant, a picture of a saint, and a tiny horseshoe, *una herradurra de caballo* that would put me in a better position for a *fortuna fabulosa.* In the pyramid's center, topped with an ornate gold cross, was a water-filled inner bubble. Inside the bubble lay a tiny head and torso of what looked like the pope or Buddha or a Chinese Jesus carved in the deathly white of a plaster Madonna statue. Cast in a marine light, broken from its base, the torso floated around the bubble when the pyramid was upside down, then sank to the bottom when it was right side up.

I walked back across the border to El Paso, stopping to look at the river again through the chain-link fence. I leaned against the barrier with arms raised in let-me-out-of-this-place prisoner style. Who was the inmate, the river or me? Three white plastic grocery bags and I plastered ourselves to the fence. It broke my heart to see a river strangled in steel mesh and coils of razor wire.

The day grew hotter, and my shins ached from walking on hard pavement. I strode into a small plaza and bought a cone of lime sherbet, then sat on a park bench under a canopy of trees, shaded from the fierce sun of the Chihuahuan Desert. Something out of the ordinary was happening in this plaza. There was a speaker's podium, several rows of folding chairs, and a fountain crawling with bright fiberglass alligators with torqued, animated bodies and open jaws. The plaza began to fill with the well-dressed officialdom of El Paso. Someone told me they were there to dedicate the new fountain, *La Plaza de los Lagartos,* by sculptor Luis Jiménez. At one time the central plaza held live *lagartos,* lethargic and abused alligators that everyone said for years merely lay in the pool and did nothing. Today the new misting fountain kept their replacements shiny and wet.

A few plaza derelicts held their turf, mingling with the VIPs. One carried a neatly tied bundle of what looked like hundred-dollar bills. The *viejos* resting on the benches, the plaza regulars, appeared mildly disturbed but curious about the invasion, perhaps remembering the narcoleptic alligators from their childhood. More Spanish was spoken than English. The border seemed fluid and unimportant. My sherbet melted down the side of the brown-sugar cone in neon-green drips, and one of my wildest dreams came true. Into the plaza strolled a mariachi band.

Mariachi music seems to flow into Place with the snug fit of irony. It is a musical map of revolution and love. Sugar-sweet love. Monumental love. Monumental grief. Betrayal. Machismo. Animals. Death. The El Paso mariachi band had twelve musicians, robust and dignified in white shirts and charro suits—short maroon jackets and matching pants with gold braid down the leg. A pale film of Texas dust coated their ebony cowboy boots.

The music went on, all that moonstruckness in trumpets, violins, and guitars. I grew homesick for my husband, who was back in Utah on our salsa farm, tending the beds of tomatoes, chiles, cilantro, and onions. Here I was in Texas, remembering that I was conceived but not interested in Texas and instead was once crazy to go to Egypt or Persia or the Arabian deserts to live on a caravan and how such dreams, as forlorn as they now seemed, were fed by light. The plaza vibrated with sound and sun, no fears of collision between scarlet lipstick and cobalt alligators, the canary-yellow dresses of twin girls, the raisin eyes of the *viejos*. The geography of aridity is a prism for brightness, the eclectic partnerships of a fiercely articulated palette. Deserts share a kinship of color. You know you are home and the world is not so large.

One of the mariachi players caught my eye and smiled beneath his Clark Gable mustache. While the others wore black string ties, this man wore a turquoise bolo. He was sixtyish with slicked-back mahogany-brown hair, a face of leather, and ultramarine eyes.

If you see a Mexican mestizo with eyes the color of bands of evening sky, you will not easily forget him. I was so startled I could not release his gaze. I had seen this same man a few years before, miles away in La Paz, in Baja California Sur, playing in a smaller mariachi band. I did not know if this was a coincidence, if musicians commonly roamed a circuit, or if he was a ghost who insinuated himself in every fiesta and by his eyes made you remember him. Those eyes promised clarity. They gathered waters. I was thrilled to see him. I held my holy pyramid on my lap, letting the Buddha Jesus Pope rest at the bottom of the bubble. *Una fortuna fabulosa,* I thought. Alligators and ice cream in the Chihuahuan Desert, a mariachi band without asking for one, a ghost, and a kind blue gaze that filled the heart with its beauty.

IT IS THE STONE of the desert. It is the color of yearning.

Turquoise is not a common mineral, but everywhere it is found, there are signs, back to times history can scarcely reach, that people have extracted it from the ground and taken its beauty for themselves. It comes from arid, dusty, stripped-down, skinned-earth places. It occurs almost exclusively in the geography of asceticism, in broken lands of bare rock and infrequent green. Set against the palette of desolation, a piece of turquoise is like a hole open to the sky.

Turquoise is the wealth of the nomad, portable and protective. As a prized gem, it advanced quickly and deeply through the Near East and pre-Columbian America while Europeans coveted their cold and lustrous rubies. Turquoise, *dootł' izhii,* anchors a corner of the four-cornered Navajo universe, it guards desert springs, it is itself water and sky. Nobles hoarded it, peasants wore it, the faithful inserted two thousand words of the Koran on a two-square-inch slab of it.

For the ancient Egyptians a square held the angle of failure, the pyramid the angle of success. Sedentary and not easily dislodged from their valleys along the Nile, they instead took their journeys in the afterlife, loading themselves with goods and turquoise and lapis ornaments (what is a pyramid if not a giant suitcase?) and leaving behind glimpses of themselves through the density of time. These people of the desert went through life with their *ka,* a spirit that came into being with one's body and resembled the body in all aspects. Body and *ka* coexisted in death, as in life, and thus preparations were made for a proper *ka* abode: a carefully preserved, mummified body or, should the mummy perish, a statue of the deceased. The "suitcase" was loaded with miniatures of weavers, bakers, painters, and other provision makers, lists of commodities, instructive texts, and small, functioning models. Paintings guided body and *ka* life in the hereafter with stories of body and *ka* life on earth. In these paintings blue appears as a most precious pigment, painstakingly extracted from copper.

For the Egyptians the blues of turquoise and lapis lazuli were the colors of faith and truth. For her death journey three thousand years ago, a woman of wealth wore a bracelet of linked flat plaques the size of small stamps, turquoise alternating with gold, each plaque mounted with a delicately carved hawk until her wrist was a circle of blue-green, gold, and twenty-five birds.

In other graves of antiquity Sumerian women were buried with elaborate vessels and jewelry, crimson garments, and ribbons of gold and silver. A silver hair ribbon found in the pocket of one young woman's robe—tucked away as a spare or forgotten in the rush to the afterlife—distills an ordinary gesture in the extraordinary business of jewels and finery, the desire to make a magnificent display of the self for the delight of others.

The Chinese declared turquoise unfit for women but by the thirteenth century changed their minds and used it to decorate their icons and their wives. Tibetans crushed turquoise, gold, silver, and lapis into ink and wrote prayers on pale blue paper made from the palmyra tree. Reflections on Himalayan lakes gave the color of turquoise back to them. The Aztecs placed *chalchihuitl,* turquoise or jade, in the mouths of the dead to "supply the heart." The woman of the *chalchihuitl,* a goddess of water, wore skirts of blue-green, like the skirts of the Caribbean that flare from island and Yucatán shores, waters the color of solace and serenity.

Turquoise changes color. Sometimes its color vanishes—one early source calls it "air green." The wearer can influence these changes. Turquoise is a sympathetic gem.

It is prized not for hardness or translucence but for its color and its color's effect on the heart. The stone "brightens and refreshes the vision when it is looked at fixedly," noted an Arab mineralogist in the late thirteenth century. A hundred years later, in a natural history of precious stones, Persian scholar Muhammed ibn Mansur wrote, "The eye is strengthened by looking at a turquois [*sic*]. If one sees a turquois early in the morning, he will pass a fortunate day. One should view a turquois at the time of the new moon. The turquois helps its owner to victory over his enemies, protects him against injury, and makes him liked by all men."

The Persians cut their gems on a wheel and polished them with willow and a white stone. "Moisture, oil, and strong odors impair the luster of the stone," Ibn Mansur wrote, while "mutton fat strengthens its color, therefore on the hands of butchers are turquois always beautifully colored."

Since antiquity the Persians lorded over the turquoise mines near Nishapur (now Neyshabur), believed to be among the oldest on earth—some of the beads from these mines date back to 2100 B.C. Nishapur lies in the northeastern Iranian province of Kho-rasan, in a wrinkling of earth west of the deep folds of the Hindu Kush. Its history, like the history of the entire region, is the history of upstart dynasts in ascendance and decline and invaders spilling out of central Asia. Hellenistic and Islamic conquests took deeper root and enfolded their influences into an Indo-Iranian tribal cul-ture. The great trans-Asia trade routes funneled through Khorasan, carrying Persian turquoise to India and Russia and feeding to the peoples of the Mediterranean dyes, perfumes, silk, rubies, and the lapis lazuli of Badakhshan, a likely source of the lapis coveted by Egypt.

Nishapur turquoise once set the world standard for gem quality: hard stone, sky blue, no hint of green, no impurities. The Persian turquoise is said to hold its color better than stones from other deserts. To preserve their color some miners carried the stones in their mouths before offering them for sale. Others put them in earthenware pots, moistening the clay. On religious holidays the shahs showered their harems with handfuls of stones. Turquoise was prosperity and beauty. It was the equivalent of a bulletproof vest. *Ferozah,* Persian for turquoise, means "victorious." Against a threat or in battle the wearer of this stone was in no danger of being killed. Against scorpion stings and reptile bites there was no better protection.

Treatises on mineralogy in fifteenth- and seventeenth-century India echoed Persian and Arab views on the medicinal virtues of turquoise. It drove away pains caused by demonic influences, they said. It banished unpleasant dreams. A turquoise ring eliminated the chances of drowning or being struck by lightning.

The Afghans cured cataracts with turquoise applied to the eyes and a chant to Allah while you waited. Greek physicians claimed that turquoise prevented death by accident and cured eye problems, epilepsy, and intestinal troubles. When turquoise turned pale or dim, the wearer could expect illness, warned John Swan of England in a 1635 work with the modest title "Speculum Mundi, or a glass representing the face of the world; shewing both that it did begin, and must also end: the manner how, and time when, being largely examined."

Poke a shish kebab skewer through a globe at the Colorado Plateau and it will come out the other side on the Tibetan Plateau. More than all others, the cultures of Tibet and the native American Southwest have absorbed turquoise into their traditions, ceremonies, and folklore. In Tibet the stone *yü* shares with humans the common dualities of life and death, wealth and beauty. The *la yü*, or vital spirit of turquoise, keeps one's life in proper balance. If the *la* abandons the body, it can be recovered by a ritual that involves milk from a blue-haired goat, turquoise wrapped in white silk, a medium, a trance, and "a sling with nine eyes." Tibetan turquoise came from local sources, the treasury of the spirits who protected lakes and springs, and from China, where it had less value. In China, superstition described turquoise as a transmutation of the fir tree into a blue-green moss. Thus, the name for a light-colored specimen of the stone translates as "fir tree ears."

To protect yourself from lightning, the Navajo say, wear a bead of turquoise in your hair. The Navajo divinity Changing Woman, so named because she is life springing from nothing and a woman who renews her youth each season, lives in a house with a turquoise door and four footprints of turquoise leading to a turquoise room. Changing Woman looks through binoculars of rock crystal, the stone of light beams and fire and a natural ally of turquoise. Carried on the tongue, rock crystal is the word in a prayer that means truth. In a Navajo legend of the first world, First Woman becomes so intrigued with a distant fire that she goes to it, where she finds a man. "Your fire is rock crystal," he tells her, "mine is turquoise." In this declaration there is reason to live together.

Turquoise carries itself into every aspect of the Navajo's fluid lives. Like their rose and amethyst desert, it changes color for no reason and cannot be taken lightly. It is both family wealth and sacred, for oneself or for sale. Southwestern tribes like the Navajo and Zuni wed turquoise to silver, to the trading post and reservation system, and to an Anglo economy that calved off some of their work from tradition into the realm of the tourist market, where, to paraphrase one ethnologist, design became the Indian's idea of the trader's idea of what the Anglo thought was an Indian's idea of design.

Family heirlooms kept for personal adornment still make it to pawn for goods or cash. Most of it is reclaimed, but dead pawn, ready to sell, can come to the market from thieves or poverty or heartbreak. The people who once wore the Navajo pawn in her possession seem to haunt it, laments an Indian woman in *The Antelope Wife,* a novel by Louise Erdrich. Of a glacier-green turquoise and silver piece, she says, "I have to tell you, I can hold that piece only a moment, for when I polish the pattern on some days it seems to start in my hands with a secret life, a secret pain."

My first turquoise was a plain, Zuni-made silver ring from Arizona with two rows of channel inlay, pieces of stone fit into a flat mosaic. Less fussy than the customary seed-cluster ring or beetle-back gem in ornate bezel and band, this ring likely was a man's ring, though small and subtle. I wore it in the summer, for turquoise is symbiotic with skin and seems to need much bareness to conspire with its color. Because jewelry snags and smashes during the acrobatics and labors of outdoor life, I wear little of it. I envy those whose bodies carry just enough. I have never owned much turquoise nor loaded my fingers, wrists, neck, and ears with it, a fashion that, unless you inlay your teeth, too, announces that you have recently moved to Santa Fe from New Jersey. In those days, however, along with the Arizona ring, I wore a second, cheaper turquoise ring.

Off my fingers the rings lived in a jade dish by the bathroom mirror until the day I took pity on a couple and their teenage daughter when their Volkswagen bus, painted in mescal colors of fuchsia and lime, broke down near my home in the California mountains. I let them use my telephone.

Back then we all dressed like hippies, we acted like hippies, but I was too terminally confused to be an *actual* hippie and too terrified to hitchhike all over the place like most California hippies, unless, I thought, I could play it safe like one of my friends, who always hitchhiked with her hang glider. At my house the woman called a tow service, then put the phone down, looked in my refrigerator, and asked me if she could make omelettes for everyone. The man nibbled hashish brownies from a plastic Baggie and wore no shoes even though it was February at 5,355 feet above sea level. He never spoke. He stared avidly into my unlit fireplace as if it were a television set or an altar: the Shrine of Our Lady of Perpetual Brain Damage.

Turquoise and silver rings covered all but two of the teenager's fingers. A neighbor, who during the week worked in distant Hollywood as a stuntman, stopped by and asked me, "Who are the hippies?" The Arizona ring disappeared from the dish. Somewhat unassertively I held up the cheap ring and asked if they had seen its mate. No, they said with righteous indignation, and before they left, the cheap ring had vanished too.

Soon after the theft, one of my brothers, who worked as a silversmith while he was in college, gave me a ring he had made with a Persian turquoise. It was the palest turquoise I had ever seen, a robin's-egg blue, which is not the color of leaves or sun on a spring day but the color of the space between them, the pool of light beneath the greenery that envelops and camouflages the nest. Because I feared losing this ring, I wore it constantly, letting it adapt to rough days in the mountains, where I eschewed fuchsia vehicles and fell in then out of love with the stuntman.

What route had this pale stone traveled, I wondered. Who were the keepers of the mines at Nishapur, birthplace of Omar Khayyám and Farid ud-Din Attar, two of Persia's greatest mystic poets? Were there still harems to shower with jewels? Was being in a harem like being a pet, worth the rain of turquoise? There was a village in the remote deserts of North Africa, I recalled, where men and women lodged separately. The men did not understand the women's language. Once a year they joined in a rite to preserve the balance between the male and female forces in nature. On these days the women made sure to use a language the men could understand. Perhaps they explained the solace of songbirds, the press of virtue, the way women are given by destiny to a man, and how life, love, and death are not linear in time but live side by side. Perhaps they said, Give us silver, *give us blue.*

I pulled from the shelf an old geography book plump with dust and imperialistic fervor. In this 1928 text Persia was not yet Iran, Iraq was Irak, and everyone outside of Great Britain, in the eyes of the author, was Backward and Unproductive and In Dire Need of Leadership. Nevertheless, the geography of desert turquoise inflamed a certain restlessness, names with old atlas spellings like Derreh-i-Safid (white valley), Derreh-i-Siyah (black valley), Derreh-i-Sabz (green valley); the mines of Khaki, Khuruj, Ali Mirzai, and Aghali, positioned close to caravan routes, the arteries of commerce between Eurasia and Asia proper. Another book source graded Persian turquoise as *shirbumi* or *shirfam* for whitish stones, *tufal* for flat pieces used in amulets and bracelets, and the greenish *gul-i-kasni* (chicory) favored by the Afghans.

I tried to imagine the places, the air, the smells, the color of the rock that held the blue—places of extreme heat and light and nights with a deep, black cold. I took to wearing multilayered, gauzy skirts, bead anklets, and an entire forearm of silver bracelets. I listened to scratchy tapes of Middle Eastern singers, their ululation wafting through the incense cedars around my cabin. I envied a belly-dancer friend who could arch her back, move her hips, and ring bright sounds from her finger cymbals, all the while balancing a saber across her forehead. I will go there, I thought, muddling in my fantasies nearly every culture from Morocco to Saudi Arabia, faithfully mispronouncing the names of my destinations.

My hand carried the stone of the desert into a different life and a complicated land, the life of a starving artist with random jobs and a rage for wandering, a land of malachite forests thick with ponderosa, sugar pines as graceful as dancers, and lodgepole pines with "insurance" cones that could hoard their seeds until after the intense heat of a forest fire released them. The streams and rivers ran with water so clear it pressed against my heart like a hand.

Nothing but occasional daydreams could pry me from this place. This was where I set down my crazed years, fighting what I thought threatened every young woman: an intolerable and crushing onset of adult blandness.

Along a bend of river that slowed into a deep pool, my friends and I attached a heavy rope to the branch of an enormous black oak. The tree stood on a steep slope above the flow, giving the height we needed for our swing. None of us questioned the act of grown-ups with recently acquired college degrees flinging themselves through the air on a scratchy length of hemp, but I was too cautious to test it, to be the one to go first. One of the others did the honors, the rope held, and, if you chose the right moment to let go, the river was deep enough to hold the plunge of the heaviest body without injury. After the trial run I was urged to be the next person to take the swing. The other men and women were far more daring than I was, but I had earned an accidental reputation during an earlier incident on the river, a reputation which I vehemently disavowed and hoped never to maintain.

A FEW WEEKS BEFORE we made the rope swing, my tribe of friends and I had spent a ninety-degree afternoon on a stretch of river lower down the mountain, swimming in a gorgeous catchment pond below a waterfall. Not content with the languid inertia of a summer day, the men felt compelled to jump off the waterfall into the pool. The waterfall was fifty-five feet high.

A sun-fried brain or a bored *ka* propelled me to the top of the falls after they made their leaps. Treading water below, they yelled frantically. The roar of the water drowned out the meaning of their cries, which, I learned later, were cries of pain. They had jumped naked and were suffering scrotum impact problems. I knew the leap was scary but safe, so at the time I interpreted their screams not as a warning but as encouragement. They knew me to be reluctant and not enamored of danger, but thrilled once I crossed a threshold of risk, especially if it involved the river. "Your nerve endings are too close to the surface," they told me, which apparently accounted for both the fear and the exhilaration.

I waved at them and took position. Two black-chinned hummingbirds flitted out of a patch of manzanita and hovered at my fingertips, their needle bills poised at my turquoise ring, their emerald backs and obsidian and violet throats iridescent in the bright sun: gem clusters with wings and beating hearts.

The river threw itself off the precipice, as clear and slick as liquid glass, a mesmerizing band of curving water. Below me the reassuring jewel-green of depth lay well away from the paler shallows and the surrounding shoulders of rock. Around me the mountains of my mother and grandmother and mothers before them rose high into the wide blue air, flanked with the blunt chaparral, then high timber and the keen polish of glaciers across their granite bulk. The sparest of the palette—emerald river, pale ecru stone, sapphire sky, and the unnameable color of their clarity—struck the deepest nerve. The ache of it all nearly made my knees buckle. I felt as if I was already beneath the waterfall, its weight pressing against my chest. "It is sheer beauty, so pure that it is difficult to breathe in," wrote poet Rupert Brooke, and there on the waterfall I had no breath. I knew the Sierra better than I understood love. The least precarious thing in my life was my appetite for the sensuous.

"I will do this once," I said aloud to no one. Just once.

Then I lifted my bare feet off the lip of flood-polished granite and plunging river, and I fell through the clear mountain air to a glittering pool of water the color of a hummingbird's back.

THE SWING WAS easier. I braced my feet against the knot and grasped the rope with arms above me. I kicked off the slope and flung myself across the water, the trees and bank blurred in flight. Timing was everything. I found the right moment on the swing's arc to let go and drop, letting the river swallow me with a joyous splash. The men thought of me as brave, but they, after all, had jumped from the waterfall without their pants.

The thrill did not make me crave the rope swing. There were other distractions, like tequila and books and the mustang clover that grew in a meadow near my house, tender blooms of purple and white rising straight up to the sun, or the stuntman and the Saturdays he came looking for me after a week of crashing burning semis. Always on my finger, the Persian turquoise slowly darkened from its air-green, the color of the light that hovers over robins' eggs.

Once in a while, at night, I hiked alone to the river to scare myself witless by swinging on the thick hemp rope outside the safety of daylight and visible depths. With shapes and forms dimmed by night vision and an uneasy, never-to-be-trusted moon that turned the river from liquid to solid—a scrim of silver mirror, a ribbon unfurled—I rode the swing and let go. In those days my friends and I strode through an uncertain world, strong-limbed and reluctant to settle. Our emotions were nearly torrential but not very durable. In our young lives, in those glorious mountains of summer, this swing was, like the waterfall, a necessary flight from the sheltered to the wild.

TURQUOISE IS ORNAMENT, jewel, talisman, tessera. It is religion. It is pawn. It is not favored for pinkie rings. It did not likely come from Turkey, its namesake, but took the name of the land it crossed on the old trade routes from Persia to Europe.

The extraction of turquoise requires caution, the Zuni claim; the guardian of turquoise makes his home on a mountain protected against disrespectful collectors by angry white and black bears. In the 1850s something like angry bears chewed up the karma of an obscure Scotsman who spent twelve years seeking his fortune at ancient mines on the Sinai Peninsula, where chunks of raw turquoise reportedly spilled out of the black rocks and washed onto open alluvial gravels in abundance. Under his tenure Sinai stones hemorrhaged to London. His native helpers secretly hemorrhaged even more shipments to Suez and Cairo, and eventually the venture collapsed. Some gem dealers can look at a stone and by its color tell you where it comes from: this is Persian, this is Sinai, this is Nevada, this is cheap chalk buffed up with epoxy.

The chemistry of turquoise: $CuAl_6(PO_4)_4(OH)_8 \cdot 4H_2O$, a hydrous phosphate of copper and aluminum. The copper and aluminum—along with iron and other mineral traces—join with a phosphate radical, a group of oxygen atoms so clustered around nonmetallic phosphorus that they behave like a single atom.

Phosphates are known for their bright colors. In turquoise, according to some mineralogists, the blue comes from the copper; the green comes from the presence of iron. Dark, spidery veins reveal the matrix in which turquoise participates; the veins are usually limonite, iron-stained quartz, metallic oxides, or other minerals.

Turquoise occurs in limestone, batholithic and feldspathic granites, shale, and trachyte, rocks that are found nearly everywhere. Unless they are in an arid environment, however, they are not likely to bear turquoise. Although turquoise has more than one origin, most types formed million years ago, when groundwater seeped into alumina- and copper-rich mineralized fractures in zones of igneous rock. What has been said about gold can be said about turquoise: turquoise is the burden of waters.

The physics of turquoise: soft, porous, inclined to spontaneously dehydrate, semitranslucent in thin slices, opaque and refractive in chunks. Mild abrasives, like fine sand, will polish it. A lighter stone is more porous and will soak up the sheep fat that gives a butcher's ring its porcelain gleam. Turquoise is often confused with chrysocolla and variscite, one of the only other phosphates to be included among precious stones. Turquoise has no taste but the taste of its beauty—not an illusion if you recall the imperial Roman who loved a cup of glistening fluorspar so much he chewed the rim to bits.

The dignity of turquoise: Ancient southwesterners gave turquoise, the greatest wealth, as offerings to water, the desert's greatest gift. They left tokens of turquoise at canyon seeps and springs amid emerald mosses, maidenhair ferns, creamy blooms of columbine, crimson monkey flowers, dragonflies the color of flame, and heron-blue damselflies with bodies as thin as a vein. From turquoise they carved tadpoles a quarter-inch long and set raised turquoise eyes in toads of black jet. With turquoise they traded for copper bells, macaw feathers, the skins and plumes of parrots, and pearlescent shells from the Pacific and the Sea of Cortez—the stone of the desert for the glories of sea and forest.

The Spaniards in Mexico and Central America in the sixteenth century were so feverish for gold, they executed anyone who lied about its whereabouts. Chain shackles and angry dogs deterred tendencies toward reticence. The Spaniards' gold delirium may have confused their notation of *chalchihuitl,* a term they used to describe turquoise, jade, malachite, or all blue-green stones collectively. In the late sixteenth century, the Spanish priest Bernardino de Sahagún recorded the natives' descriptions of turquoise: "Some are quite smooth, some roughened, some pitted, some like volcanic rock. It becomes round, it becomes pale. It smokes. The fine turquoise smokes. It becomes rough, it becomes perforated, it becomes pale."

The bulk of the turquoise in Mexico came from Pueblo Indian mines in the Southwest along trade routes that extended from Arizona and New Mexico to Chichén Itzá in the Yucatán. For the cultures of Mexico, turquoise acquired the status of divinity, elaborately manifested by turquoise-encrusted skulls, masks, bones, beast figures, and other religious objects. True to their on-the-edge, wigged-out, possibly exaggerated reputation (penis skin-cutting, hearts ripped out of chests, etc.), some ancient Mexicans reshaped their teeth and inlaid them with bits of turquoise. In 1519, the Spanish conqueror Hernán Cortés is said to have encountered a group of Indians "rather aloofe" from the rest, "higher" and of "differing habit." These people wore rings of jet and amber in their noses and, in their pierced lower lips, gold and turquoise rings so heavy, their lips hung over their chins, baring their teeth.

While the Americas took turquoise to great heights of art and ritual, it did not gain value in Europe until after the Middle Ages. Even then turquoise was considered medicinal and talismanic, secondary to diamonds, rubies, sapphires, emeralds, and other gemstones, whose richness remained so locked in their transparence, one ended up wearing only his or her own lust for it. "Many strange things beyond faith are reported concerning the vertues of this stone, which nothing but excesse of faith can believe," wrote Thomas Nicols in a 1652 treatise on precious stones.

The Persian prescription of turquoise as a pacifier apparently followed it north, prompting the English to believe that it dissolved enmity and reconciled man and woman after estrangement. "Out upon her!" an angry Shylock exclaims in *The Merchant of Venice* when he learns that his daughter has taken his turquoise ring, a long-ago gift from his betrothed, and traded it to his creditors for a monkey. "I would not have given it for a wilderness of monkeys."

Is turquoise green? Is it blue? In recent times Europeans and Asians have preferred the purest, veinless sky-blue. In a period display of cultural chauvinism in his classic natural history of 1915, *Turquois,* Joseph Pogue noted that "semicivilized" and "savage peoples" (that is, aboriginal Americans) were less picky about color, to the extent of paying high prices for "unsightly pale green." More likely the astute natives turned the turquoise around as jewelry, offering tourists and trading posts the stones—the green ones—that they valued less, keeping the blues for themselves.

An attraction to a certain turquoise, even to the color of the ubiquitous artificial stones, is subjective. The craving for turquoise is universal. Turquoise is capricious, it is alluring, no one leaves the Southwest without it, although its life seems to flee from it when it is removed from the bare, blood-red sandstone of its native land.

◆　◆　◆

I ONCE TRIED to visit raw turquoise in the belly of its homeland. On that day rain showers slipped off the Sandia Mountains and pushed me along the old road between Albuquerque and Santa Fe. Islands of broken mountains floated on a rolling sea of pinyon-juniper forest, low-slung and soft-edged in the spring squall: the Cerillos Hills, also known as the Turquoise Hills, and behind them the Ortiz Mountains. These mountains held the sheer antiquity of turquoise.

From mines that dated back more than twelve centuries, the Cerillos Hills fed turquoise to the known world. Cerillos turquoise adorned the pendants and prayer sticks of people in the nearby Rio Grande pueblos. It turned up in California and on the masks of the Aztecs and the wrists and throats of the Maya. It was mined with bone tools, stone hammers, mauls, adzes, and plant-fiber baskets used to carry tons of rock debris away from the mountain to reach the veins of blue stone. One of the mines, on the flanks of Mt. Chalchihuitl, produced turquoise of a quality and quantity incomparable to any other.

On my way to the old mines I passed a town that seemed to have spilled paintboxes all over itself. Galleries and studios in buildings dating from New Mexico's gold-mining boom bled art into the main street, behind bright signs and banners. Two men with fluffy, weaverbird-nest, ZZ Top beards sat on a porch and stared into space, a position they appeared to have assumed around 1978. Where the town left off, the pinyons and junipers took over again. In Cerillos, a quiet hamlet of adobe and cottonwoods, I drove by an herb shop, the Clear Light Opera House, and a petting zoo. Then, because a chill wind had joined the rain, I postponed a walk in the hills for a visit to the local museum.

The museum filled a wing of a trading post, although one concentration of eclectica avalanched seamlessly into the other. Here was the fallout of an accidental taxonomy of artifacts alongside trendy Balinese scarves and jackalope refrigerator magnets. To reach a homemade diorama of mining chronology, I waded through an undergrowth of bullets, bottles, antlers, potsherds, gem collections, break-open geodes, a plastic replica of the USS *Nimitz*, a Subaru hubcap painted in psychedelic colors, an icon of Christ stumbling onward with the Cross on his back, and two-thirds of a plaster Madonna. There was an assemblage of rock conglomerate in the shape of Texas, red trinkets from Red tourists (pins, bookmarks, and tour pamphlets from Russia), and a newspaper clipping with the header "Saving Our Past from the Jaws of Subdivision." Among rusted, frontier-era utensils and other domestic items resided a three-piece chicken dinner (a box with three kernels of corn) and "A tip from the host: Keep your hands off my wife."

I fantasized proprietors who had dropped the iconic spoor of their journey from ship and airplane-model–building to counter-culture then straight to Christ, which is not an uncommon story. More likely they were simply hoarders of things who took the ini-tiative to load their ark with the random relics of local knowledge.

The diorama showed mining technology through the ages, beginning in the fourteenth century with a homemade mannequin with cotton-wool hair and a loincloth made from the pelt of an apparently neurotic mammal. The mannequin was posed to beat a rock with a tomahawk. The 1870s miner mannequin panned gold against the papier-mâché backdrop of the Never Mine. Roy Rogers, Dale Evans, and Trigger beamed benevolence upon them from a nearby photograph. Narrative descriptions explained that gold miners uncovered old tunnels in the Cerillos Hills in the 1880s, where they found stone tools belonging to the early Pueblo miners. Historians believe that shortly before the 1680 Pueblo Revolt against the Spaniards, the Indians filled the turquoise mines with rubble to hide them from their oppressors.

Amid the chisels, picks, coffeepots, and bits of rusty metal stood a display case with starfish, sea urchins, scalloped shells, arrow-heads, scorpions, the horn of a bighorn ram, seafood deli crab claws, buckeye seedpods, mouse skulls, sharks' teeth, one coconut, and a gold egg. Other animal parts appeared as a lamp supported by four deer legs amputated at the knee joints and a stuffed, moth-eaten peacock whose neck was nearly severed.

Nothing in the museum bore a particular order, only a compounded, weightless curiosity. There was nothing unfamiliar to the average westerner and nothing arcane like elephant hair balls or the face of Rush Limbaugh in a pancake. Perhaps you had to be a Russian to marvel at the Apache tears or shriek at the disturbing crunchiness of dead scorpions. Like most of the small, motley, but well-kept museums in the deserts of the West, this one left an impression of something badly furry, of terminal dust. I sensed a slippage into the mute.

In the trading-post wing of the building I was thrilled to see that the rock-collection boxes of my childhood back in the Oligocene had not gone extinct. There they were, small nuggets of fool's gold, quartz, chalcedony, zircon, and other mineral specimens glued to a hard foam liner, neatly labeled, and updated by a reassuring postnuclear enlightenment: no chunk of the once mandatory, so-harmless-you-can-eat-it, uranium-bearing carnotite, whose death rays combined with routine suburban fogging with DDT to make us who we are today.

In the printed material about mineralogy I liked the metaphors buried in "sibling faults" and "a dense, confused mass of minute irregularities" and grades that "show no cleavage." From a jumbled box of stones I chose a sliver of agate to take home to my husband. Wearing the soft fabrics and gem colors common to southwestern style, the kindly woman behind the counter looked all the better for having fled from someplace, maybe the bearded guys' porch in 1978. When I paid for the agate, I still held my notebook open against my ribs. She smiled at me with intense interest and asked, "Are you journaling?"

Although the sky threatened more squalls, the wind bit my face, and NO TRESPASSING signs confined my route to peripheries, I managed a short hike in the skirts of Mt. Chalchihuitl. The outlier hills occupied a wrinkle in New Mexico. The Chihuahuan Desert pushed up from Mexico, the eastern plains rode in from Texas, and, in the center, the Rio Grande spliced a rough jumble of tablelands. The land's spare qualities rendered an unexpected intimacy, comfort against a pervasive sense of estrangement.

Under the cover of spring clouds, the Cerillos Hills rose in muted browns and blond-gold dotted with the quiet green of junipers and pinyons. If you knew turquoise against the rich terracotta slickrock of the Colorado Plateau, these hills would seem too drab to hold the blue. Yet this mountain range, this block of intrusive monzonite porphyry, carried considerable quantities of gem in its seams, veins, and fractures.

Played out after their gifts, the Cerillos mines remain inactive and blocked off. I walked back to my vehicle dodging traffic, a caravan of clamorous, dusty trucks bulging with gravel, the latest spoils of the human compulsion to turn the earth inside out and carry it off, load by load. The flank of the turquoise mountain was a gravel pit.

THE EGYPTIANS, for whom blue was truth, saw the color of daybreak in lapis lazuli. They considered lapis as precious as gold, partly because of its scarcity—and why not, if you worship Ra the sun and consider each dawn a tenuous miracle after night's darkness? In some prayers the words for turquoise and water were interchangeable. Many buildings had green floors like the meadows of the Nile and blue ceilings like the sky. *Nila,* Sanskrit for "blue," named the great river of life, the place the oldest homebodies on earth would not leave until they embarked for the spirit world from their tombs. They packed up their riparian home with them, they filled their story paintings with lotus blossoms, palm fronds, egrets, kingfishers, geese, cranes, butterflies, red-eyed hawks—all the splendid plants and creatures of the Nile Delta.

When I was a teenager living in England, my mother occasionally allowed me to skip school and leave behind the cold, gray London days to go to theater matinees, art galleries, or museums. Inevitably, I ended up in a favored place, the Egyptian rooms at the British Museum, which house a formidable collection of antiquities, everything from mummies and perfume spoons to papyrus books with figures drawn in the trademark Egyptian style: two dimensions, mostly in profile, torsos torqued to frontal view, and a notable absence of butts.

The fragments of two ancient mural paintings from Thebes always drew my attention. One showed a circle of trees in the deceased noble's garden: Sycamores, date palms, and mandrakes surrounded a rectangular pool filled with serene blue water, birds, and fish. Except for a goddess sitting on a sycamore limb, the garden pond reminded me of a California swimming pool.

In the second painting the noble and his family hunted waterfowl in the thickets of a papyrus swamp. Bright tilapia fish swam below the hunter's boat. Butterflies and birds burst from the flowering reeds. The hunter's cat perched on a bent papyrus stem, holding the wings of a bird in its teeth and two more birds in its claws. A goose sat on the boat's prow and more birds hovered over the stand of reeds, birds so thick there was scant space between them, each one drawn with recognizable colors and markings. In his hand the hunter clutched the legs of three long-necked pale blue waterbirds—cranes or herons—with wings outspread to escape, every feather defined. The scene seemed bathed in light the color of pollen. The instructions for the extraordinary life after death were simple: Delight in the lush natural beauties of ordinary life. The story paintings sent the river along with the traveling body and *ka*. The river: What more would they need?

By far the most striking of the British Museum's Egyptian collections housed the smallest treasures, and there I spent many afternoons. The profusion of turquoise and lapis scarabs, beads, amulets, bracelets, collar necklaces, clasps, armlets, and other ornaments cast the entire chamber in blue-green: all that luminous serenity, then the shock of their displacement, these fugitives of the desert plucked from northeastern Africa and arrayed in a small room on a far island of rock in the North Sea, miles and centuries away from the wrists and throats that once wore them.

Conjoined with silver, the blue light also collects in case after case in trading post after trading post in the Southwest, in tasteful showrooms with track lights and Kokopelli flute music wafting out of the air ducts, and in the oldest, crumbling sandstone-block structures, whose wooden plank floors still creak with the weight of generations, the fluidity of pawn. In the old trading posts, the blue and silver wealth resides alongside horse tack, refrigerated mutton, Pennzoil, stacked cans of Hills Brothers coffee, pinyon cream for burns and dry skin, and Blue Bird flour packed in twenty-five-pound sacks of bleached white cotton. Cluster necklaces, manta pins, bolo ties, key chains, concha belts, and ketohs, an archer's bow guard that evolved into a wide bracelet decorated with silver and topped by an asymmetrical slab of turquoise with matrix veins like a map to water or heaven. Brooches and pendants crafted by contemporary Indian artists of superb talent. Sky-blue plastic beads strung with coral-red plastic beads. Barrettes, cuff bracelets, money clips, rings with channel inlay, rings with single cabochons, and heavy watchbands, some of them with the watch intact, the glass dial yellowed by years of harsh sun and the hands frozen at half-past eleven sometime during the Eisenhower administration.

In the trading posts lie the sherds and scatterings of the south, the sacred Navajo quadrant that holds the brightness of the day. Here, as in the Egyptian rooms at the British Museum, there is the need to revel in their collective luminosity, and there is the frantic desire to buy a single disk the size of a communion wafer and run off with it as quickly as you can, to take it away to the sandstone, as if to bring one small prism of sky to all that red heat. Look at it in the morning. View it on the new moon. Perception itself is the embrace.

◆ ◆ ◆

IN THE DESERT there is more dust than gold. Most of the world is expected to desire gold, for it is rare and it does not burn; it is eternal. Like gold, precious gems also dazzle us into full chase, as if their capture beneath our gaze could bring happiness.

In *The Conference of the Birds,* an epic mystical poem written in the late twelfth century by the Persian poet Farid ud-Din Attar, the birds of the world gather for a pilgrimage to Simorgh, an almighty king. Attar, a perfume seller from Nishapur, the city of turquoise mines, puts tongues in the mouths of birds. He chooses a hoopoe, a bird with an erect crest and long curved bill, to lead the journey and expound wisdom through anecdote and fable, forming an allegory of life's passage from the secular to the divine.

When the hoopoe describes the journey as hazardous, the birds make excuses to stay behind, each according to its kind (and a parallel in human character). Among them are the loyal turtle dove, the nightingale bound by transient beauty, the parrot that mistakes its cage for paradise. The timid finch fears she is too fragile for the journey—*I am less sturdy than a hair,* she exclaims. The heron cannot leave the seam between shoreline and sea, which transfixes its gaze. Another bird claims to be a prisoner of desire.

> . . . my love
> Has loaded me with chains; I cannot move.
> This bandit, Love, confronted me and stole
> My intellect, my heart, my inmost soul

The partridge resists the journey because it cannot tear itself away from its obsession with gemstones. The bird declares:

> . . . My one desire
> Is jewels; I pick through quarries for their fire.
> They kindle in my heart an answering blaze

The hoopoe then tells the partridge that the precious gems it so craves are its own; it wears them in its crimson beak, eyes the color of rubies, claws the color of flame, in its glossy plumage, richly barred flanks, and ebony throat. The gems, the hoopoe scolds, have only hardened the bird's heart.

> Without their colours they are nothing more
> Than stones—and to the wise not worth a straw.

Some among us cannot fully rise to the craving. For me gold holds the greatest aesthetic appeal when it is the painted aura of Byzantine saints, set against a lake-dark blue. Gold's history is the history of mining at a high pitch of fever and entire mountain ranges gutted. Silver takes on moonlight better than gold. I cannot help but dive headlong into the mystery of pearls and the way one's throat warms them into a lustrous heat. How can I know the provocation of a ruby if I have never been near one? Can my bracelet of twenty-five birds for the afterlife be the lapis flutter of blue grosbeaks along a jade river?

It is said that Saharan traders of a thousand years ago drew stars on their jewelry. Their constellation amulets were maps to water. Each "compass" was passed down through the generations. From our mothers, from the family of women, many of us today fall heir to our adornments. In my collection is a strand of pearls from a great-aunt, who brought them home to me from her travels around the world. With a dearth of soirées in my rural life, I wear the pearls with sun-bleached cotton shirts on strolls to visit cliffrose in bloom, renewing their luster with my skin, remembering a stalwart lineage of pearl-wearers, their necks bearing strands of perfectly matched spheres on every occasion that mattered in their lives, from college graduation to tea dances for the war effort and weddings in dresses the color of gardenias.

In classic Persian literature the stringing of pearls on a necklace is a common metaphor for the writing of poetry. The pieces I inherited are not so much jewelry as stories and maps, incomplete and uncertain narratives bound by an elemental sensory contentment, a common empathy with bright bits of mineral and their "answering blaze" in the senses. Precious stones speak of status and power, it is true, but also of how humans hold great space in their souls for color.

From simple bits of rock arise metaphor, mystical properties, and marvelous virtues—or the sheer pleasure of ornament. Sometimes the reason for ornament falls away to memory, belief is honed to a simpler faith. The pastoral nomads of northwestern India stitch tiny mirrors into the fabric of their skirts and bodices. The mirrors scare away tigers, the women say, even though their people have not seen tigers there for over eight hundred years.

In its home deserts, in the American Southwest and the Middle East, turquoise is an amulet of the wanderer; it is the carrier of culture and myth. It is not a burden in land so spare and open you give up early on any hope of restraint. The people who wear it most handsomely are the native peoples who consider it holy—not preachy holy but instinct holy, like the taste of a spring hidden in acres and acres of flat-out, bone-dry rock and sand.

The turquoise I wore in the mountains? I wore it because I thought I was brave or in love or going to Arabia. Now I wear it simply because I am too forgetful to take it off. The turquoise I carry into the canyons of home weighs little more than the fear of tigers. Against the burnt stone and wind-rippled sand dunes, the oxblood-red walls of the Entrada Formation with their Tyrian purple shadows, turquoise is a jolt. It is irrefutable proof of the proximity of heart to beauty. The intensely articulated blue seems, like desert light itself, beyond all wealth, even when you know that to breathe light, the sweetest scent, the finest taste, is simply enough.

Despite their distance from one another in time and place, people of diverse desert cultures invested turquoise with similar properties. This stone was universally benign, it soothed the vision, it bound eye and color like no other. The virtues of turquoise are available only if it is a gift, the old books say. The thief of my rings in California left herself unprotected, perhaps subject to lightning bolts and many scorpion bites. The Persian turquoise ring that sits in a satin Chinese box on my dresser does not grow destitute of its native color. It is, without me, yet the burden of waters and, as Thomas Nicols wrote, "it doth recover its own lovely beauty which ariseth of the temperament of its own naturall heat, and becometh ceruleous like a serene heaven."

I will pass this ring to my niece, daughter of the man who made it, and though she may not find cause or desire to tease her own reckless courage, she will know that the ring flew with me on a hemp rope high over an opaque night river, in the cusp of youth with no hazard of thought, only the sheer suppleness of sensation.

Azul Maya

There are nine different words in Maya for the color blue
in the comprehensive Porrúa Spanish-Maya Dictionary
but just three Spanish translations, leaving six butterflies
that can be seen only by the Maya, proving beyond
doubt that when a language dies six butterflies disappear
from the consciousness of the earth.

EARL SHORRIS
"The Last Word"

The sound of the Yucatán Peninsula is a low hum, the emanation from a thick cover of green that stretches far into the horizon like giant broccoli gone berserk. A road splices this jungle. Along its edges lies a fortress of slash—trees cut and piled as if there could never be a peaceful transition between closed and open space, between green wall and pale tarmac. The slash heaps parallel the road for miles and miles south of the airport until we meet the slashers, the work crews that move down the coast along a two-lane road, leaving a four-lane highway behind them. In their wake sprout resort hotels as big as Luxembourg. The construction is not unlike an industrial excavation for mineral wealth: land shaved to reveal a rough and raw nakedness, infrastructure installed, laborers swarming the premises. Here the ore is a spectrum of color that feeds a human longing for bliss. Here is the mining of Caribbean blues.

The road-jungle edge was not the edge I anticipated. It takes more driving, a camping layover, a bone-jarring dirt road, and entry into a coastal nature preserve to truly arrive. At last, in front of the small beach house we have rented, I feel as if I have crawled through an aperture in one of my horizon bands and emerged on the other side into turquoise writ large. The world layers itself in chromatic resonance from the horizon to my toes: deep indigo, aquamarine, turquoise, then water as clear as glass, ruffled with tidal foam on sand so pale that, like Navajo Sandstone, it takes on a rosy hue when the light is low.

We occupy Casa Rosa, a worn-out, cement-block cabana with two large rooms and a porch on the side of sunrise and a porch on the side of sunset. Rosa's twin, Casa Azul, sits next to us, empty of tenants at the moment. There is no electricity, only solar-heated water and a stove and lamps fueled by propane. The neighbors are scant, scattered down the coast. The broccoli forest surrounds the cabanas on three sides. The fourth side opens to the palm-strewn beach and the sea.

To this place we brought groceries, which, because of a moment of accidental hysteria in a local market, turn out to be mostly avocados and papayas the size of soccer balls. I cast my eye on other possible forage in the yard off the sunset porch, all of it at least visually edible—almond and jacaranda trees, blood-red hibiscus, fat coconuts, and a geranium tree, genus *Cordia,* with burnt-orange blossoms and branches filled with yellow-gold birds with black bibs on their necks, the orange oriole, an endemic to Campeche, Yucatán, and Quintana Roo, the three states of the peninsula.

The piece of continent underfoot is a vast sled of coral and limestone underlain with sinkholes and caverns and pockets of rainwater in the hard, calcitic rock. The tropical forest takes purchase on a thin skin, its crowns topped with orchids and air ferns that climb to the light. At land's edge, our habitat, the shelf breaks up into lagoons and mangrove swamps, then meets the Caribbean with miles of white beach under the protection of the preserve. Here we will lapse into the simple roles of fisherman and color-eater, with no anxieties beyond one projectile barracuda and a dead man under a coconut palm.

The Yucatán's Caribbean coast drew us because Mark was here once, pre-me, pre-Luxembourgs, and because both of us love Mexico. So much blue, he thought, would lure me out of the Southwest without the usual reluctance, my dire fear of leaving my bighorn sheep, my random cairns of river rocks in the bathroom, or of the world coming to an end if I missed the greening of one single leaf of cliffrose.

We saved our money. We practiced our Spanish with lesson books and tapes. On the label of a jar of salsa I found *"Se habla español"* next to a toll-free number. When I called to try out some conversation, I reached a taped sampler of salsa recipes. Mark wore his flippers in the shower. I jettisoned any hotel publicity that offered Mr. and Mrs. Bikini contests, and I imagined ourselves— but only for three lunatic seconds—at Club Med in disco clothes or sidled up to a seafood buffet as long as a supermarket aisle. Resorts with golf divas aroused this many neurological impulses in our brains: zero. We sought options of self-sufficiency and packed snorkeling, fishing, and camping gear. Through a chain of inquiries we found this vintage cabana inside the coastal reserve. Even before we arrive, there is a sense that this sanctuary is growing more precious each day, so certain is the press of the industrial riviera against its borders.

On our first full day at Casa Rosa, Mark and I awaken before light, the stars limpid in air saturated with humidity. Off the east porch the sky grows bands of rose and lavender. Suddenly, an enormous crimson disk lobs up over the silver ocean. The sun rises and I am confused. I turn and twist and stand on my head. The low morning sun over the sea defies an imprint, *If the sun is over the ocean, the sun is going down.* I cannot quickly undo a lifetime of

Pacific sunsets. *Atlantic* is still a new world to me. Its rhythms and forces demand attentiveness. How do the storms move? What gravity bulges the tides? Where are we fixed on the earth's lissome curve?

The gyre that pulls this sunrise ocean moves west from Africa across the equator then caresses this thumb of land on Mexico's flank. The Gulf Stream carries the warm waters farther north. Like the ocean currents, airflow also moves in a circular pattern, captive to the earth's rotation, pulled one way or the other on either side of the equator: the Coriolis effect. This force can act upon the spiraling of water down drains, counterclockwise if you are in the Northern Hemisphere, clockwise if you are south of the equator. We are still in the Northern Hemisphere but just barely. My quest for drain behavior reassures me that we will not be flung off the spinning globe—you can never be too sure. On a flight to Australia once, when the airplane was precisely *over* the equator, I rushed to the airplane's lavatory and filled the sink with water. Then I pulled the plug to see which way the water would circle the drain, hoping for some sort of momentous turmoil in the physics of deflection. When you venture well beyond home, it is important to assess the territory.

On the beach the shrill, high-pitched whistle of a great-tailed grackle in a coconut palm anchors me to this exotic ground. Everyday one of these gregarious black birds will give this cry at nearly the same time, just as the molten orb appears on the shimmering scrim of sea and sky. Such markers as these must teach me where I am.

I know I am not in the desert because the pages of my book ripple, my hair is an inch shorter with curl and wave, and everything I own has gained weight by swelling in the damp, salty air. A T-shirt now weighs as much as a sheet.

When I sit on the sandy beach, two stalks pop up from a hole. Spheres on the end of the stalks rotate, then stare at me. When I move my hand, the eyestalks retract, and on the other end of them is a small crab nearly the same color as the powder-white sand. I sit quietly until a dozen crabs send up their periscopic eyes. I feel compelled to moon them. I build a few crabs of my own. The sand is like *masa harina* wet down for tamales, easily shaped into detailed sculptures. A real crab emerges boldly and mounts one of the sand-built crabs, knocking the eyestalks right over.

The crabs scurry sideways into their holes when a military Jeep-truck whizzes down the beach, its open bed packed with soldiers. Automatic rifles at the ready, they appear to be on their way to a coup. Later a helicopter flies the same route. Its open bay reveals a machine gun on a tripod and the soldier who mans it. In this way the Mexican *federales* keep vigilance against drug smugglers, commercial fishing operations (limited if not banned on the preserve's shores and lagoons), and poachers of the sea turtles that lay their eggs in the warm sands. Like the cry of the *zanate* and the backward sunset, the morning patrols will become a daily marker.

Mark takes a small kayak out to the reef, armed only with his fly rod. His plan is for us to live off the sea. He will catch dinner every-day, he says, something to balance out the papaya-avocado food pyramid. At one point he is out so far and paddling so resolutely I think he is heading for Africa. Then he returns to shore with a magnificent frigate bird over his head, a gliding seabird with an eight-foot wing span and absurdly small feet, the proper proportion for a creature that flies more than it perches.

After his reconnaissance to the reef, Mark and Israel, a neighbor and the caretaker of Casas Azul and Rosa, motor out of sight in a *panga,* an open boat made of molded fiberglass. They are headed for Serious Fishing. Israel is an athletic Mexican with a streak of mischief and an endless collection of baseball caps and T-shirts emblazoned with a repertoire of international logos. For most of his forty-some years he has been a fisherman. He speaks little English. Mark and I speak cassette-tape Spanish, but, because of trips to Baja California, my vast knowledge of salsa recipes, and French and Italian in my previous lives, I understand quite a bit. It is as if I have ears but no tongue. We get by.

My walk on the beach soon turns into a run "upstream," a direction my river-headedness assigns to the north, the ocean on my right, because I come from life on the banks of a canyon stream. Israel has warned me that dogs will chase and bite me if I run downstream, or south. The run is comfortable, long, and easier than any run at home. As soon as I am rising nimbly off the balls of my bare feet, breathing without strain, feeling quite fit and that I should probably enter a marathon race or do a shampoo commercial, I realize that I am running at sea level, not a mile above it as I do at home. I am further humbled when I encounter a young Mayan, one of the soldiers from the truck, perhaps, who is jogging in head-to-toe olive-green military fatigues, automatic rifle, and combat boots.

The day unfolds below palm trees and *mariposas;* for a while, the butterflies outnumber the birds. Mark and Israel are gone so long I begin to worry enough to imagine them far out to sea, dividing up one granola bar. I take an afternoon stroll downstream, braving the dogs that turn out to be impostors. Several miles down the beach, beyond the mouth of a lagoon, I am so filled with fresh air and curiosity I feel as if I could walk all the way to Belize, where, I once read, a group of Maya near the border still hopes that the British will help them oust the Mexicans.

I must use all my senses to find out who inhabits this piece of coast, what swims, flies, or crawls, who eats who, who has power and who does not. It is up to me to discover what to avoid and how to get lost, what is present and what is missing. Local knowledge reveals change and certainty, the wild and the tame, the abundant and the rare, the layers of history that haunt and the stories that people tell. With only three weeks in February to be here, I will attend the feast but leave after the appetizers.

Someone said that if you want to understand an unfamiliar piece of the American West you look at the fences. Fences punctuated the mass trespass against native America. Fences carve out the individual from the communal, they announce, depending on your point of view, what is kept in or what is kept out. As a desert dweller, I believe that water is a truer entry to Place. In the West, aridity defines us.

There is abundant water here in the Yucatán—ocean, marsh, lagoon, underground rivers, *cenotes* (natural wells where freshwater surfaces), a tropical forest swollen with transpiration. Storms bring a hurricane's eyewall of torrents or nothing at all; even jungles have droughts. By invasion and sheer presence, the sea pushes itself into what is drinkable and what is heard, or what you miss hearing when you are distant from the surf. The sea holds an abundance of comfort and inspiration and danger, all that a person needs in order to rise to the full largesse of beauty. It seems that if you allow this beauty to become a blank, if you turn your back to the blues and deny your dependence on them, you might lose your place in the world, your actions would become small, your soul disengaged.

At dusk Mark and Israel return with a bag of silvery, finger-sized bait netted on the reef and a quarter of a jack, a kind of ocean perch. I have a knife, and I want to open the fish myself because I am always curious to see what is inside a fish, its swim bladder and heart, the things that it eats. In the bellies of freshwater fish I have found tiny intact fish and, once, a whole grape. The interior of a sizable creature of the Caribbean pricks my interest. However, this one has empty space behind its pectoral fin.

"Where are the other three-quarters?" I ask Mark. Israel is jumping around the beach making fang marks out of his fingers.

"I donated them to a shark," Mark replies. He holds up the intact fish head. The colors run from dark green-black on the top to silver on the cheeks and throat. There is a faint olive band that would extend from eye to tail—that is, if there were a tail. "I hooked it and started to reel it in, thinking it was a big one. Then the fish suddenly lost lots of weight. I reeled in a head and shoulders."

From the ragged flesh it is obvious that large teeth ripped the jack apart in a single bite. *El tiburón!* Israel had yelled in the boat, doing the fang gesture so Mark would understand. Once we cut off the jack's head there is no further gutting because the shark's end of the fish had all the guts. Whole, the fish would have weighed over eight pounds. We are left with four steaks. This, I tell my stalwart provider, is plenty.

DAWN CASTS a rosy light over a quicksilver sea, washing out Venus. Along the horizon the sky appears bruised. The sea mirrors all the colors, its turquoise translucence absent until the sun climbs higher. When the crimson orb appears, its edges ripple against the thick atmosphere. I wonder how the Pueblos of the Southwest would view it, the marvel of a rising god that can be looked at straight on without blindness.

A *zanate* begins the day with its shrill dawn whistle and some mischief. Against the spring-green striping of palm fronds his feathers iridesce jet-black with a purple sheen behind his head. The females show necks the color of dark chocolate. The eyes are bright yellow, the long tail keel-shaped. A member of the same family as blackbirds, orioles, tanagers, and meadowlarks, the great-tailed grackle, also known in the Yucatán as a *k'au,* prefers to be near humans and cultivated land. It seems to occupy the niche of magpies; it is like a raven with a motor mouth. I wonder if Heckle and Jeckle, our home ravens, e-mailed the news of our arrival to the grackles: EXPECT USELESS BUT AMUSING GRINGOS. SEND MORE PAPAYAS.

After their sunrise cry the grackles are all *clack* and chortles and creaks and yellow eyes casting much attention on the roof of Casa Rosa, where Mark threw the fish head. During the night we fully expected a jaguar, but the only predator is the gray house cat that will spend most of the day on the tin roof making raspy gnawing noises.

This cat and two puppies are the resident composters. Irma, Israel's wife, has taken in two stray dogs, one black, one liver-colored, with prehensile bodies and legs as thin as chicken bones.

They wobble on miniature feet, stomachs distended by malnutrition into tight balloons. Their tails are like thin strands of linguine. They emit croaky yips then fall over and pass out with the effort. They will not come near us, nor do they move away quickly, they are so weak. Irma's fattening-up project is not yet apparent. In a stupor they chew on one another, oblivious to the morning's helicopter. It cruises the shoreline at a predictable nine o'clock. All you need to do is smuggle your booty at noon.

Every morning Israel pushes his wheelbarrow to the beach and rakes up fallen palm fronds and debris washed in from high tide: bits of black seaweed, air-dried blades of turtle grass, errant pieces of trash. I love to sweep or rake—something about the motion calms and paces me—so I often help. Whereas we Americans would drive a utility vehicle within a millimeter of every labor task and hope we would not have to get out of the car to perform it, the Mexicans use their wheelbarrows. They pile them with laundry, garden tools, outboard motors, palm fronds, sacks of oranges, children, cases of bottled water. Up the coast we saw the Winnebago model: a wheelbarrow covered with a square canopy of blue-and-white-striped canvas. Inside the tent were shelves to hold supplies.

Midday, Mark returns from a trip to town with more fruit, postcards, a butcher's chicken with feet as yellow as egg yolks, and a four-dollar Cuban cigar. He also bought several cups of a red paste, spooned into a wrap of plastic by one of the market vendors. It is as red as paprika. The red comes off on our fingers. The paste has an exotic, earthy scent. Neither of us knows what it is.

After lunch we venture out to sea in the sit-on-top kayak, a yellow, two-seater craft that looks like a banana. We head for Africa on a fruit peel. Above the reef the water lies in dark bands of cobalt fingered with turquoise. Beds of turtle grass and kelp sway beneath us. We manage to put on masks and flippers and swim, slithering back and forth from the banana peel without capsizing. I paddle close by while Mark explores the reef. I wonder what I will do when a shark bites his legs off.

The forests of coral are visible through the clear water but nothing like the view with the mask, a dreamy, liquid world brought into sharp focus. Blue chromis and blue-green parrot fish drift past my nose. Through shafts of aquamarine sunlight swim gaudily striped angelfish, fish the color of canaries or orioles, fish so small and bright they look like luminous chips of topaz, emeralds, sapphires. Underneath them lies a landscape of every shape and pattern imaginable, from the most stolid brainlike mass to a fan of ochre coral veined with scarlet, as delicate as lace.

I understand nothing. I lose my tongue.

It occurs to me that the entire reef is one giant digestive tract made of millions of intricate parts. Pores, polyps, and tentacles, stomachs and spicules and spines. Tubes, valves, feet, fins, filaments, filters. Creatures that squeeze, squish, or squirt, creatures that mate with others or mate with themselves. Water moving inside, through, and around animals that look like trees or flowers, plants that look like animals, some drifting a few feet, others floating all the way to Belize, still others fixed and going nowhere, all of it vastly carnivorous and omnivorous, pulsing with the unceasing motion of the sea. I have no voice for this complicated landscape, no language of perception. Little smell and scant hearing. Only keen sight, imperfect taste, faint, watery touch, and the ethereal muscle of currents pressing against me.

Mark spots a sea turtle feeding in the underwater garden. By the time we switch places and I am in the water, the turtle has disappeared. I watch for the toothy barracuda. We have heard wild tales about this formidable open-water predator, tales likely calculated to unnerve the average radio-collared tourists and keep them close to their discos and credit cards. Barracuda want to steal disabled fish—for example, the one you have just caught and should not cradle in the shallows if you do not care to have your calf muscles torn off.

For reasons that are not clear, barracuda like orange swimsuits and, when they approach head-on, they probably want to look at themselves in your mirrorlike mask faceplate rather than bite your face. Shiny objects attract the barracuda's attention, and the charge is a split-second, powerful rush—no nosing around to distinguish a pinkie ring from a sardine. The mostly exaggerated attack lore suggests legions of bejeweled snorkelers soon missing their hands, necks, or ears. To be safe I hold my left hand and gold wedding band over my head and out of the water while I float facedown in the gentle swells.

There is a lagoon behind the cabanas, nearly as large as a bay. At one point it narrows to a handle-shaped mouth and runs out to sea. The channel is fringed with mangroves and rich with fish. When we drive down the rutted dirt road to the small bridge that crosses the channel, a handful of *federales* stop us at their checkpoint. We stand outside the car while one of them searches it. The searcher is quietly polite, but another soldier stands alert, gun across his chest. He stares at us coldly, as if we had stuffed the bug-sized rental car with cocaine and turtles. Suddenly, his face relaxes. He points to himself and says proudly, "*Corredor, el corredor.*" He is the runner on the beach, the fellow who jogs in his hot uniform. In my wretched Spanish I tell him he is strong and runs far, praying to the river gods that I used *fuerte* (strong) rather than *inarrugable* (wrinkle-resistant) or have not said "There is only one thing smaller than your pea brain and it's below your belt" to an eighteen-year-old who is holding an AK-47.

Mark fishes from the bridge like one of those old guys on city piers, with no boat, boxes of bait at their feet, and more conversation than concentration, but the conversation is with a couple of Italian tourists who pass by—from Livorno, they say, and they are lively and rather fun and soon I am dredging up Italian words from remote, unused sectors of my brain, explaining that I once lived in Rome, went to school in Florence—*Firenze!* we all cry, remembering the Uffizi, the Raphaels and Cimabues, Brunelleschi's dome—and they politely tolerate my ruthless verbicide and a rust-covered recitation of Dante. *Nel mezzo del cammin di nostra vita, mi ritrovai per una selva oscura.* So delighted are we to be in Mexico talking about fish and *La Divina Commedia,* soon they are calling me *l'americana romana* and so much Italian is floating up from the memory banks that I feel I must tell them the story of my entire life since Italy, and we laugh in the bright sun and hold one another's shoulders and air-kiss both cheeks as we say goodbye. In the clear water under the bridge several barracuda move along the mangroves with quiet stealth. Mark catches and releases a fish with a pursed mouth full of fused teeth and a line of chartreuse dots from eye to tail fin.

At dinnertime Israel shows me how to cook the remaining jack in the red seasoning that Mark brought from town—*achiote* paste, a Yucatecan specialty made by mixing garlic, cumin, cilantro seed, oregano, allspice, vinegar, and other aromatics with the crushed seed pulp of the annatto tree. The annatto pulp gives the *achiote* paste its bright red. Israel adds fresh lime juice to the *achiote* and spreads it on the fish. We take over from there, grilling the fillets on a barbecue set up on the sunset porch.

When Israel or Irma speaks to us, I understand nearly everything but can say so little. It is the way I felt on the reef—tongueless, mute, lost without a verbal map to nuance and detail. Words clog my head, swelling, pressing into every crevice, surging forth but unable to come out. It is even worse after the conversation with the people from Livorno. Now, whenever I speak, it is a mongrel Spanish-Italian-English. When I get stuck, I draw pictures on a piece of paper to explain.

The moon rises over the palms and our fish blazes bright paprika red over the coals. I sketch mountains and mesas and cactus. Babies in California and Montana explain where Mark and I were born, where our families live. I put a little beard and skis on Baby Mark. Israel adds a fishing rod, for he is now calling Mark *el pescador.* Using an orange as a globe, I draw clumsy continents and make a map from this beach to Utah's San Juan River. All of us are amazed at the distance. Somehow we explain whitewater rafting.

◆ ◆ ◆

OFF THE COAST OF Campeche, on the Gulf of Mexico side of the Yucatán Peninsula, lies Isla Jaina. Over a century and a half ago the Maya made the island of Jaina a necropolis. *Hanal,* they called it, the "house of water." The Jaina cemetery was filled with ceremonial objects and everyday utensils. The tombs also held an abundance of statuettes made from painted earthenware.

Jaina's clay statuettes depict aristocrats, artisans, and actors, priests and ballplayers, dwarfs and the blind—a broad spectrum of Maya society from the richest nobles to the most humble villagers. In gesture and ornamentation the detail is extraordinary. Detachable helmets with feathers and flowers; headdresses of birds, monkeys, and fish; masks, shawls, and *huipiles,* woven clothing with floral embroidery. Dangling earrings, necklaces, bracelets, slingback sandals. A fan resting on a knee, fingers resting on a knee, a hand outstretched, a hand on the hip. Beards, scars, tattooed cheeks, teeth filed to fine points. A thin man carries a fat man on his back. Two ballplayers lean into their game. A figure with holes in the joints of his limbs (a puppet?) wears a costume adorned with parrots and jaguars. Mouth open so her mutilated teeth can be admired, a woman believed to be a worshiper of the wind wears a *huipil* and thick strands of beads.

According to Dr. Román Piña Chán of Mexico's National Institute of Anthropology and History, the burial relics were produced between A.D. 600 and 1000. They have "given Jaina its fame," he writes, "for they depict the people of the island with such fidelity, it seems as if they have returned from the dead."

The many Mayan gods were multipurpose gods. A goddess of the moon, for instance, also served as the patroness of sex, birth, and weaving. The weavers formed a guild in her honor. Like the Maya farther south in Central America and the indigenous Peruvians along the Andean cordillera, the weavers produced textiles of incomparable technical skill and pure, singing color. They wove their world into "radiant cloth," as Chilean poet Pablo Neruda called the textiles of the Incas, to attire "the lovers, the burial sites, the mothers, the king, the prayers and the warriors" of the pre-Columbian Americas.

One of the figurines from Jaina is a weaver. She carries a loom carved with a bobbin of yarn and a two-headed snake. Her long braids fall down her back, interwoven with ribbons. Although the figure's red clay has been exposed over time, there are still remnants of blue on her skirt and tunic. It is a particular blue, now in its age slightly chalky with turquoise hues, the color of certain feathers on a pinyon jay's throat or a band of twilight sky against terra-cotta sandstone. This was a color the Maya could not get enough of. On this end of the visible spectrum lay their fascinations and their faith. One after another, the clay statuettes of Jaina were painted in blue pigment. It is as if someone placed the figures in the graves, then let loose a dense blue mist.

Azul Maya is distinctive and pervasive. It is found on murals and temple ornament as well as ceramics. Despite heat, humidity, and age, the blue pigment remains deep and rich in color. Its stability, considering its organic content, is remarkable, and the Maya knew the sophisticated chemistry that made it so. Contemporary science has successfully deciphered its properties.

The paint consists of *sak-lum,* in Maya—palygorskite, a white, powder clay mineral—and indigo, a dye extracted from the leaves of *Indigofera suffruticosa.* Through manipulations of heat the Maya locked the indigo into the clay's channel-shaped molecules, forming a chemical bond that cannot be easily undone. The clay has fingerprints, impurities so unique to certain locations that it can be traced to its source—clay from the coastal Yucatán, clay from the inland plains. The alchemy, not the clay, gave the pigment its blue, the color of divinity that outlasted the mortals.

On the beach at Casa Rosa, the sun strong and high in the sky, everywhere I look, the blues assert themselves. The turquoise sea forms an all-consuming horizon against which everything else stands—shells known locally as pea strigillas, ice-white with the palest of pink interiors; the cool blue-violet jacaranda blooms; hibiscus with reckless throats of sizzling red velvet. In the sea there are more colors than anyone has names for. Pliny the naturalist tried—aquamarine, he said, is the color of a calm sea, a not-storm blue. I can say aquamarine or ultramarine, turquoise or cerulean, yet words soon run thin and deficient for what is, after all, the simple apprehension of light.

In an essay about language Earl Shorris describes the world's many dying tongues, most of them the tongues of indigenous peoples. Although the estimated 6 million descendants of the ancient Maya speak twenty-five languages, a number of them are destined to disappear with the deaths of the last speakers. The Maya have at least nine words for blue, all with certain attributes, most without translation. The absence of those words, Shorris says, is far deeper than silence. "It is not merely a writer's conceit to think that the human world is made of words and to remember that no two words in all the world's languages are alike," he writes. "Of all the arts and sciences made by man, none equals a language, for only a language in its living entirety can describe a unique and irreplaceable world."

The cry of the *zanate* and the faithful witness of each sunrise fix our days. The rest of the clock goes thoroughly mushy, with languorous barefoot hikes along the beach to the mouth of the lagoon, coconuts dropping around our hammocks with dull, avuncular thuds, endless swimming, forays to the reef in the kayak, smoky tamales wrapped in bright green banana leaves, sold from a truck by women in white cotton *huipiles* embroidered with scarlet flowers. Lamplight and dark surf lie at the farthest margins of the days. The moon waxes into fullness, rising violet behind a heap of cumulus, then amber as it climbs. Fireflies flicker yellow-green amid the palm trees and a high tide spills onto the gleaming sand disks of lapis lazuli and crescents of amethyst with sapphire threads—hundreds of jellyfish. It is as if we have come to the place described in

Hindu cosmology as the "essential island," an island made of pulverized gems and sweet-smelling trees.

If language is frozen, if I am mute in this part of the world, then it will be a synergy of senses that saves me, the unconditional inhalation of light into something audible, its complicit touch on my fingertips, eyes, and tongue. I swim in the warm, erotic, turquoise sea and fully expect to be undone by a color. This water, these transparent blues, I want to burn them into my vision so deeply that no matter where I go, they will always be with me in their spellbinding pitch of purity. It is, after all, mostly a hunger of the senses that puts the love and terror of life into radiant cloth and on the enshrouding paint of hundreds of figures who exclaim themselves in inert clay.

MOST BIRD-WATCHERS — a sensible lot with crisp lists and clothing whose appendages zip off—do not usually find themselves in crowded, confined spaces trying to keep a barracuda from biting their ankles.

We are sitting on the beach. Gulls swarm indolently over our heads. Papaya rinds surround our lawn chairs. Pushing a wheelbarrow loaded with a monstrous outboard motor, Israel walks by in his flip-flops and IRISH FOOTBALL baseball cap.

"*Vengan mis gringitos!*" he calls to us. He is mounting an expedition.

We have not wandered far for hours, days, years, whatever, so devoted are we to the dazzling fringe of white sand on the turquoise sea. We are not likely to move unless a hurricane blows in and plasters us against the coconut palms. The beach life has kept us in the bird-watcher's realm of fish eaters—gulls, pelicans, terns, cormorants. A sooty tern swoops to the water's surface and grabs a fish without landing. Like the magnificent frigate bird, sooty terns work hundreds of square miles of ocean by aerial predation. Their feathers are not waterproof. We believe it is our duty to watch the terns until one misses its plunge dive and ends up a soggy mess. We feel we should sit here until we witness a moment of natural selection, one bird blowing its gene pool. It might take a long time.

Neighbors have joined us in the adjacent cabana, Casa Azul. Friends from Montana arrived with an intent to live off the sea and their groceries, which strangely turn out to be sacks full of papayas and avocados. We are amazed that Tony, Joan, and their young son, Lander, have dropped out of the frigid northern steppe into this envelope of sea and time. They, too, have come a long way around the global orange.

The speed of delivery—all of us—to this distant place gives me a kind of geographical vertigo. The only way to recuperate is to swim, walk, and visit Mayan ruins in jungles filled with luminous butterflies. Once in a while, we send Tony and Mark off with their long, agile rods to pursue bonefish, the apparition of the Caribbean shallows. When the army chopper flies over, we brandish our Frisbees. Lander covers himself with sugary white sand as soon as he has enough sunscreen on his lithe little body to make a good glue. The gumdrop look will remain his terrestrial guise.

Tropical languor has fully seized us. We are now stuck in our Darwinian tern study.

Israel slowly coaxes us into a vertical position. We think about bolting for the hammocks. "*Vamos a la lancha,*" he insists, pushing us and the wheelbarrow toward the boat that is docked on the edge of the lagoon. Mark grabs a rod, but we are not seeking fish. We are going to the *isla de los pájaros.*

"*Por todas partes hay pájaros,*" explains Israel. Birds everywhere. An island of birds.

All six of us pile into the open *lancha.* Israel motors along the shore, then weaves through broken patches of mangroves. The lagoon is the size of an enormous lake; we cannot see the opposite shore, only a straight, shimmering line of water on the horizon, dotted with low clumps of islands. The low afternoon sun marks the west, more or less, but without our guide none of us could find our way back to the dock in this maze of mangroves and water.

Mark trolls a fishing line over the side of the boat, the end knotted with a tarty-looking metallic lure, a faux sardine in Day-Glo drag. His rod rests low against the hull and half-forgotten. There are sights to see: an osprey nest made from a mass of twigs and a snarl of green nylon string, a small Mayan ruin, its base nearly flooded by the estuarial tide. The boxy, one-room structure has a single doorway and what look like holes for *vigas,* or roof supports, along the face. It leans slightly and sprouts greenery from its roof and a crop of moss across the gray limestone blocks.

We know that the ancient Maya were a people who loved jewelry, wrote poems, tracked planets, and predicted eclipses. They perfected the mathematical use of zero and figured out the chemistry that made balls bounce and a certain blue pigment resistant to fading. "They were devoted to perfume, having bouquets of flowers and odorous plants, arranged with much care and art," wrote Fra Diego de Landa in *Relación de las Cosas de Yucatán,* a book about the Maya written in 1566 by a man who, in the name of a Christian god and colonial imperative, also burned twenty-seven rolls of hieroglyphs and destroyed over five thousand "idols."

Yet this small, enigmatic stone box on the lagoon, whose doorway frames a space of the blackest emptiness, seems to underscore how much we do not know about the Maya. Israel turns the boat away from the ruin and opens the throttle to full speed. We crane our necks toward ancient history. Our minds dwell on mystery and enigma. Lander, being a healthy ten-year-old boy, dwells on bloody sacrifices and gods with the masks of jaguars. Then all hell breaks loose.

Mark's filament line whizzes out from his reel. He catches his rod midair, before it departs from the boat, and clutches the cork grip as the rod bends into a tight parenthesis. When Israel cuts the motor, it is as if he is braking to a screeching halt to avoid a head-on collision. The sudden drop in speed swamps the bow. There is no time for Mark to play the fish. At the very moment the motor reaches idle, the fish arcs out of the water toward the boat, sending a split-second message to six brains: aerial barracuda.

Tony, Joan, Lander, and I flee to the bow and stack up like a pyramid, our fists clutching each other's shirt fabric. The barracuda flops around the middle well and disengages the hook. Fifteen pounds of untethered fish muscle with spiky, flesh-ripping teeth explode on the floor of the boat.

The huge barracuda thrashes against a thwart and appears quite capable of flying, which sends Mark and his bare, vulnerable shins to a tightrope walker's position on the gunwale. He and the human tower on the bow threaten to topple and capsize the boat. The barracuda nearly has the entire place to itself. Its slender, torpedo-shaped body throws back the sunlight; the whole fish is blinding silver chrome. In a kind of gasping, the curved plates of flesh over its gills open and shut in the waterless air.

I think about how, in Montana, I have held a trout by the tail end and thwacked its head against a rock for a swift, humane kill. I remember a sense of relief and dread if the trout went limp on the first hit. Limpness meant instant death. A pulse or twist of flesh against my palm meant I had to deliver another blow. I am wondering who will thwack this three-foot-long barracuda. Its massive head is shaped like needle-nose pliers. Its belly is likely filled with earrings and Rolexes.

Somehow Mark and Israel manage to use the spare oar for a fatal stroke. The fish lies still. The human pyramid disassembles. Already the men are growing the magnitude of the barracuda battle exponentially between capture on the hook and the tales to tell over a cold *cerveza*.

Muy grande!

El pescador!

Quién es más macho?

With eyes and fingers I take in this breathtaking predator, its body a landscape of the Atlantic. The sleek skin curves in a reflective mirror, dimming in death to burnished stainless steel. The dark and light dorsal bars are olive-green to near-black, a pattern that mimics dappled underwater light in the shallows or amid turtle grass. Close up, the chrome flanks have opals in them. This fish can change its colors selectively—darken and lighten pieces of itself, not only for camouflage but also as communication, using flesh and light, water and color, as language. Aqueous and round above a formidable jaw, the barracuda's eyes drain themselves of clarity. You cannot fix the colors quickly; they ask you to hold the present, and that is impossible. Lander stares at the sharp, sharky teeth and whispers, "Barracu-uuda."

We motor across the water again. Mark trolls a fresh line and lure. We glare at him. Deeper into the lagoon Israel approaches another island and kills the motor just off its shore. The entire island, about two acres in size, is covered with a gallery of trees the size of mature cottonwoods. So thick are the trees and the mangroves at their feet, the island appears to be without purchase in any soil. It is held by the weight of leaves, branches, roots, and birds. *Isla de los pájaros.*

The egrets of my home desert are as white as snow. The egrets on this island bear the colors of the desert: bodies the slate blue-gray of summer monsoon clouds, shaggy neck plumes in the cinnamon-red of sandstone, pink bills with a black tip, legs of cobalt blue. Unlike many other creatures, birds have color vision. Evolution favors them with the ability to see each other's vivid and diverse plumage, for communication, camouflage, courtship, perhaps for sheer pleasure. Of what value would these cobalt legs be if another bird could not see them?

Israel points to one of the long-necked birds. *"Garza morena."*

Like its heron cousins, the reddish egret (*Egretta rufescens*) is a wader of the shallows. It "canopy feeds"—extends its large wings to form pools of shadow over the water to more easily spot prey, which it stirs up with its twiglike toes.

A halo of cormorants surrounds the crowns of the trees, very black and busy. A few ibis work the mangrove fringe with the egrets. The trees themselves are hung with fruits of outrageous boudoir pink, heaving and fluttering. Each pink fruit—there are nearly a hundred of them—is a roseate spoonbill.

This island is a rookery for *Ajaia ajaja,* and many of the nests hold fluffy chicks, pastel pink with an outer flush of blue-gray down. Like all young birds that are nearly ready to fledge, they are too stubborn to leave the nest even though their overgrown bodies spill over the sides. They look like pink chiffon prom dresses standing in little ashtrays. The spoons on their faces are miniatures of the adults' spatulate bills. The parent birds perch close to their offspring, preening themselves in the growing dusk. The roseate spoonbill, wrote Roger Tory Peterson, is "one of the most breathtaking of the world's weird birds."

Like the ibis, the spoonbill is a tactile forager. It stands up to its knees in the fecund shallows and sweeps its flat mandibles from side to side, detecting prey and creating small whirlpools that suck minnows, shrimp, and aquatic insects into the water column. In *The Birds of America,* John James Audubon's spoonbill feeds at the edge of a marsh. He used dead spoonbills as his portrait models. "When the Spoonbills are by themselves and feeding, they can be easily approached by those who, like yourself perhaps, are expert at crawling over the mud on hands and knees, through the tall and keen-edged saw-grass." Audubon himself crawled and pulled the trigger for art. He shot two. A third spoonbill "might, I believe, have been as easily shot, for it stood . . . looking with curious intensity as it were upon its massacred friends" before flying off.

A century ago the spoonbill's nun's-blush pink screamed "target" for plume hunters, and the bird was nearly decimated by hat fashions. Its existence today depends largely on the protection of mangrove ecology against forces intent on draining estuarine wetlands for development.

The kitchen-implement nose, the ice-cream colors—much about the roseate spoonbill feels silly, a view jaded by a culture that relegates gawky pink birds to lawn ornaments and shower curtains. More so, the spoonbill on this Mexican *laguna* seems impossible and vulnerable. Why are they pink? Why not? Are they antidotes to emotional monotony? There is nothing desert-spare about the tropics' palette of pure, shameless color, the splintering of a prism of Place into thousands of resonant pigments. From behind a lace of green leaves, an adult male shows the scarlet highlights across his silky pink wings. The throat feathers are the pale rose of a pea strigilla shell.

"*Chocolatera,*" Israel whispers. The name of the bird.

The light is diffuse and moist over emerald water with a metallic cast. *La isla de los pájaros* croaks and clicks and quivers as the birds settle in for the evening roost. In a slow-motion, Pleistocene lift of broad wings, the egrets leave the mangrove shallows for higher perches. All avian eyes are on us, yet the birds remain unalarmed.

The search for birds, says an ornithologist in one of my books, will take you to places you might not otherwise visit. Birds make you step out of your life and into theirs. They move about under your nose or on the other side of the globe. Sometimes, at home, I long to feel the deep currents of their migrations, a motion of air well beyond our senses, something to take us back to the beginning of things. There is no better description of utter desolation than Roger Tory Peterson's: a world without birds.

Israel edges the boat away from the island. I watch it recede into a daub of green indistinguishable from the other islands that dot the lagoon. On its heap of twigs and string the osprey notes our passing with a stern gaze. More birds arrive at the lagoon for the night's roost. Mark pulls in another fish, a jack, the same kind of fish that he shared with the shark, but smaller at about two pounds. This time we can inspect the entire body: white with a dark olive back and bright yellow fins and tail. The *pescadores* dance in the boat, exuberant about the fiesta we will have at the cabanas. We throw the jack into the front hold with the barracuda and motor to the dock.

For a brief moment, on the lagoon in the languid sunset, I sense what must be close to an instinct between this land and the people who are born to it, something that I feel when I am driving home in the evening desert, the river on one side of me, on the other side twin buttes so familiar I am utterly desolate without them, a notion that *I live here* and it is the right place. I am quite sure that I could not stay forever in this coastal paradise in Mexico, but the glimpse of one of its purest moments is intoxicating. Gentle, humid air, an orb of crimson sun that can be looked at without going blind, mangrove thickets forever on the waterline, the distinctive lime-green undersides of breeze-swept coconut palms on the horizon, announcing the coming burst of turquoise sea.

In the dusk we walk from the dock with motor, oar, and fish piled in the wheelbarrow. The barracuda hangs over the side like a limp tree stump. There is the driveway of white sand, the almond tree, the sunset porch and table where I set a clear glass bowl of water floating with hibiscus. The two skeletal puppies. Irma on her porch with tortilla dough on her fingers. Familiar things. At the edge of the yard grows a low hedge of plants that are opening their enormous blossoms for the first time. Their lilylike petals are deep pink on the outside and the color of zinfandel wine on the inside. They fill the evening air with a sweet fragrance that the evening sea breeze cannot blow away.

OUT ON THE REEF in the *panga* Israel anchors the boat in the rhythmic swells of ultramarine ocean. With noisy splashes we drop over the side in flippers and face masks and kick around the boat like satellites. Face down in the blue deep: the dream world. Royal-blue fish with fins like silky feathers. A school of black-and-gold-striped fish rising in a pillar from organ-shaped, lemon-yellow coral, then turning as one, like a swarm of Technicolor starlings. Starfish the color of strawberries. Fish with kabuki eyeliner, fish with spikes. Dark shapes on open patches of white sand that are not fish but our own shadows cast in the clear water.

Why is there so much color in the tropical seas, why this wild Baroque of shapes and forms? It reassures me that no one knows the answer, that this is simply what this turquoise water does with protein and cells and sun. Some theories suggest that the kaleidoscopic patterns and pigments help creatures recognize their own kind within a wildly diverse field that teems with different species.

There is also a need to conceal and attract. Patterns can supersede actual dimensions or overlap the edges between creature and ground so that the creature looks bigger or invisible against a surface. Curved bodies absorb or contradict the light source or mimic the fluid patterns of water—here, above the reef, water that breaks into quivering hexagons of light. All of it is language, words spoken in pigment. Yet even among fish with no eyes to see them, there are brilliant displays of luminescent color.

I no longer want to know the names of things. I do not care if I am mute or if my tongue is useless for everything but the taste of salt. The verbal map is the wrong map. It is a labyrinth to false treasure. This exotic, wholly liquid place lies outside words but well within the realm of the sensual. The colors come forth for their own sheer ecstasy.

I flipper my way around pieces of reef full of fish that cannot possibly be fish, they are so drowned in color. In the near-absence of gravity my hair spreads around me in a halo of wavy tendrils. Against my body I feel a great and heavy pull of water, as if the entire South Equatorial Current from Africa, not just the tides, was handing me off to the Gulf Stream. I swim close to the turtle grass, letting the tips tickle my bare belly. Then the ocean floor and coral forest fall in a sudden, vertiginous drop, depths so terrifying that I swim back to the boat. I climb out of the water and shiver in the hot sun.

We will soon pack up Casa Rosa and leave barracuda leftovers to the roof cat. We will not see a jaguar nor start a *guerra pequeña* with the helicopter. Tony, Joan, and Lander will leave the coast for home, marveling at breakfast in the Caribbean dawn, and sleep under the stars of the northern Rockies.

Mark and I will also leave the preserve. The four-lane highway, the equivalent of Sherman's March in asphalt, will have furrowed deeper into the broccoli forest by a ferociously quick paving of several more miles, heaping slash on either side and erasing the two-lane behind it. We will spend an afternoon in a trendy international beach village, walking a gauntlet of souvenir shops to reach a fruit market and hardware store. There will be ATM machines and telephones. There will be the latest in industrial riviera chic: a very tanned German man in a lilac nylon thong bikini and a carpenter's tool belt, loaded.

Neither Mark nor I will be accustomed to restaurant meat that is not fish. We will be ready to bolt up from the table, wade through the surf, and swim out to sea with a knife in our teeth. Are there enough fish for another generation of *pescadores*? We will savor the delicious cold of coconut ice cream served in a half-shell of coconut. Someone will have spent the day hacking up *los cocos*. My envy of the beach-raking job will extend to envy of the coconut hackers.

I will hear the *zanates* open the day. I will dream that the San Juan River runs turquoise against the blood-red Halgaito Shale that enfolds the canyon walls. I will see a man pedaling an orange bicycle with his wife sitting on the carrier unit attached to his handlebars. She wears a white cotton *huipil* with orange and scarlet embroidery and a shawl of silky chocolate brown stitched with highlights of silver thread. She has the broad, smooth face of the Jaina weaver.

That handful of days between Casa Rosa and departure will be spent at a small hotel buffered from the resort Luxembourgs by two-mile-long beaches on either side, but not for long. One day we will walk up the beach toward a *cenote* and the mouth of a small river. We will pass a construction zone the size of a city block, a forest of rebar and walls erected with Mexico's inexhaustible supply of pale gray cement. One of the cement walls bears a loopy spray of gangish graffiti: STAR BOY.

The crew that is building this new resort hotel—already taller than the palm trees and with more floors to come—is a surly lot. They turn their backs to our *Buenos días* or make rude noises with their lips. They reap wages from the boom that lures North Americans here for weekend stays in hotels with marble-lined foyers and seafood buffets as long as supermarket aisles. The laborers move from villages to towns with schools and health clinics, and from thatch-roofed palapas to apartments or houses with running water and sanitation facilities. For the first time in Mexico I will feel the sharp tension of so much resentment affixed to so much need.

The construction zone will make me uneasy. I will want to turn around from our walk before we reach the river, and there under a palm will be a man in rags lying on his back in the heap of dried seaweed and international shipping garbage. His shirt covers his face. Mark will tell me he is napping or sleeping off a hangover, but it is not siesta time and I will think that he is dead, something about the stillness of his feet—no muscles seem to hold them inside his thin, frayed canvas shoes. If he is dead, his corpse resembles a desert casualty—tight, dark, and sunken rather than drowned, bloated, and washed up on the sand. He will seem dried out and frozen of motion. What will I know, having never seen a dead man?

All this will come on another day. Today, on the reef in the boat with Israel, I am resting from my long swim. Everyone else is still in the water snorkeling. Tony and Joan swim with Lander in between them, their hands in his. He does very well with his snorkel. He practiced in the bathtub in Montana.

"*Tutta la famiglia,*" I say to Israel, not realizing I have spoken in Italian.

I try to explain the solace of the familiar, how I walk the desert, how I know the desert as if it were my own heart, but that here beneath the turquoise I am so lost. Although I do not understand everything he says and I can say so little, it is clear that we have told one another that underneath the boat lies a wilderness like no other, one far beyond comprehension.

Four pairs of hands grip the side of the boat. Tony, Joan. Lander's small, sun-browned hands, Mark's big riverman's hands. Before they slither into the boat there is laughter and splashing. Israel smiles and says quietly, "*Toda la familia, Elena, toda la familia.*"

A few yards from the boat the sea floor drops off into a fathomless cleft. It is as far as I am willing to go. In shallows or depths, the tongue tricks the eyes in the telling of it. It may, after all, be terrifyingly simple. At one moment in his novel *The Stone Raft*, José Saramago brings his characters to a brink. He writes, "My God, happiness exists, said the unknown voice, and perhaps that's all it is, sea, light, and vertigo."

Tilano's Jeans

> Why have men always possessed the exclusive right to a
> sense of humor? I believe it is because they live out-of-
> doors more. Humor is an out-of-doors virtue. It requires
> ozone and the light of the sun. And when the new
> woman came out-of-doors to live and mingled with the
> men and newer women, she saw funny things, and her
> sense of humor began to grow and thrive. The fun of the
> situation is entirely lost if you stay at home too much.
>
> LILIAN BELL, 1897

I have just stapled my hair to the roof.

I was unfurling heavy rolls of black felt over plywood
sheathing. Then I would lean into the pitched roof and staple the
felt in place with tin caps, thin metal disks that prevent rips. This
required grunt labor rather than skill, but I was daydreaming about
snowy egrets and leaned too far into my work.

The roof covers our modest, owner-built home in the desert.
The house, with me affixed to its south flank, faces a river bottom
and a sheer escarpment of rose and beige sandstone. Beyond the
cliffs lies a piece of the Navajo Reservation known as the home of
hadahoniye', the mirage people, so called because it does not rain
there often. On the roof I am my own boss. I am in no rush. The

sun beats down with a delectable bite. Without unstapling my hair, I can twist my body and lie on my back. It seems a good time to enjoy the view and contemplate the dazzling spectacle of women awakening to their full powers.

The builder of this house, my husband, went walkabout for the weekend, leaving me with the roof job. We are advanced enough in our construction partnership to have avoided the tool conversation, which between a man and a man goes like this:

"Staple gun. Tin caps. Roof."

"Urmph."

But between a man and a woman goes like this:

"Staple gun. Tin caps. Roof."

"Staple gun? Which model are we using? When was it invented, actually? How did people attach felt to roofs before the staple gun was available? Do you mind if I hang some Sheetrock and decode some fractals before I get started? Man-oh-man, with a few thousand whacks of this thing I could turn these hamster muscles of mine into some mighty impressive biceps . . ."

The sex planets lob about in alien orbits, and one of the most popular venues of separation of late is the "wilderness," including vast tracts of backcountry beyond my roof. During the hiking and river-running season a number of outfitters guide recreational forays into canyon country. Many of these trips are for women only. As an unreconstructed wayfarer myself, I have been pressured to join up, don clothing that wicks, surrender to an imprecise but apparently omnipotent goddess, and hike my butt off with a social ensemble.

Although I often share—and savor—recreation time with women friends, my reluctance to participate in formal, goal-directed expeditions has been misconstrued as arrogance, even sniveling cowardice. When I leak the tiniest bit of cynicism over the therapeutic value of validating my female divineness, I have been voted the person most in need of therapy. I failed to show up at my own croning ceremony. About goddesses I have said all the wrong things.

I travel in wild country a great deal, often alone, and my friends find this to be fatally eccentric, although they use the more polite term "stupid." They feel sorry for me because I miss the fun of camping in groups, same-sex or mixed. Perhaps I am too cranky to know any better. I go afield to calm myself, to sort out the demonic squirrels in my head, a self-indulgence that lasts about thirty seconds, or as soon as the first petroglyph or curve of canyon wall comes into view or a ravenous swarm of gnats eats my entire skin or heatstroke finishes off what the lobotomy began. Then I succumb to pure sensation. I try to notice how the desert is put together, with the expectation that if I look hard enough the land will open up to me, spilling an endless stream of color, light, and living things in bright ecstasy.

In company I would likely remain completely silent for two days straight and everyone would take it personally. I would try my best to troop down a slickrock trail with a gynocentric agenda. I would fall flat on my face with strong women walking over my back in single file. Perhaps in a herd of gazelles there is always one animal that faces the west when all the others face east, one animal that drinks backward at the water hole and is actually not very gazelle-ish at all, but rather awkwardly assembled and inclined to involuntary utterances such as deranged hiccups when the lions are eating its compadres.

When I explained my limpid wilderness feminism to my friend Penny, she dismissed it. She flipped open her journal, a fat tome with an old-fashioned diary lock, and read a quote from Margaret Atwood. " 'She was taught to crochet, to set in zippers, to polish silverware, to produce a gleaming toilet. This was baggage she'd discarded as soon as she hit Spinoza.' "

Lacking any living brain tissue for "homemaking arts," we were not quite sure of the part about the silverware polishing. But we understood the essence of a breakthrough.

"Ecofeminism is liberating, a kind of postmodern baggage-shedding," Penny continued. "It opens you to the entire metaphor of landscape as woman, the earth as mother or sister, fertile and intuitive, cyclical and nurturing."

"I thought ecofeminism was when I wear my black leather miniskirt to the gynecologist," I said. I liked the way it accessorized with the steel stirrups.

"Ecofeminism is also about social justice," she explained patiently. "Ecofeminists see the environmental costs of domination, aggression, and exploitation, and they blame the ideology of a patriarchal society. They find parallels between the mistreatment of women and the mistreatment of nature. They invite men and women to enter a different relationship with nature, one of kinship rather than control."

Here, it seemed to me, ecofeminist theory gained meaning in the field. Treating nature as a pet or a therapist ends up little better than treating it as a slave. Kinship demands reciprocity. Every nature girl and boy should be prepared to defend the places they love. Otherwise we have not earned them. When we march in from the starry nights and dazzling rivers, we must argue on their behalf, pressure politicians and other moronic invertebrates to wean themselves from their unsightly addiction to corporate blubber and for once act in favor of things that matter, like air to breathe, water to drink, and space to roam. We must exalt the biocentric paradigm, speak for the creatures that have no voice, staunch the lunatic hemorrhage of wild lands from the face of the planet.

But first things first.

"When do I become a goddess?" I asked.

"Celebrating female divinity gives ecofeminism a spiritual dimension," Penny said. She told me that although there is no hard evidence that humans have lived under a pure matriarchy, where women ruled over all, archaeologists have described prehistoric societies with a distinct egalitarianism. These ancient cultures lived in close harmony with nature and included female deities in their pantheon, many of them allied with the earth and animals.

The prehistory angle reminded me of a wild-woman manual

that had achieved mass popularity in the mid-nineties. An acquaintance of mine, obviously delirious with envy, called the book *Women Who Run Their Panty Hose With Wolves.* In the vast marketplace of identity quests, female-centered spirituality had also spawned such curious subtexts as witches and she-god shoppes that sold Victorian corsetry. Bumper stickers proclaimed GOD 3000 B.C.—GODDESS 10,000 B.C.

My recreation advisor abandoned the cosmic mother tack and turned to practicalities. "On all-women camping trips the dynamics are different than with men," Penny said.

What a relief, we thought, to not feel compelled to walk eighty miles in five hours, uphill, carrying drums and guns and listening to endless sports analogies.

"When you're with women, there's less competition and more cooperation. Your physical strength becomes spiritual strength. You begin to feel your power."

Then Penny launched a final effort at persuasion. She liked me, but she thought that I was a rather pathetic individual. "Hey," she insisted, "goddess trips are just a hell of a lot of fun."

And now I am thinking of my roof situation as a kind of crucifixion. I am a nature girl who is clueless about ecofeminism, impaled to the dominant-subordinate duality paradigm with a heavy-duty roofing staple.

ONLY A FEW GENERATIONS AGO, social mores, not women, kept women inside. The clothes didn't help much either—girdles, psychotic footwear, personal responsibility for the breakdown of western civilization if you bared your knee. Far too many women must have simply been too exhausted to break the trance of life inside four walls. For them "nature" was the flooding river that destroyed the crops, the drift of red sand that choked their doorsills and sifted into food and bedding, or the wind that blew the dirt off their family graves, simple graves which they had adorned with wreaths of silvery buffaloberry and sad wild peas.

Fueled by their faith, the pioneer women who, at the turn of the century, settled the difficult, marginal canyon country in the vicinity of my roof, denied their "selfish human cravings" and struggled to live up to their divine purpose: reproduction. Nurses and midwives taught them to keep themselves healthy for ten or more years of childbearing, to avoid the poison to their fertility that came from a husband who smoked, and to avert the "precocious menstruation" that could be induced by indolence, luxury, acting on the stage, naughty thoughts, hot rooms, and "novel-reading." Outsiders often noted the courage and loneliness of these settlers. Shortly before World War I an Indian trader and his wife passed through the tiny frontier towns of southern Utah on their way to their trading post in Arizona. The wife later wrote: "I shut my eyes and see the faces of the women we met. They were tired always, but determined, and had a look that made me think they were more isolated by something inside them than by geographical conditions."

In the real world, women—hundreds of women—worked alongside men on an often harsh western frontier. In the myth they were invisible. As long as society saw wilderness as an object of conquest or a place for defining virility and unleashing aggressive impulses, women had few roles in it. A woman's perceived biological shortcomings, her "natural inability" in the masculine domain, kept her at home with the children and the laundry. By the late nineteenth century the nature archetype shifted. What was once hell then became Eden, wilderness a spiritually uplifting rather than forbidding place. No one responded to "scenery" quite like the Victorian tourist, and women joined men in its appreciation.

The feminist movement of the 1970s deconstructed the wimp myth, exposing "natural inability" for what it truly was: inexperience and lack of choices. In some arenas experience came without stone-cast gender roles. When I traveled in the Sierra Nevada backcountry years ago, the hiker's world was not, at first, solely a place of men, then, as gender barriers fell, a place where more and more women entered a traditionally male field. Instead, both sexes moved freely in the outdoors. Blisters, busted camp stoves, and gorp-thieving mice practiced no discrimination.

We donned heavy packs and chunky waffle-soled boots and somehow made it up the mountain without a miniespresso maker. We tiptoed through groves of giant sequoias with our heads tilted back to take in trees as tall as God. In high meadows lush with silky green grass, blue gentians, blood-red paintbrush, and shooting stars with delicate magenta petals swept back like the tails of comets, we laid down our sleeping bags in an integrated tumble and slept with the inert fatigue of igneous rock. Any hint of machismo was obliterated by the shared pain and ecstasy of making it over a 13,000-foot pass without our hearts bursting, into a drainage wilder than the one left behind, the mountain air saturated with blue.

Sometimes I hiked alone, sometimes with brothers, girl-friends, boyfriends. I trekked in the footsteps of my mother and grandmother and her mother and grandmother. In the years that followed, some of the outdoor women would come to prefer recreational sojourns with other women. In the comfort of sisterhood you could calm down and toughen up. You could purge appearance anxieties and surrender to primitive behaviors. There were wolves to run with.

Other than possessing the social finesse of a dentist's drill, what, then, is my problem? I consider myself eco and feminine, ready to kick up dust against humankind's abuse of the natural world. Like most women, I know how to adapt without surrender. I probably have an animal self.

The problem may be a semantic one. The incomparable joys of women together, a mutual empathy with other living things—turning these and other emotions into a commodity seems to overload them with a hollow sensitivity. Who among us could ever reach meaning when manufactured stimulation is peddled as instinct, our animal selves shrink into a seminar, and centuries of matriarchal dignity boil down to a corset? These are noble ideas with a wretched vocabulary. Language traded for iconic babble suffocates truth in packaging; it opens authentic need and experience to mockery. Say "The patriarchs seem to be recklessly inventing new ways to junk Earth like some inner-city ghetto and venture off in sterile techno-womb machines for ever more vainglorious conquests on the cosmic plane" and you may have a point, but you sound like your mouth is full of overfed tarantulas.

Some sort of speech impediment is operating here, leaving us to grope for an eloquence with which to elicit genuine spirit. In the end, perhaps, the eloquence may be nonverbal. It may come as a simple, almost metabolic knowing of the currents that bind the company of friends—friends outdoors with blisters and nuts, opening themselves freely to nature's blissful ecstasies.

ON THE ROOF the sun pours down in a white flood. The black felt absorbs the heat just short of a meltdown. Along the river bottom beyond the roof, the coyotes sing with great fervor, perhaps a grand opera celebrating the delicious flavors of grasshoppers, rabbits, and mice.

Across the river my Navajo neighbors enter yet another century of their matrilocal society. A Navajo's clan is the clan of his or her mother. Daughters traditionally remain with their natal group. A son disperses and upon marriage resides with his wife's people. Bone-tired or not, the local pioneer Anglo women took care of business. They raised roofs, corn, kids, and occasional hell. Yet these days we speak of women marching into equality as if it were a different country. No, I think, as two turkey vultures circle above the roof with their beady *Cathartes aura* eyes on me, we are simply occupying the rest of what has always been home territory.

Beyond the awkward semantics, in actual lives, lie threads

between the wildest deserts and women who have moved outside the four-walled trance. Such a woman will simply proclaim "This is my life" and let gravity hold her to it—barely, for as stark and desolate as the dry provinces may seem, they constantly overcome a person with desire. With a woman like this, it is hard to talk. So you end up listening. You want to understand how her life cultivated such depths. You try to feel how her muscles balanced and pulled across all those years in her chosen place.

To one side of me stretches a line of tin caps already stapled to the felt. The shiny disks throw back the sun in bright coins of light. I think of a story told by an Australian aboriginal to Daisy Bates, who, as a middle-aged woman in the early 1900s, lived on her own among outback tribes. The storyteller, a woman with fourteen consecutive husbands, told Bates how a man uses chips of mica to capture a woman. He directs the sun's glare off the mica into her eyes like a sharp needle of lightning. She runs to escape, loses herself in the bush for days, then follows the glint of mica to her man. The storyteller gave Bates a piece of mica, thinking Bates had no one to kiss.

For nearly thirty years Daisy Bates lived on various reserves in a white canvas tent with a few belongings and the unshakable conviction that any and all aboriginal Australians were her family. At her first reserve post she watched white settlements grow and block or obliterate the hunting and migration tracks used by people from the oldest cultures on earth. Rather than be cut off or detour from the routes of their ancestors, some of the migrating natives tromped through drained swamps and suburbs and gardens anyway.

Bates spent the bulk of her years at Ooldea, a desolate, sparsely populated post in South Australia, a few miles from a station on the transcontinental railroad. Tribal groups appeared out of the red desert to set up camps close to hers and to the railway supply line that fed them. Some came by foot across ancestral tracks from the north—this took a few years—and others were already there among the sandhills that edged up against the Great Victoria Desert, their thirst quenched by ancient water holes until everyone went thirsty because within seven years the steam-driven trains nearly sucked the aquifer dry.

Bates gave the aborigines food and basic medical attention. She attended ceremonies, studied their language and customs, and tried to put their mysteries into her notebooks. When people died, she helped bury them. When too many died, she and the natives moved camp. When she moved to a new camp, some of the local whites protested. She attracted too many blacks, they complained, she made too many graves in the sand. For three decades her life was self-contained and orderly. For nine of those years, Bates said, it never rained.

Daisy Bates was an Irish-born, stiff-backed keeper of lists. She dressed like a royal personage in dark, birdlike suits and wobbly hats. She married one man before unmarrying another. Then she more or less abandoned the second husband and her young son. She recorded aboriginal customs, songs, and stories in *The Passing of the Aborigines* and other books. She kept a kangaroo skin on her bed, packed a revolver in her long skirts, and once sat for a photo with a human skull on her lap. She claimed to have seen aboriginal women eat their newborns, but no one believed her. Her anthropology was sound, but her own life history, as she told it, was not. According to Julia Blackburn's biography, *Daisy Bates in the Desert,* Bates was an incorrigible liar.

Daisy Bates blended the most imaginative tales of her origins with the starkest reality of her old age: life in a tent at the edge of a fiery red desert, one of the world's most extreme landscapes, among people who were not considered human. The family life in Ireland that she invented was far more splendid than it likely was, Blackburn says, and she changed the details often, each time making them richer and happier.

The logic of fantasy made Bates believe her own deceptions. Blackburn writes, "A child somewhere in Ireland talking to a gathering of invisible friends is slowly transformed into an old lady in the desert, still talking to people whom no one else can see." Ironically, "whom no one else can see" suggests that Bates may have formed the habit of talking aloud to herself. It also defines Bates's aboriginal family, among them the woman who gave her the mica, the men who collected certain stones and sang into them big prayers and small curses. Everyone believed the lies about Bates's invisible youth. Few thought the people in her wholly unimagined life were visible.

Bates's dwindling companions danced the old dances, beating up clouds of dust with their feet, opening their continent to its dreamtime trails. Alone or in company Bates held fast to her camps, the land spread around her in a blaze of sun. The only green thing in the land of red sand was a cabbage stalk, which she set against an acacia tree near her tent. "I wonder how long that cabbage stalk managed to keep its colour and did the woman ever laugh when she realised it was still there, a sentinel standing guard over her after everyone else had gone home," Blackburn writes. "Or did she not feel there was anything to laugh at, sitting in the doorway of her tent and gazing out, mesmerised by a fragment of green?"

Bates's sixteen years in her black clothes, in the white tent set among bleak red sandhills, drew to an end in the late thirties. Of the aborigines remaining at her camp most were elderly. She had filled notebook after notebook with native words, then made more notebooks by stitching together brown paper used to wrap flour. Years after she left Ooldea her people were reluctantly relocated to a reserve close to what would become a site for testing nuclear weapons. The gray earth at the new reserve, the natives said, was the wrong color. During the years that followed Ooldea, Bates made camps in other places, but she forever spoke of returning to the red sandhill desert. She wanted to go back to her old home camp. What she wanted more, she said, was to move to a place where the sand was even redder.

• ◆ •

ANOTHER WOMAN OF this era crosses my vision. Born to Russian émigrés in Switzerland, a young Isabelle Eberhardt left Geneva, labeled as a hysterical female for her antisocial behavior, "radical individualism," and insistence on wearing the men's clothes in which her parents had always dressed her. From 1897 until her death in the western Sahara seven years later, Eberhardt roamed Morocco, Tunisia, and Algeria, recording her adventures as a diarist, reporter, and aspiring novelist.

Sympathetic to Muslim rebels, Eberhardt partook in uprisings against the French colonial regime. Her enemies called her a troublemaker and a woman of questionable morals—in other words, not a European woman. Officials harassed her. Someone tried to assassinate her with a saber. Deep into her North African years she was inducted into the Qadiriya Sufi brotherhood, an Islamic religious order that through strict laws and discipline established a path to God.

For Eberhardt, North Africa was the "land of fever and mirage." Within her: sometimes the fever, sometimes the mirage. She admitted simultaneous desires for hard passion and soft somnolence, much like a nomad's double pleasure in motion and stasis, not unlike a day in the North African desert itself, with its fierce, paralyzing heat followed by evening's rebirth.

At Kenadsa, a religious center on the Algerian-Moroccan border, she embraced monotony. "I am losing little by little all feelings of agitation and uncontrolled passion," she wrote. "It seems to me that everywhere, men and things ought to be as still, as sleepy as they are here." Then came the swift scorch of restlessness. "But the inner voice that drives and disturbs me, that will tomorrow push me again along the paths of life; that voice is not the wisest one in my soul, it is the spirit of agitation for which the earth is too narrow and which has not known how to find its own universe."

Eberhardt's most striking writing is found in "Sud Oranais," brief travel sketches included in *Departures,* a collection of her work. When her prose is not dizzy or waxing purplish or polemical, she deftly overlays the desert's vivid colors. Moroccan soldiers in blood-red clothes, dissidents in dark blue. Deserters who sell their red clothes and the men who buy and wear them, adding necklaces with small yellow copper bells. Camel drivers in scarlet sashes worn over white cotton uniforms set against the pale dust and heat. Clusters of fat brown dates high in the stately palms and tied with bone fetishes to protect them from sorcery. Silver, coming to Eberhardt as the glint of sun on steel rifles or as a sound: the jangle of silver jewelry or the bleating of sheep at dawn in a nomad camp. The tripod of a Saharan well, topped with purple, although it was only a mirage that colored it so, just as a mirage covered the stolid horizon of inert red sand with a shimmering sheet of blue water lined with date palms. Of Arab women emerging into public venues she writes:

> Draped in veils of red or blue, laden with gold and silver, with hairstyles of braids looped high then laid along their cheeks, covering their ears with heavy earrings, they wrapped themselves, to go out, with the dark blue cloth that concealed the brilliance of their jewelry.

At the death of her mother, whom she called the White Spirit, Isabelle Eberhardt was nineteen. It was said that when she wept at the funeral and expressed her desire to join her mother in the grave, her father calmly handed her a revolver. In 1904, in Ain Sefra in western Algeria, she drowned. As a flash flood descended a riverbed in one of the driest places on earth, the waters trapped her in her room. She was twenty-seven.

If Eberhardt had lived longer, would she have outlived her "spirit of agitation"? What if the spirit quickens just as the body can no longer carry it? What if the legs give out on the best part of the journey? If you have spent the preponderance of your life out-of-doors, in motion, with what rage do you greet the reduced mobility that age brings? Where did all those women go when they came out of the Sierra?

One of my friends, a Forest Service ranger with a lifelong career in the backcountry, came down long enough to have her knees replaced, then went back up again. Another friend, who once rock-climbed like a spider, goes slowly now, behind a pack of hikers she cannot keep up with, convinced she will make it or happily become buzzard food if she does not. Other women came away from mountain, forest, or desert to raise families and pursue careers or find a way to do both from homes close to their recreation meccas, in places like Jackson Hole, Boulder, Santa Fe, and Missoula. As they came down, they met heavy traffic going up—developers, Jeepers, dirt bikers, fleets of robust young cyborgs with backpacks, marching up the switchbacks, and a host of new rules to control the crowds. They found themselves muttering their parents' mantra about changing times and too many people and things not being what they once were.

Many women kept on hiking and skiing and running rivers, proving ourselves no different from everyone else who craved fresh air and nature's glories and a respite from life's ordinary constraints. We vowed to stem our pride and come indoors before things turned ugly, before our limbs buckled and we fell facedown in the dirt and couldn't get up again or the oars broke our kneecaps merely by their own weight or someone steered us off to a modest, cat-infested bungalow, where the doors rusted shut and the weeds grew clear up to the fascia board and there we were, inside with a lot of candles.

While you are raging about the tricks of the body, the injustices of old age, says a tribe of hiking women in my neighborhood, you walk. You walk with a stick for balance and a bloodstream coursing with pain relievers. You walk to the yucca plants outside your door or you walk the length of the Escalante River, alone or with other men and women who understand that raging against the desecration of mountains, rivers, oceans, and deserts makes more sense than she-god shoppes.

You explain that the few remaining wild places in the Southwest need not be open to off-road vehicles, all-terrain vehicles, dirt bikes, trail bikes, Jet Skis, snowmobiles, and motorboats on your behalf. Against proposals to make small remnants of unroaded public land off-limits to machines, some recreationists use discrimination as an argument—the handicapped and the elderly, they say, would be shut out of these lands if they had no motorized access. However, most of these critics are hiding their expensive, noisy, often damaging sport behind a bunch of little old ladies. Most of the little old ladies do not like to be hidden behind. We are still out there walking, limping, or crawling or, with a bounty of wild times already under our belts, we simply want our grandchildren to have the chance for similar experiences of solitude, peace, and quiet even if we have to stay home strapped to our sofas, sobbing with envy while they go.

At the close of the breeding season certain birds, such as male ducks, become covered with dull or colorless feathers. Zoologists call this phase *eclipse plumage*. Among humans, perhaps a "duller" demeanor is a deliberate truancy, the wearing of dried seeds instead of rubies in Eden, a respite from one's own outward brilliance despite the wild elixirs of living that still romp inside the head. There is no need to relinquish splendor forever, knowing that, visible or not, it remains bound to the secret language of cells.

When age fixes me to a chair on the porch, as I am fixed to this roof, I hope I will have the courage to wipe away the drool and pay attention. Shuffle my bent back and hummingbird bones down to the river to see what is flowing there and weep over the memory of how oars felt in my fists when I ran a raft through a high-water rapid, how a person can carry the river's muscle in her own. Adapt an experiential shrewdness that tricks everyone into believing it is wisdom. Crack some land vandal over the head with the collected works of Henry David Thoreau.

When you can no longer power your way through it all, when an active life slows down to prayerful attentiveness, is there still room for both the fever and the mirage?

LIKE AUSTRALIA'S DAISY BATES, Edith Warner of New Mexico arrived in the desert by virtue of departure from convention. Unlike Bates, who left husband and son, Warner did not renounce the joys and demands of conjugal and maternal love. She came to live her life as she did not because her own hand guided her, but because "[s]omething—what, I do not venture to say—has prevented what I thought I wanted to do and pushed me into what I eventually did."

After several trips to New Mexico in the 1920s, Warner, in her late thirties, left the East for good and settled in a small house on the Rio Grande in northern New Mexico. At Otowi Bridge she minded a river gauge, a small store, and a supply depot for a boys' boarding school on the mesa above the river, a place called Los Alamos. To her shyness New Mexico's lucent air was becoming. Her uprootedness sprouted roots. Her letters to friends and family had in them clouds, mesas, juniper smoke, wild geese, the river, the Puebloan dances that held each season to a curve of time. She spoke of some underlying puzzle "very near to the source of things." In a journal entry she wrote:

> This is a day when life and the world seem to be standing still— only time and the river flowing past the mesas. I cannot work. I go out into the sunshine to sit receptively for what there is in this stillness and calm. I am keenly aware that there is something. Just now it seemed to flow in a rhythm around me and then to enter me—something which comes in a hushed inflowing. All of me is still and yet alert, ready to become part of this wave that laps the shore on which I sit. Somehow I have no desire to name it or understand. It is enough that I should feel and be of it in

moments such as this. And most of the hatred and ill will, the strained feeling is gone—I know not how.

Warner befriended her neighbors at the nearby San Ildefonso Pueblo and, in the early 1940s, opened a tearoom. During the World War II years her guests were the people who had displaced the boys' school and worked at Los Alamos. Although no one in the region, including Warner only a few miles down the mesa, knew about the lab's secret mission to build an atomic bomb, they indulged in rumor: The military was running a submarine base, a Republican internment camp, a place where the front ends of horses were attached to the rear ends. For J. Robert Oppenheimer, Warner baked a chocolate cake whose flour you had to sift three times. Like so many others who lived near the mesa and knew the animist Pueblo cultures well, she later wondered how the atomic bomb could have been born at the center of so sacred a world.

Most insights into Warner's life come from journal remnants and Christmas letters to her friends, assembled in *The House at Otowi Bridge* and published in 1959 by her friend and neighbor Peggy Pond Church. Church says that Warner recorded little of Pueblo life because she found herself "unable to speak of her deep friendship with her Indian neighbors. . . . In all her years at the bridge she allowed herself to learn only a few playful words of Tewa because she wanted the village people to keep, even from her, the privacy of their language. She never asked an Indian what his cere-monies 'meant' any more than she ever asked me the meaning of the poems I showed her, knowing that the ritual, like the poem, must be its own communication." Against this, imagine Daisy Bates scribbling word after word in her notebooks as the notebooks fell apart and the language itself unraveled into silence even as it was spoken.

To the Indians of San Ildefonso and other pueblos a middle-aged woman living alone was a mystery. Theirs was essentially an urban culture. They packed themselves atop one another in their adobe cities, small islands in a brilliant sea of mountains, mesas, and pale, rolling desert etched with pinyon and chamisa. Solitude seemed alien to so communal a culture—alien, too, the idea of wrestling with the human dilemma on one's own rather than living by the group's epic rituals and the clan relationships that so carefully imposed social order. Perhaps, like Pacific Islanders crowded on their tiny atolls, they feared that a person alone is preparing for suicide. (Some do—they climb atop palm trees and fling themselves off.) For the San Ildefonso people, however, Edith Warner's very reticence earned their friendship. As Church said, her wisdom came through her silences.

Not long after Warner arrived at Otowi Bridge, Tilano, a Puebloan in his sixties, slipped quietly into her life. Church does not recall when or why he came to stay. To her the precise relationship between Tilano and Edith did not matter in the least. Their lives simply joined. Like most Pueblo men, Tilano devoted himself to the ceremonies that united the lives of his people. During the dances men became animals—buffalo, antelope, eagle—then gods, then men again, and in him Tilano held all three states of being. One day he was a deer, the next day a gardener of tomatoes. He shared his life with Edith for nearly twenty years.

SOME WOMEN COME to the desert to erase previous lives, to seek a different way to live in the world. Others choose home not by familiar ties but by color and light. *Something prevented what I thought I wanted to do and pushed me into what I did.* These women are not mystics but introverts. They are not crusaders but lost. While an outsider sees myth and stereotype, they see flesh and blood—men, women, children—in desperate free fall from cultural if not literal genocide. Some of these women are obsessed with the frightening squalls that rage between their own ears. Do they arrive this way? Do they pour into the sparest of spaces the edgy heat of their own shivering imaginations? Do they open themselves to sheer loneliness and fall too deep into self?

Throughout Edith Warner's calming days, Isabelle Eberhardt's restlessness, and Daisy Bates's eccentric life flow the desert's immutable cycles. You must drop your head squalls and open yourself to them. Even as the sun and sand burn her eyes to near blindness, Bates's vision grows keener. Warner gains solace in the things—geese, mariposa lilies, moons, the births of San Ildefonso children—that reoccur.

In my desert there is an unveiled lust, a "conflagration of clarity" in the essential shape and color of the land. It leaves you rolling around in the moonlight and feverish on a curve of sun-warmed slickrock. In *Lost Borders,* Mary Austin gives a metaphor of the desert itself as a woman: "[A]nd you could not move her, no, not if you had all the earth to give, so much as one tawny hair's-breadth beyond her own desires."

In the lives of some desert women there is solitude, chosen freely, even though solitude is not always a mental paradise. An ephemeral loner does not have a pueblo. No matter how keen my senses, I may still get nature all wrong, find no perfect fit between the dream of a place and its actual experience. Friends will try to extricate me. Some will offer the enticements of womanhood outings. If we end up taking a goddess along, it would help if she knew how to fold a map.

Above the roof the circling turkey vultures do not see the geography of human possibilities. They see me, a two-legged smudge on a plywood platter. I extricate my hair from the staple and return to felt, tin caps, and staple gun. I pocket a flashy disk for the man who will soon be home to kiss me. Before I finish my work, two parties pass on the nearby road. They pull over and watch a while, then they offer me jobs. But there is work of my own to do, a salsa farm to plant, a thousand canyons to explore, eclipse plumage to mend and hem.

In the winter of 1951, Edith Warner became seriously ill. She eventually refused treatment and set her house in order. For the octogenarian Tilano she ordered a two-year supply of blue jeans from a mail-order catalog. She returned borrowed books and wrote letters to her loved ones. In the spring she passed on.

Tilano died two years later. He ran out of jeans.

Heron Bay

The deeper the blue, the more it summons man into
infinity, arousing his yearning for purity and ultimately
transcendence. Blue is the typical celestial color. Blue
very profoundly develops the element of calm.

VASILY KANDINSKY,
On the Spiritual in Art

The giant bat moth alights on a wall map outside a Bahamian
rum bar. Hand-painted on rough white plaster, the map
shows an archipelago of mint-green islands in a turquoise sea. With
wings spread flat to eight inches across, the moth cloaks an entire
island. Now there are mint-green islands and one dark brown
island in a turquoise sea.

In its actual form the island under the moth is over sixty miles
long and less than three miles wide, a string bean of limestone
fringed by white sandy beaches and sliced across its throat by the
Tropic of Cancer. To see the land beneath the moth I must lift the
moth's wing. The insect remains still. It parted the warm air over
the earth's surface and pinioned itself to the wall for the day. The
Cubans call these moths *brujas,* or witches. The local islanders call
them money moths. If one lands on your head, they say, you will
become rich.

The wings feel like pollen on silk, powder stretched to gossamer. The wings are fretted at their edges and strewn with a faint moiré of eye spots and soft whirls against dark chocolate-brown. From up close I can see that the venation is not the overall brown but the color of amethysts. The hair-thin lines between the wing cells are veins of iridescent purple. This is where I have seen these colors before: on stones cast across a rugged terrace in the Mojave Desert, stones weathered to a patina of brown-black with blue-violet in their shadows and fissures.

On the wall map the moth's wings spread north to south. Its head and thorax face west to Cuba. The north wing—I lift it gently—rests on the site of an old plantation overlooking a shallow crescent bay the color of Persian turquoise. On this land a family once farmed cotton and raised livestock. They built a sturdy house and outbuildings of blocks hand-cut from the native limestone, structures that are now engulfed by the thick tropical scrubland.

You must thrash through the bush to reach the ruins of the old house, then assemble in your mind the way it all fell together so long ago. The best way to imagine the lay of the land is to look for the stones. Where at first you see only a tangled curtain of trunks and branches and leaves, and the layered detritus beneath them, soon the lines will appear: low walls of dry-laid stone, piled by hand to define the yards, paths, and raised beds of earth that imposed order on the unruly surroundings. The highest, broadest walls run straight through the bush like ley lines, all the way to the bay, there to meet the color bands of beguiling serenity: the palest beige sand, white surf, turquoise water. Many of these stone walls delineated property lines. Follow one and you would find your way home.

The place is over two centuries old, abandoned and swallowed by the green. But those who built and tended it, who moved the stone with their hands, might be known by name, their one and only name: Harry, Tulip, Gonk, Quamina, Jack, Hercules, Ben, Adam, July, and others. They were African; they were property.

Like most of the British planters in the West Indies in the early nineteenth century, the planters on the land beneath the moth's wing condoned and buttressed the unassailable edifice that was slavery. They were slaveholders; they were my ancestors.

The giant bat moth does not move. It holds itself as an island. It will not stir until it finds halos of light in a slur of darkness.

THE CHROMATIC BANDS of serenity, the equatorial light that lures a desert homebody with its geographically discordant but oddly familiar resonance—all of this would easily seduce us to the tropics but not necessarily to the resort-heavy, package-travel Bahamas. In this place, however, I was dealt the card of blood.

Mark and I flew from the American Southwest to Nassau in a single day. The flood of refugees from a North American winter parted into dozens of rivulets, each flowing toward warmth and refreshment and, we hoped, the casinos or the resorts with the bungee towers, trampoline clinics, and Girls from Brazil swimwear shows. This would leave the remaining territory to the motley pool of tourists like us.

We arrived in Nassau after dusk and took a halfhearted walk down dim, nearly empty city streets, our only foray during a quick overnight between islands. Sugar-pink colonial buildings edged to the harbor, where a cruise ship had parallel-parked against the wharf, disgorged its hordes, then sucked them back in for the night. The ship loomed high above the streets, its seven decks of lights ablaze in the velvet dark. So compressed was the ship to the city, the water around its berth was nearly invisible, giving one of those odd perspectives of miniature buildings and, behind them, foreshortened and flat, a monster skyscraper.

We stretched our legs, ate a fish dinner, and drank cold Kalik beer. More than fifteen hours in airports and airplanes gave us such a drugged look that the street vendor of "Smoke, mon?" did not press his case. These thrown-switch transitions, these jet-propelled lunges through blank air across a vastly complex continent, wreak havoc on a person's bonds between time and place. One minute the Grand Junction, Colorado, airport, the next minute a cruise ship in your face.

Survival meant an intense study of details—purple blossoms of rampant bougainvillea, warm, soft air from an offshore squall, the smell of fried conch, the Bibles stacked on the taxi dashboards, my growing apprehension about the connections between family and this city, where buildings bore their name and their stories. One nineteenth-century landmark in particular—we came to it swiftly and unintentionally, on our way to dinner—threw a hard punch.

The squarish structure sat with its back to the harbor. A second story had been added above the ground floor. Window frames and glass now filled what were once tall archways open to a traffic of buyers and sellers of the goods within. The night view, under street-lights and cruise ship glow, did not do justice to the paint job. The building was as pink as a flamingo's rump.

"Maybe it's the water," I told Mark in my queasiness.

Our clothes were disheveled from travel and humidity. We looked like a couple of seriously corrupt southern lawyers in their wrinkled, cream-colored linen suits, something out of *All the King's Men.*

"Maybe it's blood clots from sitting in an airplane too long," he offered. "The clots are halfway up from your legs to your brain."

The nerves, however, came from recognition. Here before us in the sultry night was one of the buildings that I had seen only in photographs. Until recently this quadrant of family geography was not well known to any of us. The south Atlantic branch of the family tree was obscured and overpowered by a lovable cast of semi-eccentric Brits freezing their derrières in the cold, hard rock of the mother isle. Until recently I had not known that I was the great-great-great-granddaughter of an agent of unholy commerce at this landmark Nassau building.

Early the following morning we flew away and left Nassau behind us. The slow-paced rural life on one of the Bahamas' Out Islands embraced us like a tonic. We were swallowed by the blues.

THE ISLAND'S GREEN RIB divided the ocean in two: the rougher, Prussian-blue Atlantic on one side and serene turquoise waters on the other, spread over a shelf of ocean floor known as the Great Bahama Bank. Technically, the Great Bahama Bank, and the Bahamian archipelago itself, are not in the Caribbean Sea but in the vast ocean river that is the Gulf Stream. Nevertheless, many people refer to the island's shores as either Atlantic or Caribbean. You have to get up in the morning and make the agonizing choice of which sea to bask in.

During our stay on the island we used avant-garde transportation: our own feet and a pair of one-speed, vintage fat-tire Schwinns with finger bells on the chrome handlebars and reverse-pedal brakes that sometimes worked. Rust from the salty ocean air threatened to freeze the chains to their toothed rings. The wide tires remained slightly mushy. But Mark and I rode the bikes everywhere, to the beaches and lagoons, from Atlantic to "Caribbean" and back, down lanes of bright white sand lined with coconut palms and sea grape, through villages and scattered fruit farms, where people came to recognize us and wave their greetings. "Good morning good morning," they called. At first I thought the greeting was to the morning itself—and fine mornings they were—then I realized that the melodic island patois repeated words for emphasis. We waved back and rang our bells, nearly toppling over with a suddenly unbalanced load of fly rod, flippers, and snorkels, or a string bag full of coconuts or a whole chicken and packages of grits, rice, and dried pigeon peas.

Beyond the edge of the lanes the bush grew to an impenetrable thickness, much of it likely secondary or tertiary growth after long periods of fire, grazing, lumbering for boat-building, and slash-and-burn farming. This was not the wide-open, walk-to-the-horizon desert. The space between trunks, limbs, stems, and leaves was negligible, negotiated by small, agile things like land crabs, birds, bugs, and giant bat moths.

Cacti took over disturbed areas, undeterred by roaming goats and salt air or by the incongruity of a cactus in the rain-blessed tropics. The twenty-foot-high, branching, spiked columns of the dildo cactus resembled Arizona's organ pipe cactus but with a jokester rather than a churchy name. Prickly pear cactus, another desert familiar, spread its villages of thorny paddles as if it owned the world. Perhaps only a couple of yucca-bitten desert rats like us could marvel at the close proximity of cactus to orchids or appreciate the image of a prickly pear in a hurricane.

Neither elaborate nor ramshackle, the island's houses and scattered farms found their decorative wealth in paint, gallons of it spread in a pyrotechnical display of aqua, royal blue, magenta, pistachio green, shrimp pink, and daffodil yellow, swaggering, jazzy colors on every door, shutter, window frame, and slatted ventilation panel. The colors unified the landscape by their dissonance, their exuberant contrast with the saturated, unfiltered brightness of the tropical sky and the sun-burnished sea on every horizon.

Much of the paint had fallen off the old one-room pillboxes built in the "slave house" style, an island vernacular dating back to plantation times. The steep-angled, four-sided roofs wore the imprint of hurricanes in their patches and sags. Some of the houses were still inhabited by older folks; others sat unused beside modern family quarters. The old houses had neither trim nor overhang—the wind would rip it all away too easily—and their faces displayed a uniform Georgian symmetry: a doorway in the center, flanked by a pair of identical rectangular windows. Flakes of faded paint—robin's-egg blue was common—covered the rough-cut wooden shutters.

With refugees from the American colonies the plantation system came to the islands in full force after the Revolutionary War. Gentry, farmers, mariners, merchants, and others loyal to the British Crown fled the newly independent country and began washing up in the Bahamas—nearly 8,000 of them between 1783 and 1785, including their slaves and a number of free blacks. Because the Out Islands were largely "vacant" (the Spanish had swiftly decimated the indigenous Lucayans by working them to death), the new governor had no trouble doling out land to the Loyalists, who looked upon each island of size as one vast cotton farm. Over the years, through already burgeoning markets in Nassau, the planters acquired more laborers, thus opening the consequential chapter of African enslavement in the colony. The population became and remained predominantly black.

Farming the island shelf of rough limestone was like farming on bones. The long-staple Anguillan cotton grew best, yielding a winter and a summer crop, but even it could not be sustained in meager soil and ill-suited conditions. Soil exhausted, crops infested with chenille caterpillars, the cotton economy collapsed within a few decades. In 1807, the British Parliament banned the slave trade at ports and on ships throughout the Empire. Slavery in the Bahamas was abolished altogether in 1834.

Compared to other West Indian colonies and the American South, the plantation system in the Out Islands began late and was short-lived—hardly fifty years. Even before emancipation a number of Loyalist families had already turned to other enterprises or packed up to go elsewhere. Some of them left their land to their slaves. Former slaves and free blacks then farmed, fished, mined sponges, raked salt from island salinas, or otherwise eked out a living.

To reach some of the beaches and fishing spots, once in a while Mark and I abandoned the sandy backroads and took the coastal Queen's Highway, the island's main, paved two-lane. At one time gates marked each plantation or parcel of land along the road, blocking passage to travelers until they had the owner's permission to pass through. The now gateless road took us past a zinc-white church with Chinese-red doors and a buttercup-yellow house with lime-green shutters and three black-and-white-spotted goats.

In some of the yards glass bottles and net floaters—brightly colored plastic balls used in fishing—hung from the trees, "fixing" the homestead against thieves and ill-willed spirits in the tradition of obeah, a sorcery magic with African origins. Flowers grew in every yard—crimson and yellow hibiscus, orange geranium trees, white and pink oleanders. So many of the species thought to be quintessentially Caribbean actually replaced or edged in on the West Indian indigenous plants. Hibiscus from Asia and East Africa, bougainvillea from South America, tamarind from Africa and India, mango from Asia, poinsettia from Mexico.

We pedaled past an old cemetery under a grove of long-needled Australian pines that lined the edge of a bay. The trees soughed and whispered in the breeze. Exotic to the Bahamas, the pines are aggressive colonizers and smotherers of native vegetation. Some people call them casuarinas or "shee-oaks" for their seductive wind song. They covered the graves in a carpet of shed needles.

My ancestor joined the island's plantocracy in 1788 with twenty-seven slaves and title to 740 acres. A mariner and a merchant, he came by way of earlier generations already in the south Atlantic, in Bermuda and the Bahamas. He was perhaps a Loyalist by sympathy and advantage but not by dislocation from the American colonies. He was more likely an acquirer of failed Loyalist land, which he and his son added to the original land grant and raised to a total of 2,000 acres, with over thirty-three slaves to work them.

These are the demographics on this island during his first year as a planter, listed by the census record "State of the Population, Agriculture &c. of the BAHAMA ISLANDS in June 1788":

White male heads of families: 29
Planters possessing ten or more slaves: 19
Merchants: None
Number of slaves: 476

Acres of cultivated land: 2,380
Inhabitants established before 1788:
  42 white male heads of households
  12 planters with more than ten slaves
  306 acres under cultivation

The family kept strategic holdings in Nassau, where they were inclined to be born, baptized, married, and buried, as if the city and its handsome Anglican church were more civilized than the scrappy island several hundred sea miles away. They were, after all, British— colonial British, that is, with allegiance to a culture and a country that none would live in for the next hundred years. On the island plantation they farmed cotton but diversified to horses, cattle, sheep, and other livestock. A few family members died here before they could die in Nassau. Their graves are lost in the bush near the ruins of the old plantation, I was told, along with the graves of their slaves.

In the roadside cemetery under the Australian pines, many of the tombstones bore the surnames of the neighboring planter families who married into mine. Slaves, too, commonly took the surnames of their masters, so the name bearers, past and present, may be black or white or mixed race, blood-related or not. The oldest readable marker was less than a hundred years old, but nearly all of the names went back to the plantation era. Simple, straight-carved letters etched the stones' slate-gray faces. "Our beloved mother." "Clothilde wife of Mr. T.E.K."

I rode my bike back and forth along the pine grove, thinking I was crisscrossing the Tropic of Cancer at this spot. The Australian pines allowed little to grow beneath them, deflecting the dense bush that would otherwise consume the cemetery and obscure the markers. The graves barely fit between the Queen's Highway and high tide.

◆   ◆   ◆

If by your art, my dearest father, you have
Put the wild waters in this roar, allay them.

WAS IT WILLIAM Shakespeare's fault?

For his last complete play, *The Tempest,* the Elizabethan bard is said to have drawn inspiration from the account of a shipwreck off islands now known as Bermuda. According to word received in London in 1610, the *Sea Venture* was lost in a storm while sailing between England and the infant Virginia Colony at Jamestown. Its survivors sojourned in the tropics, then rebuilt a ship and arrived on the mainland with tales of wreckage in paradise.

In *The Tempest,* Shakespeare told of a storm and a shipwreck and set the story on an enchanted isle. The play appeared on the London stage in 1611. Why not imagine, in a wholly pulp-novel sort of way, that its exotic setting, its dramatic tension between rawness and civilization, struck one young man in the audience, who then and there bid his family farewell, packed his codpieces, and hopped on the next ship for the New World? *Be not afeard,* speaks Caliban, *the isle is full of noises, [s]ounds and sweet airs, that give delight, and hurt not.*

Whatever the reason—romantic seduction, primogeniture, religious persecution, the promise of land, fortune, or adventure—a William Adderlie from England by way of the Virginia Colony was, in 1612 or 1613, among the Company of Adventurers, the first English settlers in Bermuda, then known as the Somers Islands for Sir George Somers of the famously wrecked ship. Bermuda's history is then sprinkled with Adderlies and Adderleys, some of whom branched out to other parts of the south Atlantic. One of them allegedly salvaged silver bullion, pearls, and other treasures from a Spanish galleon sunk on a shoal called the Boilers. Another was linked to an ill-fated Puritan settlement and still another turned up in jail for slaughtering a whale in defiance of the imperial Bermuda Company's monopoly. A number of decades and a blank period later, the Adderleys clearly established themselves in Nassau,

New Providence, and on this out island in the Bahamian archipelago. The Bermuda "prehistory" thus places an uninterrupted maternal family line in the British West Indies for nearly four hundred years.

In genealogy you might say that interest lies in the eye of the gene holder. The actual descendants are far more intrigued with it all than the listeners, who quickly sink into a narcoleptic coma after the second or third great-great-somebody kills a bear or beheads Charles I, invents the safety pin or strip-mines Poland, catalogues slime molds, dances flamenco, or falls in love with a sheep. Genealogy is a forced march through stories. Yet everyone loves stories, and that is one reason we seek knowledge of our own blood kin.

Through our ancestors we can witness their times. Or, we think, there might be something in their lives, an artist's or a farmer's skill, an affection for a certain landscape, that will match or explain something in our own. If we know who they were, perhaps we will know who we are. And few cultures have been as identity-obsessed as ours. So keen is this fascination with ancestry, genealogy has become an industry. Family reunions choke the social calendar. Europe crawls with ancestor-seeking Americans. Your mother or your spouse or your neighbors are too busy to talk to you because they are on the Internet running "heritage quests." We have climbed so far back into our family trees, we stand inches away from the roots where the primates dominate.

For a break in home cooking at our rental, one evening Mark and I joined a buffet dinner at a local inn. We arrived to discover that the buffet would be served not in the dining room but in a limestone alcove, with a candlelit nightclub motif. The alcove had a low ceiling and deep pits of shadow beyond the candles. Compact and crowded, it smelled of dust and spilled beer. Each of the scattered tables was a stone mushroom ringed by a stone bench.

Before I succumbed to a vast array of social disorders, Mark steered me to one of the tables. Always a thoughtful man, he placed us near the entry, where I could see the night sky and stars and be less likely to shriek with panic and bolt, snagging my sarong on the jagged bench and leaving it behind as I raced for the exit in my underwear. A rock-and-roll band played a lively Bob Marley repertoire. People were dancing. I sat on the stone furniture and broke out into a cold sweat as the couple at the table greeted us politely.

"Mingle," Mark whispered to me in a smiley voice. "Don't go psycho." He excused himself to go find some rum punch.

Our table companions were vacationing midwesterners in their mid-fifties. They wore monogrammed, sherbet-colored golf clothes and wanted to party. They came to the Bahamas often, they said; it was an easy weekend trip from Ohio. He was in real estate. She was engrossed with the band. She bobbed her head and shoulders to the rhythm of the bass and ignored us as Mark returned with drinks and a plate of unshelled peanuts. Her husband turned to me and asked about our sojourn on the island. I mentioned bonefishing, beaches, and the blood relations who once ran the local plantation. He appeared to be interested, and before I knew it I was administering the anesthetic.

Well, there was the Puritan and the whale killer, I explained. The cotton planters, the bankers, and the blockade runners. The sponge magnate, the members of the colonial parliament, the great-great-uncle who organized the Bahamian and Jamaican pavilions at the grand Victorian exhibitions in nineteenth-century London, showcases of colonial glory complete with palm trees, stuffed reef fish, and insects pinned to boards. I babbled about how, for historical reference, the uncle used the 1493 Borgian Map of the New World, on which Pope Alexander VI had drawn a line in red ink, dividing the newly discovered lands between Spain and Portugal. Rivers, valleys, mountains, islands, people, creatures, parceled out like a succulent Florentine pastry by a fat man in a white dress and gold brocade beanie.

Great-great-grandmothers and uncles, sponges and popes, I threw them around like flying fish.

Mark made another round-trip for rum punch. The woman

broke her rapt attention to the music. She covered my hands with hers and leaned across the table until our foreheads nearly touched. Her smile seemed stuck, a curved ellipse between pearl-drop earrings. She looked at me with an intent, frank gaze.

"My son is twenty-three. He's our only child," she said. "I can't stand being away from him. I am in love with my son." She lit a cigarette and turned back to the band.

"Have you known the Bahamas since you were a kid?" the husband asked. He threw a handful of peanut shells over his shoulder.

"No," I replied, "this is my first visit. Until a year ago I knew little about this wing of family history. My great-grandmother was the last of my direct maternal line born in the Bahamas. She left Nassau to live in England. We were English for a while, then American when one of her sons, my grandfather, married a Californian."

I described how my cousin and her husband had assembled an exhaustive genealogy, how they scoured records, copied wills, studied land records, and sent me photographs of the old plantation and historic family buildings in Nassau.

"They did all the work," Mark added. "They built the family tree."

I sipped my drink and remembered learning of the connection to an extraordinary, often shameful chapter in North American history.

"Sometimes the family tree looks more like a shrub," I squeaked.

The music grew louder. More people left their stone cocktail tables and headed toward the dance floor. I tried to remember the last time I was in a nightclub. Back in the Reagan administration? And now I was thousands of miles from home, sitting around a Flintstone dinette set listening to "Pimper's Paradise" and a woman with a skewed Oedipal dilemma.

I watched a lithe young man on the dance floor, a twenty-one-year-old off-duty police officer and part-time scuba-diving guide. Mark and I had met him when we were snorkeling on a small reef off the Caribbean shore and again when he was in uniform, a crisp white tunic and navy trousers with red stripes on their sides, his black shoes polished to ebony mirrors. He grew up on the island and loved his home, he told us. He wanted to "see the world" but had a deathly fear of the cold. He was afraid that if he went anywhere beyond Florida he would freeze. The warmest apparel in his wardrobe, he said, was the neoprene wet suit he wore for diving. Tonight he had dressed in his hip big-clothes, baggy jeans and an oversized short-sleeved shirt of gauzy cotton. When he danced against the light, I glimpsed a set of handcuffs under the shirt, attached to his hind pocket.

"Do you still own any property on the island? Did you come here for investment?" The realtor in the man was fighting the imminent coma of listening to someone else's family history.

I shook my head. "My cousins' research made me curious, and Mark and I wanted a winter month near blue water."

Quite simply, I wanted to see the island itself, to put earth and sea beneath the stories. It is hopeless to expect to know the long-ago strangers who are our kinsmen, but it is easy to learn about their land and to seek in it some attendant continuity, of family, of life. Compared to other islands, this one remained relatively rural; no Club Med, golf palace, or gated villas obscured the old plantation grounds. I could sit on an old stonemasoned wall and see the turquoise bay much as the Adderleys had seen it two centuries earlier.

The band upped its decibels, pounding the reggae beat against the dirt floor. The policeman-diver was by far the best of the dancers. I pictured him walking around Minnesota in his wet suit. He seemed so young, just a kid, a willowy figure with a bright smile. The handcuffs flapped against his back pocket.

With a broad sweep of my hand in the direction of the plantation on the turquoise bay, I started in again. Mr. Real Estate may or may not have still been conscious. "Just as the plantation collapsed, one of the patriarchs supposedly committed suicide." The music was so loud, I was shouting. "Woman trouble. A butcher knife. His grave is lost out there in the bush somewhere and I am trying to . . ."

The woman turned toward the table again and aimed herself at me like she was chasing a priest into a confessional booth. She wanted to register me as sympathetic rather than startled, as if her mind and social ceremony were in two different places. She reached for my hands.

"You see, my son and I . . ."

Away from the music, back into the night's thick dark, I decided with some relief that the proper pacing for a nightclub visit and catching up on lifestyles in Ohio was about every third or fourth presidential administration. We found our bikes where we had parked them, in the halo of light from one of the few streetlamps. Beyond the glow we could hardly find our way. Only a pale strip of white road ran through darkness with no seam between land and sky. Perhaps I should have walked the bike, but the lashing wind and pounding Atlantic surf bred a reckless energy. Here in the deep seat of the calming blues I felt anything but calm. I had somewhat preposterously delegated myself the responsibility of righting a great wrong and had it in my head that I could not do so unless I found the patriarch's lost grave in the bush and . . . and what— pounded a stake through his heart?

Mark strolled alongside his bike, admiring the stars. I raced off, pedaling as fast as I could through the blackness, half-expecting a head-on with a fallen coconut, a collision that would launch me into the pallid gravel or a hapless flight into the bush, where I might land on a prickly pear cactus, one of the most common plants of my desert home.

AFTER A BLOODLETTING THRASH through the bush, the path barely visible and often lost, there was reason to wonder why anyone built a place on this harsh, soil-poor ridge, a place with a grand entry of walkways, walled terraces, and a weathered, foot-worn stone staircase whose intimacy allowed me neither the detachment nor the indifference of an ordinary tourist. I could climb on the limbs of the family shrub and find those who actually walked here, their birth dates, their children, their fortunes. Without stopping to look at details, I made Mark thrash farther, to the remains of the house itself, where we scrambled up an old wall and at once understood why the site was chosen: high ground, a view across dazzling turquoise water nearly to the Exuma Cays, the buildings positioned to catch the prevailing east-southeast breeze.

Little remained but the stone, and the stone—the details in the ruins—offered scant clues: a kitchen building with oven and chimney, a place of work and fire kept separate from living quarters; peaked walls that might have held a palmetto-thatched roof; the main house, with doors and windows on all sides; a number of porches and evidence of either a lower level or a cellar.

The gray building stone was likely quarried nearby, then cut into blocks that measured from elbow to fingertips, cooling the interiors with their thickness. Mortar fixed the blocks and a coat of plaster finished the walls. Water, crushed limestone, sand, and lime produced by burning conch shells provided the masonry materials. Piled stone walls, now sinking into the duff, once outlined yards, paths, and gardens and the spaces of family, slaves, and livestock. I could not piece it all together. It was too old. At least one hurricane—a powerful storm in 1926—had severely damaged it. The bush smothered it.

Three generations of ancestors lived on this green ridge forty feet above sea level, overlooking the cove they called Heron Bay— "Herne Bay" in the old documents. The dates fall from the land purchase in 1788 to the 1890s, when legends abound and the disposition of the land becomes unclear. The one known portrait of the Adderley Plantation in its prime, an oil painting remembered by one of my mother's cousins in England, has been lost.

The sequence of construction is uncertain. What is certain: Slaves built the place, people who were a wholly separate yet intimate part of my forebears' lives. The material status of African slaves of this era, historians say, ranged between poverty and destitution. They were issued food and clothes and small garden plots, one blanket every three years.

These Africans likely came to the island by way of the Nassau markets. Before that, any distinction of their home villages, their customs and beliefs, had been erased. Most Europeans labeled Africans not by their ethnic identity but by the port in Africa from which they were shipped. They were designated as Gold Coast, "Guiney," or other regions. Agrarian Congos worked the fields alongside Moslem Gambians and Ibos from inland rivers. Their New World names came from the Bible and classical myth. A few were remnants from African cultures that named children for their birth day or month. The ancestor's slaves Quamina and Cuffy, identified in his codicil, were likely named for a variation of Quaka, a male born on a Wednesday, and Cuffee, a male born on a Friday. Emancipation gave their descendants their surnames, and thus many blacks on this and other islands bear the names of early white planters.

Although other societies, even ancient ones, had slaves or rigid, often draconian labor hierarchies, no other system was ever organized in the same manner as the forced transatlantic migration of millions of Africans to North and South America, Central America, and the Caribbean. In the Hispanic Caribbean, predating the sugar and cotton economies, the African trade replaced the Lucayans and other natives, who had been worked to death in the Spanish gold mines. Argentine writer Jorge Luis Borges noted what surely must be one of history's most bitterly ironic acts of "philanthropy." Borges wrote that, in 1517, a Catholic friar, "feeling great pity for the Indians who grew worn and lean in the drudging infernos of the Antillean gold mines, proposed to Emperor Charles V that Negroes be brought to the isles of the Caribbean, so that they might grow worn and lean in the drudging infernos of the Antillean gold mines."

From atop the plantation hill we could see low tide drawing away the blue waters of Heron Bay, now known as Adderley Bay. As if someone had pulled a huge plug, the receding tide left a vast expanse of damp white sand edged with scattered mangroves. High tide would refill the bay just as swiftly, carrying with it the schools of bonefish that fed in the shallow flats. The tides and the bonefish pulled at Mark's fly-casting arm like a string on a marionette. He headed down the faint trail to the bikes and fishing gear, leaving me with the ghosts.

When I tried to envision the plantation family, I saw men with too many buttons, stiff collars, cotton stockings, maybe gout and a mouth uncomfortably full of wooden teeth. Everyone in flax or butternut-colored clothes. Itchy underwear. Frocks and bodices. Velvet-lined cases with pistols. Once in a while the lascivious food scene from the movie *Tom Jones* came to mind, and I saw Albert Finney sucking oysters or gnawing a drumstick, grease running down his chin. Maybe the ancestors ripped bodices. The inhabitants of this place were a very long time away; the biases of my own times obscured and remodeled them. I could never know their faces and, from faces, begin to ask what kind of people they were. Civil and parish registers of birth, baptism, marriage, and death—the library genealogy—told nothing of what they thought or read or loved. Much of their lives remained invisible; only a few generalities were known.

The Bahamian forebears were loyal subjects of a monarchy thousands of miles across the Atlantic. They practiced the deep-seated racism of their culture and their times, and they sought their God through the Anglican faith. They married the sons and daughters of other white planters and merchants. They married young, they died old, and their families were large, although births and burials, in the same year, record a sorrowful infant mortality. When an estate was settled and a living, grown son did not inherit anything, but his wife and children did, one might wonder about desertion or estrangement or scandal.

The will of the first patriarch, Abraham Adderley, written in 1809 and proved upon his death in 1812, was the only known will to name slaves and assign them to his heirs, at least one for each daughter and grandchild, more for each son. Amid the sheep, horses, and horned cattle, the dwelling house and farm buildings, land tracts on the island, and city lots and quays in Nassau, was another kind of property: thirty-three humans. Henry shall have George, William takes Beth. Emeline takes Rose, Caroline has Tulip, and Ann shall have Adam, July, and Beck. The "Negro woman Sarah" shall live with a daughter, "to be taken care of by her, but not to be considered as a slave." Abraham bequeathed to Nehemiah, his eldest son, my great-times-four-grandfather, eight men and eight women. In turn the codicils of Abraham's heirs passed no slaves. By the time the next generations died, the institution was crumbling.

The ancestors could read and write, but there is no story of how they learned—perhaps school in Nassau or England or a supply of anonymous reverends who were their tutors. Perhaps their natural history came from Pliny the Elder. They probably knew how to dance. They had to import everything from iron pots to a pin. They were good with boats—inter-island transport was a lifeline— and, like most of the Loyalists in the Bahamas, they modeled their farms on the white plantocracy in the Carolinas, a baronial, agrarian lifestyle, semifeudal and entirely sustained by slave labor. When the weak soil was exhausted and their crops failed, they abandoned the island. They likely left most of their African laborers behind.

The women of the plantation remain in shadow—Ann, Emeline, Rosa, several Marys, numerous Elizas, and others, the wives, daughters, and sisters of three generations. The records note marriage and baptism, usually in Christchurch in Nassau, and the date but seldom the place of death and burial. Knowledge of their most intimate lives comes only from the births of their children, five, twelve, thirteen to a family, plenty of mouths to feed but at least in these latitudes none of them needed a winter coat or mittens.

There are the names of the women but none of the spaces that bound them, the feelings that brought awe or envy, praise or hysteria, the exact topography of their hearts, the way they carried choices and grasped time. So many accounts of long ago give a narrow way of seeing, a matter-of-factness, largely about social constructs, manners, and material goods, that verges on abstraction. Landscape is missing, *what could be seen.* How the green land and white lanes sloped to the blue-green sea, how the bush was full of surprises or the heron mirrored the scallop of the bay with its line of flight. The heron flies this same way two hundred years later, slate blue amid the unsettled colors of water and sky at midday.

For the earliest generations the Out Islands lay distant and rugged, with a vaster wilderness beneath them, under the ocean. Absenteeism may have been common. With property on New Providence and this island, the Adderley women and children could have lived in greater comfort in Nassau. The husband could commute—sail from the Out Islands, tend to business—or stay in Nassau full-time, leaving his farm to a manager or overseer. Well into the 1800s and the third generation, however, the plantation was home in all respects. Children were born on the island, a most fundamental human event that cut through social and racial partitions. In *The Reshaping of Everyday Life: 1790–1840,* Jack Larkin offers a likely description. "In the South, birth often crossed barriers of color and servitude; the children of many plantation mistresses were delivered by slave midwives in a female circle that mixed black and white. This world of birth was a female one."

Out on the bay I could see Mark wading into the incoming tide, a dark stroke against aquamarine water with bands of turquoise then indigo on the horizon, blues darkened by increasing depth. I wished to be out there with him, away from the old stones and engulfing vegetation. Some primordial urge—a vestigial *Homo sapiens* fear of predators?—made me want to hack away at the bush until it was orderly and understandable. Another part of me lauded nature's persistent obliteration of this site.

Somewhere in the bush lay the old slave cemetery. Somewhere below this gentle rise of land, close to the shore of the bay, were the graves of ancestors, unmarked, unkempt. One grave allegedly held the bones of one of Nehemiah Adderley's sons, the last of the island's planters before the abandonment. He was the suicide, or so the island folklore claimed.

Everyone will tell you that genealogy serves two purposes: self-knowledge and social status, some sort of pedigree divined from names, locations, and achievements of eminence. However, there is nothing quite like an anomaly to suck attention away from the droning census records. A suicide hinted at emotion and thought. A closet door was flung open and daylight flooded a skeleton.

I sat atop the plantation house above the bay in my cotton clothes, a continent away from the high desert of the Colorado Plateau. Only a few days before, our gazes had taken in red sandstone cliffs, a sidelong aerial view of Cuba, and a marine province smack in the middle of the Gulf Stream, all within forty-eight hours. On a filament line made from hydrocarbons Mark lured bonefish to tiny, artificial shrimp hand-tied with fur and Mylar. He released the fish he caught. We were not hungry. We had never been threatened by cholera. We had no idea who made our clothing or grew the wheat for the bread we ate. We could talk to someone in Hong Kong merely by pressing buttons.

On this island in the ancestors' days, time would have been so different, so long, so visible. What kind of time would you need to grow food, draw water, go somewhere, get mail, weave palm fronds to thatch a roof, do up the buttons on your dress? Soaked in a mythology that now gives tropical islands the hedonistic allure of leisure, rinsing our winter-weary spirits in the calming blues, who among us could even begin to imagine the labor, the weight of hours?

Everything about the plantation ruins seemed solid but diminutive, as if people back then were so much smaller. When did we become tall? In England? What did a family eat for dinner in

1809? Who went fishing? Where were the cultivated fields? How did the native forest look before it was felled for cotton? Who helped the women in childbirth? What did the voices sound like, African and white? What would you do if you suddenly needed a book or a teacup?

One presumes that the English of tropical New World colonies were prudes. Englishwomen do not like heat. Even of the "heat" in the distant motherland, Jane Austen wrote, "What dreadful hot weather! It keeps me in a continual state of inelegance." Yet the sea's silken waters spread below the ridge, a peaceful enchantment of blues. Did the plantation women go skinny-dipping out there? How could they not? In the main house, the windows opened to bay and bush. Sea breezes could enter these small rooms, the luxuriant greenery surrounded them, a kind of Eden. Did they notice something delightfully indecent about the island's cloying lushness?

I thought of my great-grandmother "returning" to England to live and marry, as if England, rather than its colonies, had always been where the family belonged even though few had actually lived there for several hundred years. Was England exile or home? Did it seem miserable and dark? Was she too young to remember, to dream of turquoise water?

I have a photograph of this woman, the only face from the Bahamas-born Adderleys. It is a formal studio portrait taken when she was in her late forties or early fifties. She wears pearl-drop earrings, a gold watch and bracelet, and a wedding ring set with precious stones. Her neck and throat are engulfed in an untropical fluff of fur, probably fox. She is looking elegant and British. She gave her face shape to her granddaughters—my aunts and mother—but not to me. I cannot find any of me in her except her wrists and this blue, blue bay.

A small forest erupted inside the main house, rooted in the floor of a roofless parlor. The outside walls were less choked, so I dropped off my perch and walked their perimeter. Sharp thorns tore at my shin and blood ran down my leg and coated my ankle. A mockingbird threaded its song through the treetops. I watched a delicately shaped lizard, an anole of some sort, slip across laces of light and shadow. The lizard was the color of avocado flesh, the rim of darker green next to the skin. One exterior wall of the house still held faint coloration, as rough and faded as an old church fresco. The wall was rosy pink, like the nacreous blush inside a conch shell. Was this a rose-colored house? I squatted down and ran my hand over my ankle. With my fingertips I touched bright red descendant blood to a low part of the ancestor's wall, beneath the rose paint.

Into the gray ruins and dense, humid forest the sun came in patches of flickering light. Seasonal changes in this closed-in plant world were subtle and slight. Time was thick, perspectives confined to the middle distance. I felt panic. I needed a horizon. I climbed back up to the perch above the treetops.

Although I knew so little of these people, Anglo or African, who came before me, I knew this: Everywhere, every day, every one of them saw the turquoise waters spread before them, the bay of shimmering liquid light.

TWO BROTHERS OF the island's plantation years: Henry and William. They have siblings, but I shall follow these two limbs of the family shrub.

Henry is Nehemiah's eldest son, born in 1803. Son and grandson of slave owners, he grows up on a slave plantation. When he is nine years old, he inherits from his grandfather "a Negro Boy called by the name of George."

Although his brother William runs the plantation, Henry shares a financial interest in the property. Henry marries Mary Ann Perpall, the daughter of a Loyalist family of East Florida origins and Spanish descent, and makes his home and his fortune in Nassau as a banker and a businessman. Records note his brief tenure as the master of Vendue House, a stolid Georgian building used for the auctioning of slaves. The place will eventually become a museum, painted flamingo pink with white trim. I will stand on its creaky wooden floor, where the auction blocks once stood, and feel ice cubes pressed against my neck and back.

In 1832, shortly before emancipation, Henry and other vestry-men of the Anglican church protest the colonial government's pol-icy of weaning the Bahamas from slave labor. He is fined fifty pounds and sentenced to three months' imprisonment. He pays the fine, apologizes, and avoids detention. He is likely a stalwart mem-ber of the postemancipation commercial oligarchy known as "Bay Street," named for the city's main thoroughfare and for white Nassau's economic leverage over the rest of the colony and the black majority.

In the 1860s the American Civil War further empowers Bay Street and makes Henry and other Bahamian merchants very wealthy men. They run cotton from the South through blockades to Nassau then ship the cotton to England at great profit. They likely sell arms to the Confederacy, for that is where their sympa-thies lie. Henry owns a wharf, ships, and warehouses. His commer-cial building on Bay Street, with latticed galleries to shade the sun and catch the breeze, is so handsome that it will later be used as a government building for an independent Bahamas.

One of Henry's twelve children and a son-in-law help run the firm. They serve as members of the colonial parliament and are eventually knighted and get "Sir" in front of and a lot of capital-letter initials in back of their name. Henry will get an "Honorable" and a few initials too. The War Between the States ends and the future of the Bahamian economy remains uncertain. Henry moves his family to London. Perhaps we should not imagine him on a ship with sacks full of money.

Henry's daughter and one of the Sirs have their children in the Bahamas but move to England when their family is young. In turn, Henry's granddaughter comes of age in London and marries a Scotsman from Fife. He places on her finger a gold ring set with precious green stones. They have five sons.

When he is in his early twenties, one of the sons travels to a small ranch town in California, where he meets a woman of pioneer stock. He marries her. His father and Bahamas-born mother visit him in his home at the foot of the Sierra Nevada. They bring their cook. There is a holiday and a scurrying about for gifts. The California mother-in-law thinks to give the Bahamas-born mother-in-law an abalone shell. Of all the gifts it was the only one she takes with her on her return to England.

One of her California granddaughters bears three sons and a daughter. These four children know England and live there when they are young, but they know nothing of the long family history in the Atlantic. To them the Old South culture is an alien, wrong-minded culture, a broad sweep of nebulous geography, something they read about in Faulkner novels. To them Adderley is a name inside their late grandfather's string of English names.

These children are still wearing blue canvas Keds during the civil rights marches in Alabama, they are deep westerners, they think themselves sprung from the loins of cheatgrass and valley oaks. In a refashioned ring, their mother wears the emeralds that once belonged to a woman who came from green islands with necklaces of white sand and a turquoise sea, a woman whose grandfather, Henry, grew up on a slave plantation. The too-West daughter is now on that island, sitting ten inches from the chest of Henry's brother. She is sitting near bones.

ON DAYS THAT MARK came to the bay to go bonefishing, I explored the shore and made several futile attempts to find the plantation graveyard. The bush was dog's hair–thick, a fortress of stifling, humid air trapped by the overgrown canopy. I often lifted my eyes to the treetops to look for a bird in the full sun. Branches and thorns tore flesh even through my clothes, and I feared I might fall into a limestone sinkhole or stumble facedown into a seething mass of killer ants or angry termites. Several times during my stumblings I ended up hell-bent for the bay to swim and rinse skin that felt dipped in nettles.

Although I had a vague description of the site, no matter how carefully I followed it, I came away bloody and disappointed. Then one day I tried to see my path as a nineteenth-century path and I started from the beginning.

In my best Scarlett O'Hara walk I descended the old entry steps of the plantation. I intended to follow the original route from the house to the bay, using the faint rows of stones that bermed up and outlined the old walkway. The rows were about six feet apart and the space in between them was overgrown and tortuous. When the walkway crossed a causeway over a tidal pond, the newer trail to and from the ruins went one way and the outline went another, disappearing into the thick brush. I stuck to the old stone rows. Sometimes I lost them altogether, sometimes they forked into different directions, sometimes there were no stones at all, for the scrubland duff had buried them. Every once in a while, I came across a sea island cotton plant, a determined volunteer sprouting soft white fluff. I thrashed around like someone out of the hell chapters of a Conrad novel. Finally, on hands and knees, I crawled out to the open beach to give up.

From the beach I looked back into the bush. And of course there was an intriguing tree amid the acacia, wild legumes, and fan palms, a tree that stood higher than the others, and it was a hundred or so feet back into the bloody jungle and of course I had to crawl back in for a closer look at this tree, thinking about the tamarind trees the family had planted by the plantation house, in garden areas, and along the paths. I crashed and thrashed into the bush again. I had seen the tree's crown and now I found its roots. They had taken purchase in the corner of a vaulted tomb. Here lay an ancestor.

The ancient grave was about five by six feet and enclosed by an eighteen-inch-high wall made from a popular regional material called tabby, a mixture of lime, shells, sand, and water. The vault style is still common in the Bahamas; in maintained cemeteries the low walls are usually painted a dazzling white. Here, the tabby wall was cracked and black with age. There were no markings, no head-stone.

At the foot of the tomb vault, only inches away, lay another grave, smaller and ringed with heaped stones—no artful masonry, merely the outline of weathered stone around a slightly raised bed. I wanted to think of this smaller grave as a woman's, the woman who cherished a "continual state of inelegance" and went skinny-dipping.

There was an unabashed tenderness in the proximity of the two graves, as if they had been positioned in deliberate counterpoint to what was once the island's raw isolation, its worn-out soil and gen-teel poverty. What were the bonds between these two, I wondered. The only possible answer was *family*. Whether real lives unfolded in love or disaffection, your bones ended up together.

Old and faded conch shells lay scattered about, their trumpet shape turning inward to a wrapping fold bereft of its opalescent rose interior. A small forest sprouted from the cemetery; I could not stand up straight. I had to crawl to reach the tomb and explore its environs.

The cemetery was placed surprisingly close to the bay, just behind the seam between beach and scrubland. Through the trees I could see that the tide was coming in swiftly. High tide bore its schools of bonefish, the silvery phantom of the transparent shal-lows. Wherever they fed for shrimp, mollusks, and other prey, they left tracks in the pale sea floor, the marks of their blunt, pearly noses. Through the trees I saw a heron take possession of the shore with its imperial gait and indignant stare. It was a great blue, like my home river's great blues, the ones that fish in silty canyon waters. Spread beneath the toes of this great blue heron lay the jew-eled waters of the entire Great Bahama Bank.

Well, I thought as I sat next to the big tree that grew out of the corner of the tomb, here lies the old man. Which old man, who can

say? It is known that the first two patriarchs, Abraham and his son
Nehemiah, died at Heron Bay. However, if local legend is to be
believed, this grave did not hold their bones but the bones of
Nehemiah's son William.

Back to the family shrub: William is Nehemiah's fourth child
and the youngest son. Born in 1809, he is three years old when his
grandfather wills him "for ever a Negro Woman called and known
by the name of Beth." While his brother Henry leaves the island to
seek his fortunes in Nassau, William remains as a planter. He marries Jane Ellen Meadows in 1835. The first of their thirteen children
is born nine months later.

Only imagination can reconstruct William's years at this house
on Heron Bay, with its wooden floors and thatched roof, its big
yards, paths planted with tamarind trees, and gardens that grow
fruit, yams, guinea corn, and pigeon peas. These years will see
his brother profit from the American war and move his family to
England.

William dies sometime before February 1890, when his will
is proved. He leaves unnamed tracts of land on the island and
"dwelling House and buildings and furniture and cattle and small
stock" to four of his thirteen children. There is scant evidence to
show that any of these children remain on the island, although the
name of one of his sons appears as a district justice of the peace in
1889. The son then disappears from listings until 1907, when a
Florida town notes him as a resident.

That is what library genealogy says about my great-great-great-
uncle William and the plantation on Heron Bay. Then there is this
different history, gathered from interviews with islanders and other
sources.

William is granted Crown land on the island. He marries and
has a son, but there is no memory of his wife and child living on the
island. William may be on the property, it is said, with only his care-
takers and laborers. His heir does not claim the land on William's
death, so the ownership of the plantation becomes murky. Whether

it passes by sale, gift, trickery, abandonment, or a burgeoning squat-
tocracy in the wake of a collapsed cotton economy, no one knows.
According to this story, the land ends up, legally or otherwise, in the
hands of a local man. He is a "bright," the Bahamian term for a person of mixed black-white ancestry.

The local William story strays from archival documents when it
speculates that William Adderley came from Bristol, England, and
may have brought slaves from Africa on his own ship. (Britain
banned slave trading on ships in 1807, two years before William was
born.) It makes no mention of his grandfather's 1788 land grant or
of other predecessors, his siblings, or his other twelve children, for
whom documentation exists, and no mention of the 1890 will that
bequeathed the property to four, not one, of his offspring. If the
archival birth-death records are correct, William is over eighty years
old when he dies. The Nassau newspapers bear no notice of an
unusual death. These discrepancies can be easily resolved. More difficult to confirm or disprove is the rest of the local William story.

William takes up with a slave woman named Matula, his cook
and servant. "[C]alled 'teeny woman,'" she was a "big dark, dark
woman with white, white teeth." Matula bears him at least one
child, a son who grows up nearby and lives to a ripe old age. When
William dies, he is buried in this vault tomb by the bay. His former
slaves and laborers stay on or near the plantation. The white son
disappears and the local man uses the land. This island legend then
gives three versions of William's death, each with a common refrain.

When William's white wife confronts him about his relations
with the slave woman, he is so distraught, he "ground him a
butcher knife and cut his throat."

William's wife is the transgressor. Only an occasional visitor to
the island, she strikes up some "affairs" with local men whom she
met at church. When her enraged husband forbids her to continue
her "church affairs" and threatens to harm himself if she does not
obey, she refuses. He makes good on this threat and "ground him
a butcher knife and cut his throat."

Legend three: William's "slave girlfriend" insists on going to a local dance. Jealous and angry at her defiance, he "ground him a butcher knife and cut his throat."

In all versions of the suicide the blood of William Adderley is spilled on the white beach of the turquoise bay.

SUN COMES TO the earth as white light, hiding colors of the spectrum until it strikes a surface. Water absorbs most of these colors. But not blue light. Water gives back the blue.

In cold oceans rich with plankton the blue is deep and intensely moving, like memory or grief. The warm seas over the Great Bahama Bank support far fewer nutrients. The sediments of big rivers do not cloud them. Their warmth, clarity, and the pale floor of the vast shelf of shallows reflect aquamarine and turquoise, colors of inviting calm. These colors, of course, come with the climate of Eden.

Tropical islands enflame a tenacious romanticism in the modern soul. Their waters receive and hold our bodies without encumbrance. They are blissful realms of escapism, the places where a lusty ease slows time and suspends rules. No wonder they once crawled with missionaries.

We stayed on the island only long enough to be the romance-blinded sybarites. We did not stay long enough to figure things out. The stretch from first quarter to full moon to a few days beyond the last quarter was simply too little time to acquire the depth of local knowledge that fits people to place. Too little time to know fellow descendants, black or white. Too little time to know anything.

Much of the Adderley stock—the pre-Loyalist and planter lineage and the slave descendents—still lived in the Bahamas. I felt no discomfort with the sharing of a common ancestor, only delight in a widening arc of family. I did not believe it was necessary to broadcast my relationship to the planters of Heron Bay. People are still sensitive to a past of property abandonment, squatters, and land titles that bear greater complexity than the human genome. The real estate man at the nightclub presumed that the reason for our visit was possession. Surely you have come here to *own something*, he implied.

If we had too little time on the island to know anything, there was ample opportunity to be pitched into infinite wondering. Can a person's history be trusted, I wondered, when so much of his or her life is invisible? What kind of people were these ancestors to hold others in bondage? Where were the abolitionists when we needed them? What were the material circumstances that steered these lives in all directions? I went far back in my mind to the very stone walls enshrouded in greenery above the bay, passing through ripples of happiness and hate, sternness and humor, dreams, lust, luck, boredom, vice, fatigue, kindness. The farther back I went, the more I lost them.

Among other reasons, tracing one's bloodlines serves a desire for status, as if heredity conferred privilege or superiority. Does having ancestors far back into the substrate of the New World make me a better person than others? No, *I* make me a better person. My actions affect the future more than they affect the past. Here in my own search for "roots" I marveled at how we throw massive resources—an entire industry—at quests for the names of the dead, the paltriest hints of forebears, and how we would gladly keep up the pace clear back to our mothers the slime molds. For the future, however, our attention span is pitiable, about a week if we truly concentrate, or to the next tank or two of gas for the SUV.

What if all this fierce attention were given not to the generations behind but to the generations to come? What if we behaved as if our great-great-great-granddaughter will look back and seek the stories? She might find evidence of happiness and hate, lust and luck, great wrongs and joyous rights. She might still wade through thickets of dogma and racial prejudice. She might also snipe, *Oh yeah, Great-great-great-grandfather So-and-so and his generation, the people who gave us nuclear winter.* And so, in this density of family history, murky or clear, it seemed important to come away not with paper ancestors but with a tattered fragment of some sort of wild, unruly map of the human race.

My cousins had amassed the incomplete stories of strangers who were kin. They found this complex and entrenched family wing in the Bahamas and its detour to Victorian England. In England they found a peculiar tendency of nonbloods—spouses and in-laws—toward peculiar demises, someone struck by lightning during childbirth, another killed when she fell under a London subway train: death by "the Tube." They found a descendant's spouse who "worked for Hav-a-Tampa, where she made hand-rolled cigars," census notes of "female scholars" and bachelors and wives who "bore no issue," budless twigs on the family shrub. Reading this refrain I felt my own involuntary childlessness, my dead-endedness. *No issue.*

What if I had been born on these islands, I wondered. Could I live where there were no rivers? What if the extraordinary mobility of twentieth-century life had not branched the family shrub into dozens of scattered inflorescences, with few living in a single place in a single lifetime? When I sat on the beach below the old plantation, did I feel roots, a lost-native connection to four hundred Atlantic years? Some intuitive pull of blood?

Whether the story of William Adderley's suicide was truth or fable, or some of both, the beach below the plantation felt spooked. The beach belonged to the invading mangroves, the tides and the bonefish, the forlorn plantation ruins. The instinctive pull, a faint recognition of kinship with eight generations, the fit of place to soul, all this came from an entirely different piece of the island.

It was a place too far to reach by bicycle. Every time we went there, we had to load the bikes—and drinking water, lunch, and fishing gear—on a battered old Bluebird schoolbus painted white. We rode this shuttle to a leeward shore, where we pedaled sandy roads and walked a nearly deserted, three-mile-long ellipse of beach, a scimitar of white backed by a fringe of green. The horizons were less obstructed by land rises or the high bush, an openness that gave me a vivid sense of standing on the world.

The long bus usually carried only Mark, me, the driver, two bikes, and row after row of empty seats. Occasionally, the bus driver gave rides to elderly women in crisp, floral cotton dresses and wide-brimmed church hats with hibiscus or berries stuck in the band. The driver was a quiet, gentle man in his early sixties. I had the impression that to him we were two people who were always getting themselves into a world of trouble, that the only rescue from our own middle-aged mischief was his good sense.

He showed us where he was born, an old-style "slave house" on a hill with the Great Bahama Bank on one side and the Atlantic on the other, one horizon in turquoise, the other Prussian blue. He pointed out his farm and tidy white stucco house with red trim and a new roof. A hurricane had torn off the old roof, he said, peeled it away as he and his wife huddled inside during five hours of the storm's raging eyewall.

He raised sheep for meat. The island's goatlike breed had little wool, a selective trait for fuzz rather than fleece so the sheep did not die of heatstroke. Tamarind trees lined low walls of piled stones. Some of his fruit trees grew in "banana holes," natural depressions in the rough, bony limestone, where water and soil collected. One day he brought us coco plums, small yellow-green fruits with skin like apples and the juicy flesh of a lichee nut. Inside the kernel was an edible "peanut." He told us that his grandchildren did not know that food comes from the land. He said, "They think food comes from Miami."

From this small farm I envisioned the interlude after the plantation abandonment, when the next generations of islanders stayed on and fed themselves—barely—with whatever they could grow or pluck from the sea. They farmed with hoe, cutlass, fire, muscle, and a donkey or mule if they were lucky. Fertilizer came from bat guano in limestone caves and the ash raked up from brush burned to clear fields. They used wind for travel, sailing "up south" (against the wind) or "down north" (the wind at their backs). Supplies arrived on the mail boat from Nassau. Otherwise, not much of the world came to them. From the patience and endurance required to survive postslavery poverty rose the Afro-Bahamian proverb "Time longer dan rope."

When cotton collapsed on this island and populations reconcentrated in Nassau, many of the settlers were too poor to leave. Although in my family tree at least one of the siblings of the last farmer left (great-great-great-grandfather Henry), other people stayed and, unlike elsewhere in the West Indies, seemed to get along with less of the enculturated prejudice against racial mixing. They prospered from their coexistence. According to the Craton and Saunders history *Islanders in the Stream,* on this particular island people "of all complexions earned a long-lived reputation for enthusiastic sexual intercourse, and in many cases miscegenation was so general and so casual that family relations became extremely complex."

While Craton and Saunders say that the islanders' reputation for "indefatigable concupiscence" may be so much mythologizing, the people still bear renown for hardiness, independence, and ingenuity. I like to think that at least some of my relatives are among them, perhaps the descendants of William's children, be they black or white, who disappeared from the records but—who knows?— may have stayed on this harsh, thin-skinned limestone platform in the full caress of the Gulf Stream.

Resourcefulness remained of great value to our bus-driver friend. Whenever he asked Mark about his luck fishing, Mark would say, "I caught a few reef fish. They were small and blue. They were too beautiful to keep." The man shook his head and thought we would surely starve.

The first time we came to the three-mile-long beach, a squall spit rain and the sun dove behind an enormous raft of clouds. The diffused light erased all distinction between sea and sky so that we swam in watercolors on silk, a blue-green world with no ground, no horizon, only a rainbow over us in a perfect arc. The water at this beach was like nothing I had ever seen before. The dazzling white sand shelved into a shimmering raft of turquoise. When the waves receded, they left a glistening sheet of wet sand with a delicate pink cast. The sun moved from angle to overhead to angle again, deepening the blues and sharpening the lines of close-up things, like the baby's-tooth shells I found scattered in a lip of high tide or the shoelace blades of manatee grass in a patch offshore. But the fretted seam between water and sand remained forever in soft focus, as if the colors allowed no edges. The great heaps of cumulus, banked up for miles and miles beyond the island's flank, took the color of the sea. The underbellies of the clouds were turquoise.

Of all the things I wondered about on this island, I wondered the hardest about the paradoxical contrast and affinity of redrock desert and turquoise ocean, the seduction of certain geographies that feel like home not by story or blood but merely by their forms and colors. How our perceptions, as someone once said, are our only internal map of the world, how there are places that claim you and places that warn you away. How you can fall in love with the light.

Once while we were on the island, Mark and I spent the day in different places. The kindly driver shuttled my bike and me to the scimitar beach. Mark pedaled to the bay below the plantation to stalk the bonefish. I thought of him wading through the nose prints, the fish glyphs in the shallows. He thought of me swimming in the brilliance of refracted light. We joined at dusk under a bronze coin of setting sun, a dusk striped by the fronds of coconut palms and scented with salt air, jasmine, and bougainvillea.

As we pushed the bikes up a low hill, I told him how the clouds bore the color of the land they passed over, the blue-green sea, just as the clouds of home bore the color of the land they passed over, the red, red desert. He handed me a long, slender white bone from a heron of Heron Bay. One bone of leg, as light as air.

The Silk That Hurls Us Down Its Spine

No one can stand in these solitudes unmoved, and not feel that there is more in man than the mere breath of his body.

CHARLES DARWIN
The Voyage of the Beagle

Imagine the Colorado River Basin as if it were a grand banquet spread before you, your dining room chair bellied up to the Grand Canyon, your left elbow resting on Hoover Dam, your right elbow on the Sleeping Ute's nose, your fork poised somewhere above Canyonlands National Park.

Think not of a tectonic plate but of a sumptuous feast. Mesa tops of thick-headed pinyon-juniper broccoli, meandering banks of lush cottonwood celery and tamarisk slaw, a tangy salad of hackberry, coyote willow, and other riparian greens. Rich, teeming eddies of catfish bouillabaisse and carp carpaccio. Slickrock pools of quivering green Jell-O, sage-freckled Uinta Basin custard, Book Cliffs tortillas, frybread rolled from the yeasty mounds of Nokaito Bench. The cool slake of a pothole martini, garnished with tadpole shrimp and a Russian olive. Wingate Sandstone tarts steaming beneath a latticed cryptobiotic crust. North Rim cutlets breaded in mountain bikers. A jumbo helping of Moenkopi mud pies piled high on your sectional plate, buttressed with brave volcanic dikes to dam off the gravy of Chinle Wash. A thin ribbon of café au lait river that carries a tiny speck of a human being, although the lusty feast distracts your notice.

You gulp succulent brachiopods embedded in limestone fruit-cakes, gnaw the bony ribs of Shiprock, spoon up sun-ripened tomato-Red House Cliffs, and ice your tongue with the San Francisco Peaks' pale sherbet. You swallow Navajo Mountain like a plump muffin and bite off that potato chip of a dam on Glen Canyon. A faint tease of gluttony numbs your palate. Or is it indigestion? Still, you must eat, for each year the Colorado Plateau menu diminishes, the diners grow more numerous and their appetites ravenous.

Munch that meatloaf of a mesa, that most tender loin of Comb Ridge. Wash down Monument Valley with foamy drafts of Lava Falls. Crunch those toad bones, devour the lizards, ravage the Triassic cephalopods. Never mind the desert bighorns, who are endangered, or the ravens, who taste awful. Avoid the datura. Spit out the dung beetle. Relish bite-size canyon wren appetizers, impaled on yucca toothpicks. Slurp the dark sauces of Black Mesa coal, fend off scurvy with Lime Creek, and scald your tongue on Mexican Hat's gravel-capped uranium tailings pile, that broad, glow-in-the-dark, blue cornmeal mush wedge sprawled below and beyond the Moki Dugway, insane and forever.

After-dinner Cigarette Spring in hand, plate clean clear down to bedrock, you push back your chair and loosen your belt. You pluck a few B-52s from your teeth and launch a sated burp toward Denver. If we gourmands truly love this river basin, you sigh, we shall never go hungry.

Life as a desert omnivore, however, is never simple. The creeping heartburn returns. Underneath the Plateau's feral pelt, some pathetic, squiggling thing on the tablecloth, some fly in the river soup, catches your eye. Go back to that canyon-bound ribbon of water with the little *Homo* in it, the one swimming the river like a desperate bug.

THE TROUBLE SEEMS to be this: Although I should be in my raft, at the oars, savoring a morsel of uncooked Utah, I am not in the raft. On hundreds of trips down Colorado Plateau rivers over a span of eighteen years, I have been in the water on countless voluntary swims, but I should not be in the water now. Although I have often been stupid, I have just been extremely stupid. My need to pursue absurdity has overwhelmed my need to stay out of trouble. Moments ago I rowed to shore to investigate a pair of bright yellow objects in a debris pile. I pulled the raft's nose up on the sand and clipped my lifejacket to the frame. I walked away. While my back was turned the river nibbled the raft off the sandbar and carried it off in its swift current. The raft is empty. I am swimming after it.

The boat holds lifejacket, transportation out of the desert, drinking water, and food—real food, not some carbo-loaded physiographic province. The ghost voices of everyone who taught me anything about river running have stopped screaming *Always tie up your boat* long enough to start screaming *Always stay with your boat.* I am staying with my boat—it happens to be a considerable distance ahead of me, careening down the canyon. I am alone. I might drown. I have not finished living yet.

This must be the moment for a split-second flashback of my entire life: learning to read, eating avocados, my hamster Ned, my flannel sleeping bag with the little green turtles, climbing Mt. Whitney, falling in love. However, I shall go back only as far as morning.

THE COYOTES HOWLED the sun up the canyon rim, and when it spilled into my camp, the songbirds surrendered such lovely notes they broke my heart. So fervently did they sing, it was impossible not to separate their songs from all the other sounds of daybreak and fix on them as I lay wide-eyed and brokenhearted in my burning bed.

The canyon already blazed with heat. Sleeping bag and clothing felt like tools of the Inquisition. I donned hat and sunscreen and flicked aside the bed tarp quickly, checking for scorpions. On the campstove I brewed coffee, then cooled it down and iced it, barely surviving this rigor of Life in the Wilderness. Major John Wesley Powell, who ran the Green and Colorado Rivers more than a century ago, never had block ice in a giant cooler lashed to his wimpy wooden skiff. While today's river runners would gag on the Powell diet of rancid bacon, moldy flour, and stale coffee, they would sell their mothers for a glimpse of the Colorado Plateau before the dams and the crowds. I bore no delusions that the river beside me still flowed through Powell's *terra incognita*. From Rocky Mountain headwaters to the Sea of Cortez, the Colorado shoulders the weight of our needs, the thirsts of our farms and cities, and the affection of thousands of recreationists who ply its waters.

I daydreamed as I broke camp and loaded the raft, a routine repeated many times in my gypsy life as a river ranger's wife who spends much of the season afloat with him on his bimonthly patrols through the canyon. The packing, hefting, loading, and strapping felt so reflexive that, even after the first night out, I forgot that I had left the ranger behind. I missed him, but I did not need him. Other than keeping my tasks well within my own strength, a solo trip did not seem like a big deal.

I untied the raft, pushed it into the water, and climbed aboard. After an easy ferry the raft slipped into the main current. With an abruptness that could detach your teeth from your head, a low-flying B-52 suddenly unzipped the air between canyon rims, followed by an ear-splitting roar. The military planes flew over the river daily, sleek and darkly Transylvanian, looking as if no one were in them but bombs and robots. Around the first bend I passed a party of river runners. They waved from their camp, obviously bearing up well under the stress of the Nuevo Powell style—rancid prosciutto, stale cappuccino, Utah beer. Then I had the river to myself. It belonged to me all day long.

The canyon walls rose high, voluptuous, and red. I felt the river's muscle beneath the raft, pulling me along with little effort from the oars. It came to mind how simple river life is: Surrender all human measure of the universe to the river's own gauge of time and distance. Shed reason and frets so that what is left is a lean asceticism, a looking not at the world but into it. Let the morning serve up, as every slice of desert river will, a great blue heron.

The morning's heron stood in the shallows ahead, toes planted like twigs in the sandy bottom. It stared its Pleistocene stare. One foot lifted so slowly, the droplets that fell from it barely disturbed the water's surface. In a lightning motion the heron's stare disappeared underwater then reemerged. A few ropelike jerks of the bird's neck sent a silvery fish down its gullet. You can never get close enough to hear a heron's throat, nor can you easily identify the meal before it slides down that hose of a neck. Exotic and native fish swim these silty waters, natives whose endemism to the Colorado River basin is ancient (several million years) and now precarious. Biologists call the endangered Colorado pikeminnow, humpback and bonytail chubs, and other natives *obligate species,* creatures limited to a certain condition of life—that is, this river in which they evolved. In an ecology dramatically altered by humankind, some have become extinct, others hang on by a fin.

Unless you have been dead, you know that this is a land replete with consequence and complications. We know our own history: Modern humans came to this arid, fissured, difficult place blinded, seeing not its particularities but our own aims. Because of this blindness, the shackles were severe, our covenant with nature set in terms of conquest rather than compatibility. "Taming the menace," in the words of the U.S. Bureau of Reclamation, has transformed the Colorado into a push-button river with a queue of dams and diversions in the lower basin and a flood-poor river in the middle basin. We reap the bounties of a watershed plumbed from headwaters to mouth, and we know the environmental costs, among them the loss of native fish, the drowning of spectacular canyons under enormous reservoirs, the alteration of riparian communities. We know that our urban desert culture is quickly outstripping the Colorado's ability to support it. What we do not know is this: Have we learned anything? Would we do it all over again?

In hundreds of side canyons and washes, on semiwild pieces of mainstem bracketed by the hardware, fluid gravity still more or less makes its own decisions and follows the path of its own weight, taking with it worn-down pieces of the continent grain by grain. It is in these reaches that you are most likely to glimpse the river's fight for eternity. To witness that persistence is why many of us make our home here. For me the bond between self and place is not conscious—no truth will arrive that way—but entirely sensory. Instinct and intimacy bring the feast closer, the river celebrates things we forget how to celebrate: our own spirits, the eternity of all things.

Watching the heron brought to mind a bird-watcher's story from the much reengineered lower Colorado, where a meandering swath of sand and scrub overgrew an old, dewatered channel. Instead of flying in a straight line across the flats, a great blue heron followed the dry, serpentine curve of the ghost channel, unable—or unwilling—to disobey an ancient avian wisdom, the imperative to match its flight to the shape of a river.

As the raft approached, the morning's heron took wing and flew the river bends as I did. The bird paid no attention to the unlikely yellow objects set against a gray-brown stack of logs jammed against the bank. The attention was mine. I pulled on the oars to make shore.

I COULD USE about twenty herons now, herons to pluck me from this roiling sandstone gravy and drop me into the runaway raft like a wet noodle. The water is not cold, but the flow is swift—no rapids yet, few rocks to bash myself against. In the shallows, without a lifejacket for buoyancy and padding, the river bottom could shred me like a cheese grater. I struggle to stay in the deepest current, to reduce the distance to the boat, but my legs move like Gumby limbs, too weary to kick much longer.

What happens when I surrender to this aloof, silken creature that hurls me down its spine? What happens when I exhaust my strength and can swim no more, no matter how hard I try or how desperate I am? What happens if I let go?

How very familiar these waters feel, waters brought in from all directions over broad stretches of desert, through sinuous canyons to join their downward run to the sea. Every leaf, every riffle, every russet sweep of sandstone is saturated with memories, cut through and through with my own history. Along the river are strewn stories that make me who I am, that tell me what binds my life together, what to value and what to lay aside. We know few ways to tell the river's story other than through our own. Yet here it flows, making beauty a fact of existence, visible in its presence and absence, in flood and in washes as parched as old bones. To witness it you are grateful to have senses, to feel this one exquisite and dangerous thing that holds you to all life.

Shadows carve bands of mauve into the sun-bright terra-cotta of the canyon walls. Ripples of heat quiver against the high rims and disappear into a vault of azure sky. Ahead the water's surface splinters into a million fragments of sunlight. I try to match my swim to the shape of the river.

The river carries the raft into an eddy and slows it down. The oars no longer spin wildly in the oarlocks. If you observe stream hydraulics carefully, you will know that most eddies move in circles. The main current meets the eddy's slower water and pushes it in the opposite direction—the river flows upstream. It curls back, then meets the current again. At the top of the circling eddy I tread water and wait for the river to deliver the raft to me.

Never have I been so happy to become one with a gray bubble of inflated Hypalon. From water level the pontoon looks as high as a blimp. I find a strap end and use it to haul myself up and into the boat. Like bedraggled kelp, my dripping body drapes over the fat tube. A sudden anger rolls through me. I kick the sides of the dry box, the oars, the aluminum frame. I kiss my lifejacket. I bite the bowline to shreds. I squint and growl, *Stupid, stupid, stupid.* All around me lies the sumptuous Colorado Plateau feast. In the cooler lies a normal dinner. In the pocket of my soaked shorts lie items scavenged from a debris heap. Bathtub toys. Two yellow plastic ducklings.

IN THE LAST HOUR of sun the river that ran jade during the day runs with flames of copper and indigo. The shadow cast by a canyon wall already holds dusk, its edge a sharp clarity. Bathed in the apricot light of day's end, I watch the dark shadow move across the water. Oddly, the serenity of being beside a river induces an intensity of awareness that is inflammatory; one moves from languid calm to burning ecstasy in an instant. Inside the Jurassic walls, my frail body nearly explodes with the sheer beauty of this place. It is as if there is no air or stone here, only light.

I have guarded against theft by nearly dry-docking the raft on the beach and tying both bow and stern lines with an overkill of knots. I have arranged tarp, bed, and ducklings under a juniper, intending to inhale the tree's scent all night, and I have eaten a monkish repast. I feel no loneliness, only aloneness. Do I like being where I am, by myself? I do. I can sit on the bank and stare. If I want to, I can drool. I can absorb without distraction the bursting fullness of light and living things that give the inert sandstone a tangible pulse. In solitude you strip yourself bare, you rest your mind on what is essential and true. The canyon's shadow engulfs camp. For a while tendrils of warm air from the day-baked cliffs stave off the shadow's cool.

The river's riches, like life's memorable moments, often assume a dreamlike quality when you think back on them. Although it felt like forever, I had not actually chased the raft very far; it was not a near-death experience. Did this harsh, red-boned desert impart something besides its indifference to my wholly insignificant being? Have I learned anything?

I have learned that, skill notwithstanding, the river is always in charge. It can mesmerize and tranquilize, pulverize and tenderize, rip your limbs apart, fill your lungs with mud. The wind can turn your boat upside down on the water, the July sun can turn your brain to mush, ice in the eddies can lacerate your hands with its sherds. The river has taught me that thunder cues toad lust and a lizard I once watched turned its belly cobalt blue then deblued it before my very eyes. That ravens don't like dirty toes, so they clean them often. That the Anasazi, prehistoric desert farmers who scattered their petroglyphs throughout the canyonlands, were as interested in human genitalia as we are.

I have learned that when we dammed Glen Canyon we traded a stunning redrock wilderness for better hospitals, security lighting in Kmart parking lots, lettuce in January, and block ice in my boat cooler. That beneath the slackwater reservoirs flows an outlaw river still intending to reach the Gulf of California. That a chunk of Entrada Sandstone the size of an obese Honda can drop out of the sky and so, too, can fall the tiniest bird's egg with a shell the color of air and a yolk as red as blood. That my husband's devotion remains steady and true, to me and to the river, and that after hiking a side canyon in 103-degree heat, a cantaloupe from the cooler was the best thing we'd ever eaten in our entire lives. I have learned that on the clearest days in the worst drought, cottonwood leaves sound like rain when they tremble, and if you walk far enough you can still find prayer bundles tied to the branches of coyote willows beside a spring that gushes out of bare rock with such power it seems possessed.

I have learned that when I lie on a sweep of polished slickrock in a certain canyon near Navajo Mountain, my body and the desert are the same shape, a perfect fit of rock and flesh. The river draws off my madness and calms me. It knows nothing of my love for it; it can, like love and mystery, prove unattainable even in the moments of profoundest intimacy. The river flows downstream. Sometimes it flows upstream. The physics of river can show you endless facets of gravity made visible and fluid. It can carry two yellow ducks from God knows where or for how long or how many miles and set them down in the same debris pile, three inches apart.

The canyon takes on moonlight long before the moon itself becomes visible. The delirious bird opera that opened the day has given over to a soothing whisper of water flowing by, never stopping. The night songs come from a poorwill. Filled with formless, silvery light, the gorge floats as if weightless, then comes into sharp focus when the luminous orb tops the rims. There is no end to appetite here. This lusty feast of a province may be better suited to nourish our souls than our material excesses. We eat it to build cells and sinew, to run through our own veins and resupply our blood.

The moon shivers in the small ring of dark inside my teacup. On my two-thousandth night on the river, I still don't know anything. The best I can do is to always tie up my raft when I leave it. The best I can do is follow the serpentine curves, the dry, ghost river as well as the wet, flowing one. I am an obligate species, obligated to have this river. I can match this life to its shape. Perhaps then I might learn something.

A Field Guide to Brazen Harlotry

LOVE
She tries it on, like a dress.
She decides it doesn't fit,
and starts to take it off.
Her skin comes, too.

LOLA HASKINS
Desire Lines

For reasons that are not entirely clear I have always believed that love and restlessness are inextricably bound to a desert plant called cliffrose. The association might sound more plausible in temperate or semitropical places—all those sweaty, hothouse colors, the rising sap, the deep-throat orchids, roses with their beads of dew and libidinous landscape of lips and folds. In contrast, desert flora are sparse and ephemeral. There are spines, thorns, uncertain seeds, long periods of dormancy, and, when moisture comes, a passion of flowers so accelerated, you feel their demands on your heart, the mounting pleasure, the sweet exhaustion.

I first wallowed in botanical eroticism years ago, when the long, cold winters of my Montana home propelled me southward to cheat. By changing latitudes I could begin spring early. Beyond the northern Rockies' hard grip, the Colorado Plateau deserts were warm and soft, already engaged in rampant foreplay. The business of every plant, tree, and creature was the business of reproduction. In those years as a seasonal gypsy, on long hikes down canyons and across open mesas, I wandered through the fecund glory and tried not to eavesdrop. I committed Victorian acts of science: counting petals, defining shapes and symmetries, sorting the petiole from the pappus, the basal rosettes from the pinnately compounded. I indexed my brain with genera and spilled Latin names onto the Halgaito Shale.

The wildflowers taught me color, not lipstick or wall paint or inner-self color, but all the colors possible in a panorama of poly-chromatic reds held under a dome of azure sky—papery white prickly poppies, blue-violet flax, firecracker-red penstemon, the crimson spark of paintbrush amid silver-green sage.

The pages of my plant identification book wore thin from key-ing. My eyes lost focus in the dense undergrowth of footnotes. My sketchbook filled with portraits of rocks and plants. Next to the sketches of Anasazi pottery sherds and pinyon pine cones were notes like "Sinuous canyon, drowning in light. Navajo Sandstone? Entrada? Walls like flesh. The slickrock holds me in feverish thrall and the grip of inertia . . . 'you who beneath his hands swell with abundance' (Rilke)." Or, on sojourns that coincided with a rela-tionship in which I clung to a rather obsessive, unrequited love, "Datil yucca. *Yucca baccata.* Curled fibers on the margins of sword-like leaves. Center stalk with creamy blooms. Fibers used by the Anasazi for sandals and paintbrushes, roots used for shampoo. Liq-uid as slick as soap beneath a coronet of spikes. Extreme pleasure is a form of self-immolation, desire its leash around the neck. Do not bother to resist."

In no time scientific inquiry fell by the wayside. Phrases like "pubescence of the leaves subtomentose or tomentose" brought out a blush instead of a dictionary. I abandoned field guides, lists, and, near water, clothing. I spent a great deal of time lying down on dunes of coral red sand, shaping myself to the slip face and its crop of silky white and pink evening primrose. On one spring sojourn I mixed camp in a field of purple scorpionweed with a decision about marrying the man in my life, a very sound, un-unrequited love. There was little doubt in my mind what all these plants were up to, their wild, palpable surge of seduction best absorbed by the undermind—no categories, no labels, no conscious grasping but a kind of sideways knowing. Spring in the desert grew beyond the reach of intellect and became a blinding ache for intimacy, not unlike beauty, not unlike physical love. Even though I moved away from Montana and now live in the desert full-time, each spring still carries this craving, this weight of bliss.

And, here on the Colorado Plateau, once again the orb has slipped. The Northern Hemisphere tips away from the cold. The season is turning and, in my neighborhood, the lavish scent of damp sand, the upsurge of chlorophyll, the birds that mate in the air above our heads—all of it makes us slightly crazed. It is spring again. I have decided to live inside the sex organs of plants.

◆　◆　◆

DESERT PAINTBRUSH (*Castilleja chromosa*): A low-lying herbaceous plant with narrow leaves and clustered bracts, or modified leaves, that resemble a ragged brush dipped in scarlet paint. The bracts, not the flowers, bear the showy red. The flowers, as thin as eyelashes, lie hidden in the bracts.

AT A DISTANCE the land clings to its wan winter brown, fired by the orange and maroon forests of leafless willows along the banks of the river below my house. Close up the colors come as   *Desert paintbrush* fragments, as tendrils of green against red sand or onyx bibs on the throats of meadowlarks that change their guttural *tchuck* into the throaty melody of breeding season. The red-winged blackbirds, too, have traded winter songs for mating arias and flaming-red epaulets. Only days earlier their shoulder feathers were dark and drab. How do they grow the red?

A week of storms bears the promise of a wet season, the hope that enough rain will come this year to evade drought even though it never does. The desert feels stripped of its winter passivity, the air sharp on the edges of the fronts that pass through. Sometimes the storms walk in slowly, their rain moving across the land like a curtain of blue dust. Sometimes the storms stop short of the river valley. Heavy clouds drape the far-flung islands of mountains that ring us—the Abajos, Carrizos, Chuskas, Utes—but send only their wind to tear and whip until my hair hurts. Then more rain, more mud. Everyone's trucks turn the color of clay flowerpots. Blobs of red gumbo ride in from the Navajo Reservation on wheel wells and mud flaps.

On a clear, calm day I hike up the tilted sandstone spine that knifes through the desert, the ridge of my winter quarters, where I brought moods and crayons and watched 360 degrees of broken desert in the ever changing light. A month has passed since my last visit. I missed the thaw, the shift from frozen water and dormant wood to a softening so full that the ridge itself could have swelled and doubled in size if I didn't know better.

On the ridge, spring's colors break out of the sandstone like a hulking seed bursts from a pod too weak to contain it any longer: aquamarine lichen, the fresh, sweet green of single-leaf ash, a scattering of cryptantha with blooms the color of the inside of a lemon skin, and, in sinuous folds of slickrock, wildflowers in electrified red: paintbrush.

The desert paintbrush is the queen of slickrotica. You can tell by its fiery scarlet and early bloom, as if it wants these curvaceous sweeps of sandstone to itself before the wildflower season's full

Baroque. Paintbrush is partially parasitic on the roots of other plants. Underground, it invades the vascular tissue of another plant and absorbs its nutrients. Sometimes paintbrush nudges up seductively close to the host, a flashy scarlet starlet in pickpocket position.

In contrast to places where soil is abundant and deep—and to the neighboring Great Basin's bowl full of alluvium—the Colorado Plateau desert is earth unmasked. Weather and time remove detritus as small as sand grains and as large as hopes for a few inches of soil. On sedimentary strata with little or no veneer, plants like the paintbrush take purchase. They must adapt to different parent materials, fix their roots into substrate that varies in type and hospitality within a few hundred yards. Some plants take to sand and gravels, others to shallow silts or clay. "Edaphic endemism is rampant on the Plateau," says a statement about as tabloidesque as a botany text will dare. In other words, the range of certain endemics, or flora limited to specific localities, is often determined by soil conditions.

Paintbrush grows in tucks and folds of canyons and amid pinyons and junipers on the high-elevation mesas. A tall, gangly *Castilleja* with red-orange bracts prefers stream bottoms, springs, and other wet places. Paintbrush genera spread themselves from Wyoming to New Mexico and eastern California to Colorado. But many of them slip their lives into bare-boned sandstone. The paintbrush becomes attached to its homestead. I interpret this as affective as well as physical and take them on as allies. I admire their loyalty to dirt.

Red is common among early bloomers, as if nature wished to jump-start spring, to skip the formalities and lunge into an unfeigned passion that dissolves reason or reluctance. Red is the color of attention. Red flowers sear retinas made weary by winter, by snow or the season's low, angular light. The color prepares you for the wings of a bluebird, the shimmering violet throat of a hummingbird, sunrise in bands of pollen yellow.

There are physical reasons for the boldness of red. Light waves are longer at the red end of the spectrum of visible light. During a lurid desert sunset, layers of dust close to the horizon absorb the shorter wavelengths while the long red waves reach the eye. The iris of the human eye is a muscle that controls the amount of light that passes into the crystalline lens. The eye bears three pigments—blue, green, and red—that absorb light and signal the brain to read colors. The gene for the eye's red pigment is found on the X chromosome. Some women have two different red pigments in their eyes. They see subtle differences in color that men and other women cannot see.

In California's Sierra Nevada one of spring's first wildflowers arises from the forest floor as the snow recedes. Brilliant red asparaguslike tips press through rich black humus and grow into stout, fleshy columns with shanks of bell-shaped flowers. The snow plant (*Sarcodes sanguinea*) is full-on shock-red. It lacks chlorophyll and feeds on organic matter. It looks like a mushroom on acid. Surely it is hot-blooded, a plant with its own floral furnace, emerging like rubies in crisp alpine air inches away from a snowbank. In plant and human worlds, in mountain and desert, red flowers like the snow plant and paintbrush are visual aphrodisiacs, they signal the seasonal shift from dormancy to reproductive frenzy, from the cerebral to the carnal.

Castilleja produce nectar twice a day, when insects and birds are most active. Midday the pollinators rest. I am on the ridge at midday, greedily hoarding the red. The sun illuminates the paintbrush against blond rock. Red is the color of martyrs, blood, hell, and desire. It quickens the heart rate and releases adrenaline. The rains and this electric flower promise more red—and every other color— to come. I make a vow that each day will have in it a jewel like this one, knowing well that the desert bloom is not so much a season as a moment, given then lost. I am ready to live inside this paintbrush, but I cannot climb in. I am stuck in the ecstasy of anticipation.

❖ ❖ ❖

DESERT GLOBEMALLOW (*Sphaeralcea ambigua*) and SCARLET GLOBE-
MALLOW (*Sphaeralcea coccinea*): Common, drought-tolerant wildflowers with red to red-orange blossoms in radial clusters, cuplike
to hold bees that curl up inside them in the morning. Globemallow: the warming hut.

MOUNTAIN DWELLERS WILL THROW meadows at desert
ascetics, touting the dazzling Impressionism of so many wildflowers
in profusion. Californians will show off hills aflame with poppies.
In expanses of open desert, in wet years, the equivalent spread of
glory is a field of globemallow, one of the Colorado Plateau's few
"carpets" of color in a landscape that otherwise scatters its wildflowers in mixed, looser intervals. We will squint at such a field and
think *lush*. Globemallow in the desert will not make us think of
cotton, okra, or hibiscus, although it shares the same family.

The globemallow fields of spring could, in a reckless descent
into the deep past, recall the burst of flora into the raw dust-and-
basalt monotone of a primordial planet. In his essay "How Flowers
Changed the World," Loren Eiseley compresses this event into the
image of Earth, seen from outer space, emanating a subtle change
in light.

For several million years—the crashing reptile, lizard bird,
wimpy mammal ancestor, swamp years—plant life held little in its
palette beyond a "slowly growing green," Eiseley writes. Small naked
sperm cells bound to dew and raindrops learned to be wind-borne
pollen. Ancestral pines, firs, and other conifers joined spore produc-
ers to be gymnosperms, or plants with exposed seeds. About 140
million years ago, Eiseley continues, at the eclipse of the dinosaur
age, "there occurred a soundless, violent explosion. It lasted millions
of years, but it was an explosion nevertheless. It marked the emer-
gence of the angiosperms—the flowering plants. Even the great evo-

lutionist, Charles Darwin, called them an 'abominable mystery,' because they appeared so suddenly and spread so fast."

Over another several million years angiosperms coevolved with increasingly dependable pollinators, the insects that helped to form the anatomies, colors, and scents of flowers. Flowers made extraordinary moves to seduce them—new symmetries and shapes, refined nectar, intensified color. Long floral tubes invited long-tongued lepidopterans, red drew the butterflies and birds, bees loved the blues. The angiosperms ("encased seed") packed their progeny into tight little containers that could fly, roll, hook, attach, and otherwise travel. Creatures devoured the plants' luscious fruits or ate them as insects: nectar converted, nectar that could fly. The gift of flowers, the "weight of a petal" (Eiseley again), made a world possible for *Homo sapiens.*

Big-brained *Homos* are yet naming the angiosperms, pinning down their secret lives and their resplendent colors. In a field of globemallow the namers could get mighty picky. One observer of plant taxonomy may describe globemallow's blooms as orange, another as red, others as coral, coral-red, orange-red, or red-orange. Compromise and call it chorizo. Everyone who ever played with paints would agree that the color orange is a marriage—artist Vasily Kandinsky called it "red brought nearer to humanity by yellow." The naming is difficult because our eyes can isolate far more colors than we have words for. Variations and brilliance, culture and emotion, seep into linguistic terms for the chromatic effects, the simple physics, of light.

In a time when the enlightened rationalists wanted to apply scientific order to the life around them, color, and color naming, was considered a messy business and far too feckless if left to artists. By the early 1900s several publications in ornithology and botany attempted to establish a standardized vocabulary for nature's palette. The idea was to provide field biologists with a reliable, common reference for identifying flowers, plants, and birds. If one biologist called a leaf or a wing feather chrysoprase-green or bottle-green,

meadow-green, Tiber, or dusky green, it would be the same chryso-
prase, bottle, meadow, etc., green for everyone. Name had to match
reality, and reality could be made uniform in samples, chips, and
swatches.

A Dictionary of Color, published in 1930 by A. J. Maerz and
M. Rea Paul, ordered the pigments for commerce and industry.
One of its authors worked for a lead company. Walls, ships, and
houses, Maerz and Paul insisted, could not be painted profitably
if the names of colors were nonsense. "It has been frequently
observed that while standardization has been arrived at in prac-
tically all other fields," they wrote, "in the use of color names for
identifying color sensations a condition prevails that is usually
characterized as chaos."

In the minds of chaos-busters Maerz and Paul, the fashion and
textile industries were most guilty of a "promiscuous use of extrav-
agant color names." Nonsense words, changes in references and
origins, seasonal whims, and other names with an "ephemeral existence" only resulted in confusion and financial loss. Their list of
culprits was largely French, colors like widow's joy, chimney sweep,
envenomed monkey (sixteenth century); stifled sigh, burnt opera
house, and Paris mud (eighteenth century). There was a rash of rash
colors—rash tears, rash leap—and someone at a soirée wearing "a
muff of Momentary Agitation." The authors could not locate sample pigments for such English color names as skating, wireless,
water sprite, basketball, and the smoke of the Camp of St. Roche.
Elephant's breath eluded them altogether. Hedge sparrow egg could
not be found because all samples, and possibly the species itself,
had been lost.

A Dictionary of Color presented over three thousand entries—
three thousand standards—reproducing a sample of each color in
page after page of small rectangles. Some colors had dates of origin
(Arizona, a pigment described as "sunburned almond," appeared
in 1917). Others needed no explanation—rose de nymphe, gravel,
mummy brown, ass dun (versus horse, cow, or mouse dun), and still

more might have benefited from one—bambino, fox trot, atmosphere, and sundown Yosemite, but only if you have never been there.

Although more sophisticated science would later repudiate his physics, Goethe, the German poet and dramatist, was among the first to suggest that there was more to color than retinas and wavelengths and words that attempted to define the highly nuanced effects of light. In *Theory of Colours* he wrote that "every colour produces a distinct impression on the mind, and thus addresses at once the eye and the feelings." Our response to color, he believed, relied on sensual, aesthetic, and cultural as well as biological cues. Lustrous or dull, harmonious or discordant, colors excited particular emotional states.

Goethe noted the preference for sedate colors in sedate countries (England and Germany) and the possibility of environment—gray northern skies—as explanation. The "lively" nations (France and Italy) made use of intense colors. Nearly everyone of power used red to dignify their appearance. Goethe lumped together the usual cast of alleged primitives ("men in a state of nature"), noting that "savage nations, uneducated people, and children have a predilection for vivid colours" as well as a fondness for "the motley."

Neuropsychology has gone far in explaining perception and sensation in terms of the biochemistry of the brain. We know that the center of our chromatic sense, the neurons devoted to color and shape, lies in the inferior part of the occipital lobe, in the back of the head above the cerebellum and spinal cord, next door to the brain's center for touch and nearly opposite on the hemisphere to behavior and emotion. We know how the eyes see brightness and motion, how they manage illusion, how people with color blindness and other anomalies adapt. Experiments have shown colors' effects on the autonomic nervous system. If you put male ducks in black blindfolds, for instance, their sexual activity diminishes. Under orange-red light their testicles nearly double in size.

Linking color and human behavior, chromotherapy has been around since at least the 1870s, when insane asylums in Europe put their wards in light filtered through a violet stained-glass window to calm them. A modern, self-described "magnetist and psychophysician," who used colored electric light to treat patients' ills, claimed, "Red light, like red drugs, [has] an especially arousing effect on the blood."

Some of those who work in the postmodern buffet of emotion businesses claim that to deny feelings over color is a sign of a "disturbed, frustrated, or unhappy mortal"; to love colors too much is "poor direction." In fact, if you do not know who you are, your attraction to colors will tell you. My personal favorites—distilled from various sources—come from the seventies, the decade that saw the births of thousands of inner selves.

If you are young and irrational but act old and rational, you like taupe. Pink is sought by mistreated people in search of tenderness. Pink types live in wealthy neighborhoods. If you hate pink, you are likely an annoying person. A person drawn to purple is a teensy bit vain and inclined to prefer opera and eschew the sordid and the vulgar. Those who dread purple have a name: porphyrophobics. Orange is the color preferred by politicians and backslappers, green the preference of suburbanites, overweight individuals, and people who belong to clubs, thus validating, I would guess, the only non-government use of Government Wall Green: the golf sweater.

Schizophrenics like gray or black. Nonschizophrenics who like black hide their ages and their true natures behind an impression of sophistication. Someone should look into the color preferences of guys with blindfolds who measure duck testicles. People who prefer blue are people who know how to make money. They have a strong but controlled sex drive. Of blue-green "narcissists," one source describes them as charmingly egocentric, "probably sexually frigid," and probably divorced. Brown people are rootless and dispossessed. Yellow people are babyish or nuts. Red people project useful hostility. A dislike of red indicates a frustrated, defeated person who is bitter and angry over "unfulfilled longings." No one likes white; there are no white people.

If you were given such diagnostic comments back then, you probably need therapy now more than ever. I look at the clothes I am wearing today. I am an annoying, sophisticated but rootless nymphomaniac who is charmingly bitter and angry over unfulfilled longings. I am one of those "men in a state of nature," fond of the motley. I need help. I need red drugs. I need to climb into this globemallow, this warming hut, and curl up with the bees.

AROUND THE TIME that the globemallow is in bloom, sand verbena appears on the dunes behind our house, barely six inches high, with white flowers in a snowball cluster. Sand grains stick to the verbena's pointed, gray-green leaves, shading their tissues from heat and giving the plant a rosy demeanor. The delicate, bladelike leaves of sego lilies knife through the hardpan on the river terraces, topped by cone-shaped buds. A dry spell after the storms threatens to desiccate the buds before they open, escalating the risks of an already precarious cycle of bloom and death. If winter rains have been inadequate, if spring rains remain fickle, the desert's green promise can quickly turn brittle. A hike across the flats is like walking across potato chips. If those in denial prevail in the halls of power, this is what global warming will feel like on the Colorado Plateau: 250,000 square miles of potato chips.

Days of sharp, glittering sunshine turn the desert an immodest green and the puddles dry up in the dirt lot where the commodity cheese truck parks. Scattered among rabbitbrush and fourwing saltbush the orange heads of globemallow dot the bench on which our house sits. Heckle and Jeckle, the resident pair of ravens who keep us around for their personal amusement, perch behind the blooms. The orange against ebony feathers stops me in my tracks. The ravens quork and preen lewdly. They know exactly what each lecherous blossom and every lust-crazed pollinator is up to.

Below the bench the river rises with snowmelt from the mountains of Colorado, Utah, Arizona, and New Mexico. The flow from this tributary rushes to join its forces with the Colorado River in this heartland of canyon country. My husband, a ranger for the federal agency that manages recreation on these waters, plans a multiday float trip, one of his routine patrols down a long, wild stretch of canyon. The trip will coincide with the peak of the wildflower season.

We begin to put together rafting gear, camping equipment, and a menu for meals on the river. Somehow the season's lascivious mood permeates the menu. Somehow the menu list ends up looking like fare out of Umar ibn Muhammad al-Nafzawi's *Perfumed Garden:* artichokes, figs, and oysters. Asparagus ("It must be firm," admonishes my cookbook; "no one likes his spear wilted"), erect little mushrooms, and plump garbanzos, the bean that helped an al-Nafzawi hero deflower eighty virgins in a single night, or maybe it was the camel milk. I spend a great deal of time thinking about food love, religious love, filial love, disabling love, and raven love. I think about how in spring compulsive behavior might rise up like sap and trigger the gesture of a stranger. This stranger enters my life in an obtuse way.

In this remote part of the Southwest it is easy to fight off the ravenous appetites of commerce. The zip codes carry low priority for telemarketers, and a healthy buffer of rocks, canyons, gulches, cliffs, mesas, buttes, parabolic dunes, arroyos, rivers, and mountains lies between me and the nearest shopping mall. However, I need a new bathing suit for the river trip. I turn to the catalogues. I order a plain low-back tank in black, appropriate for the middle-aged person someone has informed me I have become. I tell myself that black is very Italian.

The package arrives. I find myself in the possession of swimwear that is not black. At first I am annoyed, then I begin to wonder if this might be some kind of cosmic awakening, not just twelve ounces of spandex. The order is in error, but I cannot bring myself to return it. How dare I? I am self-centered and clueless: I know nothing about the outside world, the loves and needs of my fellow human beings. I have not found the precise location of my television since the year 2000. I spend my days flitting about the desert, thinking about flower sex. I am destined to wear a not-black bathing suit.

I hold the new swimsuit on my lap and imagine a course of events. In my mind's eye there she was, the person who filled my order, perhaps a single mother of two kids, living on baby carrots and tunafish, sucked up in mindless repetitive tasks, her days spent at the mail-order warehouse doing pick tickets, chain-smoking Kools on the fire escape during coffee breaks. Maybe she grieves for a dead parent and a time before NAFTA. Maybe one of her kids is obsessed with lint and sleeps with a Dustbuster. The other wants new breasts for her high school graduation gift. At home a family of squirrels has taken over the upstairs crawl space. All night she hears them thrash, chew, and make toenail noises, so she spends more time at the firing range. Maybe when her kids inquire about her life before motherhood, she wonders if she should tell them about the camisoles, the night in a Fresno jail.

As I prepare for the river trip, I imagine this woman, identified on my receipt as Locator #395, pulling up a fresh batch of orders. She clung to her patch of marital loyalty as long as she could, she thinks as she works, until her husband left his job in swimming pool maintenance and ran off with a Christian fitness center attendant named Tiffany. She hung on until she felt relief at the thought of a generation that must age like any other, until she thought of all those ninety-four-year-olds named Tiffany.

When her garage door falls off, when the VCR explodes, then melts into a patent-leather pool, and the squirrels shred the insulation into floating tufts that waft through the heating vents, she ponders polyandry: seven husbands, all rather handy around the house, seven Barcaloungers, seven remote controls. Equal rights, she would tell the pudgy theocrat with seven wives, fair's fair. She grabs a newspaper and scans the classifieds under "Missed Connections." "You were crying with your sister at the Zipless Lounge on Saturday night. We exchanged glances. I'm available," says one of the ads. Another: "Albertsons. March 2. You smiled from the other side of the iceberg lettuce. You: long brown hair, blue dress, golden sun in your heart. Me: short, beard, fedora, glasses. I want to meet you." She is blond. She shops at Safeway. She invites her sister for a beer at the Zipless Lounge. She opens the next order form. Some woman in Utah ordering a black bathing suit. The zip code is totally low-priority, like zero. This customer probably thinks black is slimming or Italian or hides her age. She is probably a polygamist's wife, maybe wears those long pastel Heidi dresses with the white collars, never lets a molecule of coffee pass her lips.

At home the bills are stacking up like cordwood, Locator #395 thinks, and a seven-year-old is in bed with a household appliance. That slut Tiffany is still only twenty-four. Against the rules she lights up a Kool, hangs it from her lips, and wonders, *Why do so many people simply refuse to make their lives interesting?* She plucks a swimsuit from the warehouse rack and throws it into a packing envelope with a flurry of receipts and flyers and Styrofoam ghost turds. The suit is wrapped in clear plastic. It is not black and she knows it. The swimsuit is neon orange, the color of a highway safety cone.

In neon, fluorescent, and Day-Glo colors, electrons absorb ultraviolet light, raising an electron to a higher Bohr orbit that soon drops again, emitting lower-energy photons in the range of visible light. Concentrated at a very low range of wavelengths, the photons give the material a glowing, vivid color. These days, that's what I am swimming in: a narrow band of low-energy photons descending from the Bohr orbit. This is the first piece of orange clothing that I have ever owned. It makes globemallow look like an anemic cantaloupe. I have sent a sheepish thank-you note to Locator #395. On the river a boater will walk up to me and ask, "What are you, the First Aid station?"

◆   ◆   ◆

PRICKLY PEAR CACTUS (*Opuntia* spp.). The physique of the prickly pear, an omnipresent desert succulent, manifests the landscape: compact shape, stems in a series of jointed pads that shrink with drought or swell with moisture, shallow root systems to absorb water from brief rain showers, a bristly countenance that deters large nibblers and makes the small ones roam about its surface with numerous detours around the sharp spines and glochids, short reddish-brown bristles at the base of each spine.

The prickly pear's cup-shaped flowers are usually flamboyant magenta or yellow. In the heartland of the Anasazi, one particular prickly pear colony grows against the remains of a cliff dwelling. Each year its blossoms are an uncommon color: salmon pink, like the interior blush of a Caribbean seashell.

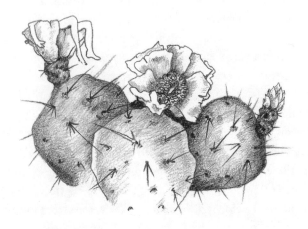

Prickly pear cactus

◆ ◆ ◆

WE HAVE LAUNCHED our trip on a river that is thick with
birds: Canada geese, cinnamon teals, mallards, phalaropes, mer-
gansers, grebes, swifts, swallows, and more Canada geese, some of
them standing on outcrops above the water in a very unwaterfowl-
like perch, pretending to be ravens but with the wrong kind of feet.
Many of the geese have paired off and disappeared, leaving loose
gaggles of juveniles wondering where everyone went.

Midday, on a lunch stop, an intent fleet of dark birds flies over
with a strange, collective *scree* and rattle, a cry between that of a
raptor and a sandhill crane. About fifty white-faced ibis land on a
sandbar. Their chests and backs are a deep purplish chestnut. The
wings occasionally flash an iridescent green. They have bright, tiny
eyes set close together, and they are in breeding plumage; a patch of
white shows behind the bill. Their curved, curlewlike bills are so
long you could pick one up by this handle and dust your furniture.
On the sandbar the ibis preen instead of feed. They are a vain
bunch.

Farther downstream we leave the ibis behind and encounter
spring's flocks of river runners scattered at camps or stopping for
side-canyon hikes. Everyone shares a giddiness over the speed of the
water—runoff through the canyon accelerates the river's velocity—
and the exhilaration of riding the swift current in rafts and brightly
colored inflatable and hard-sided kayaks. Many of the boaters have
come from ski towns in Utah and Colorado, anxious to shed their
marrow-deep cold in the warm desert air. More by reflex, a kind
of prism of sensations, than by reason, everyone is aware of the
great flood of vegetable sexuality that surrounds us—the color-
inflamed body parts of penstemon, skyrocket, four-o'clock, prince's
plume, globemallow, groundsel, puccoon, blazing star, and countless *Astragalus,* the genus of pea family plants that, because I cannot
distinguish them well, I call the wretched little vetches.

When we stop to chat with a group of river runners camped on a bankside ledge, I explore while Mark does his ranger job, which, in this case, is to answer the questions posed by two naked men in lawn chairs. The rest of their party, also middle-aged men but fully dressed in Gulf War camouflage, tends to tent pitching and other camp chores. The hot sun, the rarefied air, the river, the season—all of it evokes a feral riparian mood. Mark discusses lifejacket regulations with two guys with nothing in their laps but their dicks and their Budweisers. I am not embarrassed, but I wonder if I embarrass them or if a fleet of Mormon Boy Scouts is about to round the river bend, which makes me embarrassed over the idea of their embarrassment, so I attempt a sort of crypsis, a blending into the background, which is impossible in a neon-orange swimsuit.

I engross myself in a member of the hedgehog cactus family whose color is uncommon along the river. The Whipple's fishhook cactus usually blooms in shades of pink. In a scattered colony of small spiked barrels, these cacti bear silky cups of snow-white flowers. I am on the verge of crawling into one of the luscious blossoms when Mark returns to the raft and readies us to push off. As we slip into the current, one of the naked men shouts from his chair, "Thank you, Mr. Ranger God."

Deeper in the canyon, in our own camp alongside the swift, silty water, I climb in and curl up inside the bloom of a prickly pear cactus and think that the sex life of plants is not a simple affair. So many delicate body parts for seduction and consummation— filament, anther, pistil, ovary, stigma, style, a corolla of silky petals to enclose the cusp of love. In this blossom the corolla is a warm bath of golden light. Although some prickly pear bloom in magenta and a rare coral pink, I have chosen one with bright cadmium-yellow flowers that blush rose on their backsides, outside the cup. The thick petals shimmer with a heated luminosity; they feel like satin against my lips.

Flowers exist for one reason: sex. Sex with a flashy advertisement of their flavors and their virtues. Flowers are high-maintenance. They consume considerable energy to form and stay open for their carnal moments. In the orgy of fertilization, wind might carry their male sex cells as pollen, or bugs will crawl about their sexual parts and perform the transfer. A bee, for instance, lands on a flower's labellum, or lip. Dark patterns inside the petals—honey guides— direct it to the nectar, the bee's reward for sexual assistance. The bee departs with an abdomen covered with tiny pollen grains, which it deposits in the receptive stigma of another plant. Flowering plants keep their ovules hidden, safe inside the carpels. That's all I can say. It is rather secretive.

Botanists of the eighteenth century discovered plant sex and for obvious reasons (*Quels voyeurs!*) became a bit carried away. The Swedish taxonomist Carolus Linnaeus acknowledged nothing premarital or illicit. All was "husbands" and "wives" or *polygamia* and *polyandria* when male (stamens) or female organs (pistils) were multiple. He named a genus of pea plant *Clitoria* and was chastised for peddling "botanical pornography." He edged into plant lust in descriptions of nuptial beds with perfumes and petal curtains for privacy, tubular anatomies and succulent nectar, and "When the bed is thus prepared, it is time for the bridegroom to embrace his beloved bride and surrender his gifts to her. I mean, one can see how *testiculi* open and emit *pulverem genitalem*" (is it getting hot in here?) "which falls upon *tubam* and fertilizes *ovarium*." Inside the bloom I am surrounded by this.

After the prickly pear blossoms wither, red fruits line up along the rim of the pads like plump, miniature eggs. The sweet jelly inside the fruit is edible, as are the pads, called *nopales* in the Southwest. The pad's fleshy insides will stop a cut from bleeding. Without its showy, unpluckable flowers, the prickly pear cactus stands as a sprawling nest of thorny paddles, often in windblown, overgrazed land with a demeanor of starvation. In Navajo myth Hunger is the name of people found by the deity Monster Slayer. Hunger's leader was a big fat man, although all he ever ate was a little brown cactus. The desert provides food when it seems none can be found.

I like being curled inside a prickly pear bloom. Against the bright yellow petals the edges of the orange swimsuit blur, a kind of flame-on-flame that would provide excellent camouflage against New Mexico license plates or the fireball of an atomic bomb.

The sun-warmed pollen makes me drowsy, and before I know it I dream that a band of men trot by in pants that are supposed to look like Iraq or Kuwait from the air, former felons, no doubt, on an outdoor work-release spiritual retreat led by a recently divorced nihilist with brutal child support payments and a relaxed acceptance of his own naked body. In my dream I hear voices.

"Whatever floats your boat," the leader says to his buddies over their matched fleet of *Deliverance* canoes. He never fails to remind them, with all sorts of stabbing motions, that his ex-wife and kids nearly sent him over the brink with their shrink-wrapped pork chops, the Byzantine, not-tonight-honey migraines, a sofa that harbored lint balls the size of tumbleweeds. One minute they would be threatening to hold their breath until you bought them a pony; the next minute they would be sobbing over makeshift Popsicle crosses on the tiny graves of endlessly dead gerbils.

There was no getting out of suburbia fast enough, he thinks as he jogs along the river. All those angry little houses, all those parked FedEx vans. Maybe he and his new girlfriend, Tiffany, would pack up and move their double-wide to Montana, live on a ranchette with 2.5 horses and elk everywhere and ample patio space for Libertarian potlucks. Kmart inflatable bathtub toys loaded with Mormon Boy Scouts pinball down the river, out of control but oblivious to the fact. Lack of bloody discipline, the man snorts scornfully under his breath. *Why do people try so hard to make their lives interesting?* He trots his men along the bank in a tight, SWAT-team pod, passing a lethal spread of prickly pear cactus draped with some love-drunk bugatologist dressed like a highway safety cone. He makes a note to tell that government nose picker of a ranger to get some Agent Orange into this canyon and clean things up.

◆　◆　◆

LANGUISHING IN the deep-butter sex glow of the prickly pear flower, I let an arm drop to a pad, avoiding the spines' sharp white daggers. My hand reaches a dense mass that feels like rolled-up cobwebs attached to the cactus's waxy green pad. The wad is slightly powdery and the whitest white. I touch it and rub my fingers together. The white disappears, leaving stains of gorgeous carmine. I look like I have lolled about in a raspberry patch, not a cactus patch. I am wearing the fluids of cochineal, the dye of royal Mixtecs.

It is alarming to think that the flesh of a quintessential desert plant, an icon of drought, can be utterly transformed through the belly of an insect the size of a broken cornflake. Female cochineal insects (*Dactylopius coccus*), a type of scale insect, reside on the pads of *Opuntia* and there breed daughters who settle and males—what a life—who live long enough to mate with as many females as possible. The female feeds on the pad through her inserted proboscis, then secretes a white, weblike substance to camouflage and shade her in the hot sun. She spends her life sucking on a cactus. She is a tiny factory of pigment. The pigment, full of carminic acid and stored in her body and tissues, repels predators like ants, who cannot bear its taste.

In pre-Hispanic Mexico the Mixtec Indians farmed cochineal by farming the prickly pear cactus. They planted pads already inoculated with the scale insects and tended their crops carefully—built shelters to shield the plants from hard rain, enclosed them with walls and hedges to deter domestic animals, lit fires to keep the insects from freezing on cold nights.

Along with indigo, carmine and other shades of bright red were the colors of the highest social status. A wealthy Mixtec who wore red wore power. The color drove the conquering Spaniards wild with desire. Thinking the dye came from seeds, they called the insects *grana*. For over two centuries they monopolized all trade in the cochineal dye between Mexico and European royalty until, in 1777, a French naturalist smuggled cactus pads from Mexico to

Haiti. Cochineal textiles soon appeared in India, South America, Portugal, and the Canary Islands.

In the 1800s cochineal-dyed *bayetas,* blankets of red flannel, reached trading posts in the American Southwest. Again, the red grabbed attention. Navajo weavers, who had no such bold red dye in their traditional rugs and blankets, eagerly traded for the *bayetas,* which they unraveled thread by thread, sometimes three threads from a three-ply strand. Then they wove the red yarn into their own rugs.

And so, beneath the white web on a green cactus pad: tiny bodies like liquid garnets. The stain on my fingers dries to a dark maroon. The prickly pear's spines have not pierced me, but in the cochineal web are minute bits of the glochids. The barbed hairs give the carmine stain the long-lasting pain of splinters, my punishment for treating this plant as my *domus* erotica.

Below my enveloping cup of petals, in the spiky, jointed pads, there is a kind of breathing. To conserve precious fluids in hot sun that would otherwise evaporate them, the cactus's stoma, or pores, stay closed. In tonight's cool dark the stoma will open to take in carbon dioxide. Inside the blossom the light glows like the yellow band of sky on a sunrise horizon. I am flushed with color.

The pollinators and other visitors wallow around the sex-drenched jungle of bright yellow and green stamens, inebriated with sunlight and nectar. One of the insects is the size of a boldface comma and the same color as the flower, noticeable only because it moves. The dyed-to-match buglet, so like a pollen grain with legs, hikes up an anther-topped filament. Against any surface outside the flower, it would be a screaming, eat-me color.

Animals and insects have evolved ingenious uses of color to attract mates or deter predators. Some cryptic organisms change their environment to suit their color, like certain moths that alight on their resting tree and, to camouflage themselves, align their wing markings with the cracks in the tree's bark. The dark backs and light bellies of fish produce a more neutral density of shadow in water when viewed by aerial predators. One species of catfish with reverse countershading—dark belly, light back—spends its whole life upside down. Zebra stripes cut their wearers into pieces in vegetation near watering holes. The dark stripes appear as upward growing reeds and grasses, the white stripes as the sky between the leaves. Heat waves shimmer from the baked ground, and the zebra's stripes become as nervous as a mirage.

Chameleons and cephalopod mollusks are famous for changing themselves to match their environment. They do this by activating specialized chromatophores, or color cells. Many squid, cuttlefish, and other cephalopods are color-blind, so the chromatophores "see" neurally and instantly match the surrounding wavelengths of light. They use patterns to break up their outline so they are less visible to predators.

Creatures that want their predators to see them announce themselves in florid Technicolor. Monarch butterflies are classic examples of aposematism, or warning coloration. Their black, orange, and white markings identify them as something that tastes utterly awful. The effectiveness of warning coloration leads some organisms to mimic the colors and patterns of other aposematic creatures. The mimics do not actually have a disgusting taste or poisonous bite, but they look like the ones that do.

Color is a means to avoid being eaten. Is beauty thus ancillary to function? Ecologist Edward O. Wilson suggests that much of nature's splendid array of survival strategies, including defenses like crypsis and aposematism, was created before the earliest pre-*Homos* lifted their knuckles off the dusty savannah. Although we evolved within this continuum, we never quite fully fathom the grandiose pulse of biodiversity. "As a consequence," Wilson writes in *Biophilia*, "the living world is the natural domain of the most restless and paradoxical part of the human spirit. Our sense of wonder grows exponentially; the greater the knowledge, the deeper the mystery and the more we seek knowledge to create new mystery."

For Wilson, too, the velvet throat of a flower or the tapestry of a monarch's wing can turn humans into insatiable lovers. His term is *biophiliac*, oftentimes a dangerously lapsed biophiliac. Our essence as a species binds us to explore and affiliate with all life. We are lovers who can add up glucose, amino acids, water, fragrant oils, pigments, and other tissue and call it both a flower and a mystical gesture. We can also decimate pollinators with an unloving tonnage of pesticides, precipitating the extinction of entire populations of those mystical gestures, once and forever.

Against the grays and reds and browns of the canyon walls, the prickly pear flowers resonate with luminous clarity. Their color is made sharper by the desert's lucid, nearly transparent light. This is a place whose radiance renders its wildflowers utterly brilliant. Perhaps it is the synonymous quality of light and color that pierces the heart. Surrendering to it carries a person beyond the land's harsh extremes to acceptance, then relief.

The spring-blooming cacti of the slickrock desert cross Siren with dominatrix. The hot, satiny flowers pull me in beyond my wildest resistance. In a land of fierce edges and angles, they are gorgeous and tense, blissful and indifferent. Claret cups with blossoms of grenadine and pollen-powdered stamens, strawberry hedgehog crowned with magenta cups: To reach the color you must survive the dense thicket of spikes. When you come for a kiss you are impaled.

◆ ◆ ◆

RUSSIAN OLIVE (*Elaeagnus augustifolia*): A pervasive exotic introduced from Europe and western Asia, now naturalized throughout the Southwest. In late summer coyotes and bears feast on the fruits, leaving pale yellow-green olive seeds in their scat.

People curse the Russian olive's vigorous, unstoppable conquest and its competition with native species. Unlike the hopeless scourge of tamarisk, also a hugely successful exotic, the hopeless scourge of Russian olive can be put to use: a thorny, impenetrable wall in front of a panel of petroglyphs prone to vandals, a low-

maintenance barrier to wind and noise. In
winter, while they are dormant and leafless, dig up foot-high Russian olives from
the nearest choking infestation. Drag
them home like hostages, plant
them along a fence line, and
give them the near-negligence
that so inspires them—water and a
cake of sheep shit for their roots. In
one season they will reach eight feet
in height. Allies.

WHENEVER I LEAVE the river
after a trip, I don't quite leave the river.
Like a land-bound mariner, I feel as if I still ride
its rippled back of sand waves, the dip and rise of   *Russian olive*
silky brown folds that build with shifting sedi-
ment, then break, then rise, ripple, and fall all over again. All of a
sudden, the river's surface will surge into a long comb of waves. The
waves reach a climax of height and drop into a smooth sheet of river
again just as quickly, leaving a memory of their roaring noise. Sand
waves: the river breathing.

Off the river I will enter my own front door, painted blue.
Its color comes from an abandoned, hoganlike shelter in an old
Navajo sheep camp on the river. Over twenty years before, on our
first float down the river, the shelter was intact, a dry-laid masonry
dome of gray and brown stones with a smoke hole and fire slab
inside and an east-facing door frame of lumbered boards painted
sky-blue.

The shelter later collapsed into rubble, its disassembled blue
posts and lintel still visible in the pile. Then one year the boards disappeared. I took home in my head the color of a blue door on a jade
river and made the east door of our house the same color. From
their Moorish-Arab enemies the Spanish borrowed the superstition

that blue doors keep away the devil. The Spanish imported this belief to the New World, where the natives, too, used blue and turquoise to keep away evil spirits. Into this story I inserted the protection of the river.

Off the river I cannot leave the river because, in the potent exhalation of spring runoff, the flow is inextricable from the peak bloom of Russian olive. The combination of this river, the bare, immutable red rock, and the aroma of a scraggly tree-shrub insinuates the full meaning of home into my life. It renders an intimacy akin to lust.

The Russian olive is a somewhat annoying, nonnative invader of riverbanks. Sharp thorns adorn its polished, rust-colored branches, and the undersides of its gray-green leaves look like beaten silver. Combined with the spicy scent of river, the tree's sweet spring aroma enters the blood and touches a nerve. The bloom of Russian olive trees not only announces a rising river—a quickening of the season, a hint of adventure—it annihilates ambition. When I first inhaled this fragrance along the San Juan River in southeastern Utah, it incited an aching yearning for motion and a simultaneous swoon, a buckling of the knees. I could move, but I could also stay. This place, I thought, could accommodate the paradox.

At the end of the river trip Mark and I unpack gear, wash down the raft, and load it onto a trailer. We drive home in a gentle dusk, red cliffs bathed in the sun's last flush. Whiffs of sage and juniper come to us from the flanks of the high mesas, and the washes hold the memory scent of water in their bone-dry sand. When we top a rise, then descend into the river valley that holds town, lights spark the darkness for the first time in many miles of desert without human habitation. Thick aromatic waves of Russian olive greet us. The night fills with caressing scent.

The perfumed air is a reminder of how fluid are the boundaries between the senses. Vision, the eyes, evolved from touch, from skin that gathered light. The primitive human brain began as an olfactory organ, then smell forever allied itself with memory; it now races to the brain's limbic regions, the seat of lust and heightened emotions. All this simply because, along the river valley, we are breathing the sex life of a flower.

Intoxication seems the purist form of worship and, for another week, we are held in the Russian olive's holy trance. The fragrance remains strong even through a pall of smoke from fires in New Mexico, a haze that dilutes the valley's usual razor-sharp edges and makes the distances appear washed and limp with an uncomfortable grayness. Not even the red of the rock can shine through. Then more spring rain comes—I smell rain, smoke, and Russian olive even in my sleep—and the land is cleansed again, the blue sky and vivid edges return and, out in the canyons, the wildflowers push toward their final ecstasy.

◆ ◆ ◆

BIRDCAGE PRIMROSE (*Oenothera deltoides*), also known as dune primrose, one of a common trio that includes the dwarf and the pale evening primrose. Tissuelike flowers with broad, snow-white petals grow from a basal rosette of toothed leaf blades (birdcage and dwarf) or a taller, erect stem (pale evening). Natives used parts of these plants to help sore eyes see clearly again. In the desert the splashes of evening primrose, abundant in wet years, pull tenderness from the red-boned rock.

T. E. LAWRENCE — Lawrence of Arabia—considered the nomadic tribesmen of the Middle East to be people of primary colors, people of black and white, that is, with no halftones in their vision. They saw truth and not-truth, belief and nonbelief. They distrusted the European's doubt and metaphysical murkiness and, without any sense of incongruity, pursued the logic of several incompatible opinions to absurd ends. The Arab trait that he admired most Lawrence called "the gospel of bareness in materials."

The Arab asceticism, their resistance to matter beyond environment, seemed formed by the desert itself, the land of simultaneous silence and nothing and fierce intoxication of the spirit.

At one time Arab guides took Lawrence to the ruins of an ancient palace in northern Syria, built by a wealthy man for the woman he loved. The building's clay, the guides explained, was kneaded not with water but with flowers. This is jasmine, this is violet, this is rose, they told him as they went from room to room, inhaling the perfumed essences.

One of the guides drew him near and said, " 'Come and smell the very sweetest scent of all.' "

Lawrence wrote that "we came into a great hall, whose walls, pierced with many narrow windows, still stood to more than half their height." With open mouths they drank a desert wind born in distant Persia, empty and unbroken until it reached the walls of adobe and flowers. "The mingled scents of all the palace here combined to slay each other, and all that one felt was the desert sharpness of the air as it swept off the huge uncontaminated plains." This, the guides told Lawrence as they inhaled the desert, " 'This is the best: it has no taste.' "

The slip face of a high red dune bears a spill of evening primrose and, in the late afternoon of a spring day, this sand garden is my fragrant palace. The buds remain tightly furled in sun that still packs heat. A few purple wretched little vetches mix here and there with the primrose. I make myself comfortable on the dune and attempt a patient absorption. The fine sand is warm on my back and bare legs. In the next hour, as shade creeps up the dune, the *Oenothera* buds will open to a visible paleness that attracts nighttime pollinators. Tomorrow's bright sun will wither them. Their snow-white petals will flop over in a blushing pink. The unfurling of evening primrose happens quickly, and I intend to lie here and watch it.

In metaphorical terms the whites of the wildflower season— evening primrose, yucca, sego lily, datura—can be seen as a kind of quintessence, a mirror of how light at day's beginning and at the onset of night can come in such startling purity. In practical terms the white attracts sex aides with nocturnal habits.

I don't want to climb into the flowers of the desert's white bloomers. I want to eat them. Yucca blossoms are like thick cream, evening primrose like silken wafers on the tongue. Although the bulbs of mariposa and sego lilies fed natives and pioneers, it is their poppy-shaped flower that I am after. From the edible root of a sego lily, a hair-thin stem pushes through the roughest erosion pavement, rock chunks, or pebbled surface, an unlikely juxtaposition of *wisp* and *concrete*. Inside a white bell with hues of lavender, the base of each petal is painted in blood-red strokes against orange crescents and bright pink stamens. How carefully you would have to bite them to bits, maybe with a chaser of frosted vodka.

Long ago in the California mountains, on my summer solstice birthday, a friend announced his gift. He led me to it blindfolded. Blindfold off, there before me spread a meadow of ivory-petaled mariposa lilies at their peak bloom. These flowers, and the crimson-red snow plant before them, harbinger of a retreating cold, bind themselves to time by their own cells. They could be all the calendar a person might need. In drought or destruction, if they did not bloom, would you think that time had slipped and the world might end?

Even if no one warned you, the flowers of datura—*sacred* datura—tell you they are both gorgeous and sinister. Trumpet-shaped white blossoms grow on a mound of teal-colored leaves, each bloom tinged with a hint of violet and nearly eight inches long and about as wide, the deep, daring abode of night-flying moths and insects. *Datura meteloides,* also known as jimsonweed, delivers a powerful narcotic and, in sufficient dosage, a slow, agonizing death that turns your brain to minestrone.

Native southwesterners knew how to stop short of the poison of this member of the nightshade family. They ingested just enough to induce hallucinations; among the Pueblo, just enough to cure a person's meanness. One datura plant grows a healthy distance from our bedroom window, yet after a summer night of thick fragrance we wake up in a state of dreamily poetic agitation, which might actually be brain damage.

Another pale bloomer, the yucca, the bundle of spears with a candle of creamy blossoms, is serviced by a particular moth. Moth and yucca cannot live without one another. The moth packs a ball of pollen under her chin, then flies to a different flower to deposit her eggs and stuff the stigma with the pollen ball, thus perpetuating her kind and the yucca's as well. The complex architecture of this act results in a specialized monogamy, although the yucca flowers still excrete nectar for other insects that are not of use reproductively. The nectar and the mistresses apparently predate the yucca's dependence on the Pronuba moth as its sole pollinator.

On the sand dune the setting sun casts shadows behind every sinuous wind ripple until the surface is a sea of russet and mauve. The evening primrose buds will ripen. The grip of sepals will loosen, and the broad petals will unfurl and spread to the light. This will happen so slowly that I won't be sure I see the motion of it. For certain I will end up on a red dune that appears to be covered with a snowstorm of white butterflies. But for now a faint scent or presence hovers in the air, something a light breeze might leave as it passes. The Hopi word *siyámtiwa,* translated as "object disappearing over flowers," always intrigues and eludes me. Is it the Holy Ghost? The rear end of a bee? The rear end of the Holy Ghost?

The desert's asceticism allows the spirit to hunt for a resting place. In the minds of Lawrence's Arabs, God comes in the wind and air as the men stand in a clay and flower palace built for love. Although the wildflowers on the red dune will stay open until the next day's sun wilts them into a pale pink faint, for now I am caught in the imperfect clarity of waiting.

◆ ◆ ◆

CLIFFROSE (*Cowania stansburiana*): A small evergreen with gnarled trunk and shaggy limbs that carry five-lobed, resinous leaves. For most of the year it is unremarkable. (If you do notice it, you end up counting leaf lobes, one of the few features that distinguish cliffrose from its look-alike, bitterbrush, *Purshia tridentata*.) For a week in early summer, however, dense clusters of blossoms engulf every branch and twig until they fully conceal the leaves and the cliffrose looks like a pale yellow torch.

Cliffrose often prefers slickrock and shallow dry washes, where the embrace of low-slung rims on either side provides not so much shelter as a degree of difficulty, perhaps, to match the cracks and soil pockets in which they grow.

THE FIRST TIME I heard a Navajo say the word *gad*, I thought it referred to a deity. Instead, it is the word for juniper, the omnipresent tree that grows atop mesas and in folds of wind-smooth sandstone across the Colorado Plateau. From juniper seeds Navajo mothers made their children bracelets of "ghost beads" to prevent bad dreams. The hard, fragrant berries bear one of the desert flora's scarce displays of turquoise. Fallen, they surround the juniper in a blue-green skirt. Here with *gad* grow companion pinyon pines, single-leaf ash, Mormon tea, and, on the slickrock ledges above a heart-cleft canyon, a scattering of cliffrose in bloom.

Creamy yellow flowers cover the branches from shaft to tip, drowning the small leaves in petals. The trunk's bark is brown with a silver cast, shredding in thin dry strips. Each flower has the broad, five-petal bowl typical of a wild rose and a crown of golden stamens in the center. I sit under a dazzling mass of roses in a breeze that is nearly a wind. It gusts, then subsides with rushes of sound like airborne surf.

Bees in the cliffrose fill the quiet parts of the gust rhythm. They are delirious and so am I. The cliffrose fragrance envelopes us in a spicy musk that is stronger, yet more delicate, than the water-heavy perfume of Russian olive. It incites blatant acts of sensuality. Other plants prompt reactions that are aesthetic, intelligent, or herbal. Not cliffrose. It conspires with the sweep of slickrock on which it grows. It is nondescript when not in bloom, irresistible when it is. Sit by one and your heart will open and desire will flood into the emptiness created for it.

From this tree other cliffrose follow fissures in the rock in a somewhat orderly direction—the creases offer more moisture and soil than the acres of bare sandstone—but four or five more pale torches escape the line and erupt in different places, so there are cliffrose everywhere until the land drops off into the sheer space above a deep, deep canyon, and, below my high perch, meets the emerald-green crowns of a cottonwood bosque in the canyon bottom.

Like pale beige sand against turquoise sea, the symmetry of the desert is calming. Perhaps it is the spaces that are just right, the perfect amount of air and ground between bursts of creamy torches. Each cliffrose stands alone—or with a skirt of peppergrass and scorpionweed—and invites me to consider it the most beautiful, the fullest and most aromatic.

From my pack I take out a few objects and arrange them on the rock. Short white rump hairs from a bighorn sheep, as fine as the spines of a fish. A black feather from a *zanate,* the great-tailed grackle of Quintana Roo. A yellow plastic duckling. A Navajo *jaatl'óół,* a loop of densely strung turquoise disk beads with a piece of coral at the end of the strand. A pile of juniper berries, smoky blue-green, for Mr. Ranger *gad.* Around my neck, a necklace of pearls the same weight as a man's desiring gaze. On my hands, the red stains of cochineal.

To humble all pride I add the neon bathing suit, laid out here in its faded but ever sarcastic orange. Its jolt reminds me to make life interesting. Lives without access to sensation are lives that edge out the earth's raw, pervasive sweetness, that deeply biophilic connection to all life. Trade a scarlet desert paintbrush or a freesia in a garden for a swatch on a personal color chart and we surrender all rights to our optic nerves. We will end up being taupe people. My rock-top shrine says little more than its lovely array of color and shapes, the universal human attraction to beauty and rarity, a tendency to collect talismans for touch and wonder. The array also serves to relieve some small burden. The sheep hairs flee—a gust of wind picks them up and carries them off over the canyon.

In the years of spring escapes from Montana to the desert, I so often found myself sorting out my heart. Slowly, the senses had a way of overtaking the mind so that the perfume of cliffrose could push me into a realm of sheer pleasure. The sandstone was filled with secret veins that only the flesh could find. *Press the stone and feel its flex,* I thought, take the shape of its harrowing embrace. The sun would rise east of my hipbones. Color struck like blows. The light ratcheted up its blaze and flashed through each nerve, a net of flame, a field of exquisite friction. I was seized by something that could never be wrestled down, a feeling not unlike sorrow and ecstasy compounded. Then came the sweet drift of longing, and I hung on to the earth's curve for dear life, breathing the comfort of stone during my ride.

Pinyon and juniper

The desert in spring held such vehement feelings that I would take them north like pollen stuck to my lips and the tips of my fingers and recall a kind of insatiable rapture—sun blazing on red walls, plaintive cries of pinyon jays, a slip of jade river, the brazen harlotry of cactus flowers, all of it alluring and distant. I would walk away from that wild, heady rose, put days and distractions and the distance of three states between it and me, then, pressed against memory, the scent would become as Keats said of his lover: "Everything that reminds me of her goes through me like a spear."

Today's cliffrose grows from an island of sand and twigs and last year's woody castoffs. It is an island in a voluptuous sea of salmon-red dunes, whose petrified faces bear the whorls and ripples of their drift millions of years past. Some lines run in long curves, others cross-bed or undulate as if pushed by ragged tides. The sandstone and my skin have taken the sun's heat, the flesh of one touching the surface of the other with the warmth of each other's blood.

This land underlines flesh and bone. Our bodies take its shape when we press them to it, hips fit into a caress-minded ellipse, nothing on us but the weight of silver. The skin blushes in lambent coral air or ripples in a stab of lemony sunlight. Bones itch and wrists feel hollow, as if filled with air. This voluptuous rock is our crypsis, our protective coloration, the way a creature blends in with its background.

In the driest of lands, slickrock is the geography of water. Water resides in the shape memory of ancient seas pressed against one's bare back. Its transient, copper-colored floods carve dry, silver waterfalls on the vermilion lips of a flute of rock, sculpt the hollow that holds the palm of our hand, fingertips stained carmine with the secret of a cactus. There is the comfort that the desert's scant liquid is collected in hidden pools and in the big river—a river so enfolded in its unmitigated and difficult canyons, you never in your wildest dreams expect to see anything quite like it.

There is the reassurance that this is not a place with too much rain, that the thirst of its sandstone, of juniper and pinyon, cliffrose and scarlet paintbrush, is as true an edge as human longing. Look at these faces, sandstone and woman; both hold the history of wind. Read the heart as geological terrain, as slip faults and slow persuasions, states of ecstatic disintegration and tectonic fate, angular unconformity, angle of repose. The fierce bond between the body and this piece of earth tells what rapture feels like, how it consumes and transforms us.

The cliffrose blossoms are silky and fragile. I touch one flower-laden branch softly and the whole tree comes apart. A blizzard of petals, a shower of scent. The wild roses fall into my hair, where I leave them for the rest of the day.

My Animal Life

If comedy is essentially biological, it is possible that biology is also comic. Some animal ethologists argue that humor is not only a deterrent to aggression, but also an essential ingredient in the formation of intraspecific bonds.

JOSEPH W. MEEKER
The Comedy of Survival

Humorists fatten on trouble.

E. B. WHITE
Essays of E. B. White

The mouse died two minutes after it left the bookcase, emerging from the slot between Hopi erotica and *Remembrance of Things Past*. It sneaked around a potted cactus, hugged the base of a cupboard, then scurried across the open floor, escaping attack by all of the aerial predators in the kitchen. It stuck its skinny little doomed neck into a thin shingle of pine slathered with peanut butter. The trap's blow flipped the mouse on its back. All four feet stuck straight up to the ceiling fixtures. The sprung wire mashed its Stuart Little face into a flat triangle of blood and fur.

It did not matter that this was a mouse who spent the night with Proust. No one was the least bit impressed with its stature as the first mouse ever to penetrate the fortress that is our house. It was the first, I declared, and it shall be the last. I threw the carcass into the rabbitbrush. Antipasto for coyotes.

Let me make it clear that this war on mice—mice in trespass—contrasts sharply with a reputation for accommodating the creatures that share the open desert with my husband and me. They bring to us a world beyond our own minds and a gratitude for their animated glory. Somehow I am able to cross species lines without a single lesion in self-respect. I live my animal life in bliss.

Not that I am entirely in control around here. There is a new-found witlessness to my existence, a buckling intellect driven, perhaps, by cruel and unusual hormones. At night I dream heavily and I dream hard. Aqua butterflies swim across scarlet borscht. The Russians seek me. I dream about a flash flood in the Sahara or wearing stainless steel loafers with tassels and small hinged compartments. I fear that someone might ask me to sew something or take an exam in physics, to be the carrier of vital information: *Quantum mechanics allows an electron in an atom, say, with an energy smaller than that required to escape the atom, according to classic principles, sometimes to "tunnel" out from inside the electric field binding it, and find itself finally free of its chains.* I form a mystical attachment to two yellow plastic ducklings. I go about looking as if I ran into a door and had not quite recovered. Furthermore, some sort of intraspecific telepathy may be transmitting the affliction to the domestic wildlife.

Indeed, the neighbors are restless. They show hints of insurrection beyond the usual carnage and brutality, the cutthroat rivalry for fresh standing in the food chain, despite the fact that we have placed ourselves, we hope, in positions of peaceful coexistence. We built a house facing a river. We left many acres of habitat undisturbed, we planted no lawn nor scraped the desert scrub off the scant, water-hungry topsoil. We can smell rain five miles away. The wind rakes our hair and we see so many stars at night, I fear that merely by watching them we will lose all moorings and float upward into the deep, silent light.

After the Navajo word for "lizard" we call the place Na'ashó'ii Mesa. Technically, it is not a mesa. Technically, we cannot pronounce the word or, when we do, the way we say it probably translates as "It's your turn to feed the nuns." Nevertheless, the name fits.

In this home world there is no failure of attention to the lives of our animal neighbors. We have eaten none of them. Not one dumb bunny. We draw the line only at mice or black widow spiders in trespass and pests in the garden, the insects and rodents that threaten the salsa farm, the organic herbs, tomatoes, chiles, and other crops that give us an island of defiance against the tyranny of genetically modified Frankenfoods.

Every so often, and especially when *Homo sapiens,* in our unwavering devotion to becoming the first species to witness our own extinction, escalates the pace and level of destruction, the natural world (what there is left of it) seems to respond in a flurry of irksome mischief. This time the creeping upheaval in local biology has coincided with my own flubber-brained descent into something just short of regret.

A menagerie of wildlife surrounds our house. They think of us as their pets, a pair of unsuspecting peasants, or, at best, about as interesting as fence posts. They believe we built the house for them, creating a fascinating variety of shelters, nesting places, stones to bask on, insects to eat, flowers to sip. All of us—wildlife and Fence Posts—live in compatible anarchy.

On any given day, if the spring winds do not erase it with their aeolian roar, the desert amplifies its own audible pulse. Ring-necked pheasants squawk, ravens quork, the big Canada geese honk, coyotes yip and yowl all night. Sandhill cranes, rare passersby, rattle their throats like pterodactyls playing kazoos. A mockingbird, also uncommon, mimics the sounds of everyone else. When the pesky starlings fly by in a brown blur, lifting up my hair with the air they move with a hundred wings, I cannot scorn them because in their midst are a dozen bluebirds.

The crickets find crevices and borders and the undersides of things on every part of the deck. They tuck themselves beneath leaves of basil and silver sage and blanketflower; they love the pocket terrain, the day's miniatures of darkness. When in the year do they begin their song? When does it end? I try to place parentheses around the cricket season—note the date, temperature, length of daylight for the arrival and departure of their symphony—but to do so is futile. The crickets are simply silent, then singing. The frequency of their trills—the measure of their sound wavelengths—runs in a precise mathematical ratio to temperature. In deep summer the crickets do the math in a heightened state of orthopteran lust.

The stucco walls, the deck of sandstone slabs laid in a mortared puzzle and scattered with islands of herbs and flowers—this is the kingdom of the lizards. The lizard essentials are present: lookouts, basking rocks, open acres for quick escape without the dense grasses and brush that inhibit running if you are built low to the ground. Their cold-bloodedness requires an orbit of light and shadow, sun in the morning to start the flow of blood, shade by noon, refuge from the solar oven. There are so many lizards around here, it is like living with herds of shrunken dinosaurs.

In the lavender that grows on the deck, a young spiny lizard crawls up a stalk and tries to nab one of the painted ladies that nectar on the purple blooms. The lavender stalks are as supple as thin reeds. They bend with the lizard's weight. The lizard lunges at a butterfly, misses, then crashes into the thick bush and disappears. I hear it scrambling around in there, trying to get out.

On the west end of the deck two orange-headed spiny lizards chase and wrestle one another, the male inflated to brutish machismo, demonstrating what it might be like if dinosaurs made porno movies. Smaller, more priggish lizards hang out on the window screens like hood ornaments. They like the bugs, the ventilation, the Iranian-Celtic jazz on the stereo, the pleasant fit of their feet in the tiny mesh squares. From inside the house I sneak up close to the screen to study their bellies, powder blue with constellations of indigo speckles. One of our resident pair of ravens, Heckle (or Jeckle), dives for the lizard, nearly colliding with the screen. We are startled to see one another only seven inches apart, *Corvus corax* and I. The lizard escapes and the raven flies off to a nearby utility pole, where it and its sidekick, Jeckle (or Heckle), often perch for taking in the entertainment: Mark and me. *Days of Our Fence Posts' Lives,* they chortle.

Below Na'ashó'ii Mesa, against a sheer rise of russet sandstone cliffs, the river runs its sinuous, mobile soup. The soup's solids range from microscopic protozoa to fish the size of obese dachshunds. The big meat: Colorado pikeminnow, a now rare native that evolved over millions of years with the river itself, its migrations along the liquid veins of the Colorado Plateau rivaling those of coastal salmon; channel catfish, an introduced species whose adaptation to dams, pollution, and other human influence will likely secure its destiny as top-soup omnivore; and carp, also an exotic, and a lover of muddy shallows.

Normally, the river flows with the exuberant serenity that moving water can bring. The carp, however, suggest a disorder in river life, a disturbance in the field. Some of the fish have thrown themselves into an old irrigation ditch that intersects the mainstem. Partly silted in, the ditch is rarely used by anything other than the roots of tamarisk and Russian olive trees. The carp edge into this cleft in a search for mud food that might make sense were it not for a slight problem. The ditch is bone-dry.

Our proximity to the river also puts us in intimate contact with its airborne proteins, birds that include seasonals, migrants, and year-round residents like sparrows, flickers, ravens, and raptors. A sizable flock of Canada geese winters over on the ranches and farms along the river. The fields honk and flutter as if alive. I find great solace in these homebodies, perhaps because of their orthodoxy, their unshakable faith in one place. What if birds had religion? In their black and white ecumenical garb, magpies would be Catholic, of course. Woodpeckers some kind of Holy Roller. If I were a sensible gray chukar, I would be Lutheran. Snowy egrets must surely be the Holy Ghost herself, brilliant white against the red rock, aloof and regal atop black legs and wacky yellow feet. For several days something seems amiss. I hear the strange cry of an unseen, possibly Presbyterian bird on the talus above the cliffs, an almost raptorlike sound, but unhappy and insecure. Is there such a thing as an insecure raptor?

A red-shafted flicker abandons its territory in the cottonwood grove below the house and decides to move in with us. Heckle and Jeckle observe the drama with maniacal relish. Atop their utility pole they preen their ebony feathers and make hollow gargling noises. They know something about a relocating flicker that I don't. A chisel-billed bird with viselike zygodactyl feet is on the move, headed toward the Fence Posts' heavy investment.

For several years a pair of Say's phoebes has nested in the fir beam that supports the house's portico. We love that nest. We adore these shapely gray birds with sweet cries and a splash of apricot-colored feathers on their flanks. We think of their little families as our little families. Now, on the lip of nesting season, I expect them to make repairs and nestle down to a cozy brood. But the flicker haunts the nesting beam. No phoebes dare approach. One day, with a heave of shoulder and bill against the bundle of grasses and sticks, the flicker knocks the nest off the ledge. The nest hits the deck and breaks apart.

The next thing the flicker does: bangs away at the stucco walls as if it was hammering its way to China. It leaves huge gashes at the seam between wall and eave. It drills down to the sheathing and insulation. When Mark threatens to fill the flicker's butt with buck-shot, one of our friends suggests that he reconsider. "Flickers are sacred birds," this friend tells us solemnly.

Early southwestern Indians known loosely as the Ancestral Puebloans, or Anasazi, once inhabited this river valley in great numbers. Using the flora and fauna around them, they made beautiful things with profound meanings. Local archaeology has revealed artifacts, likely religious in purpose, decorated with the black-tipped, salmon-red feathers from the tails and underwings of red-shafted flickers.

For some of the modern Puebloans the flicker and other birds in the woodpecker family bear inferences of war and thunder. A number of Pueblo cultures associate flicker feathers with witchcraft. Fetish makers of the Keres group will not use them in their fetishes; like the plumage of owls, blackbirds, and crows, flicker feathers are taboo. The Hopi ascribe the flicker and its colors to the sun's journey. At several ceremonies poles hung with dense bundles of brown, red, and black flicker feathers are set out at sunrise and removed at sunset.

Buckshot in the butt of a war bird is not the least bit respectful, but the holes in our walls grow larger as the flicker pounds toward the Sheetrock and halfway to Shanghai. I propose a hunter's atone-ment. "Okay," I say, "after we kill the flicker we'll eat it." Flicker tastes just like chicken.

All courage for bird murder fails and the stucco flies off the walls in a flurry of hard crumbs. We try new strategies. A sprinkling of powder from homegrown cayenne chiles, based on an uncertain assumption that flickers lick their feet. A board so full of nails it looks like a hairbrush. We set the board points-up on the flicker's perch, but the bird roosts there as if the nails were a soft thatch of lawn. Duct tape stretched across the beam, sticky side up, also fails to dislodge the rascal.

One night, in the thick darkness of no moon and all of the house lights turned off, I know the flicker is on its roost, off guard and slow in reflex. The Jehovah's Witnesses have left me a weapon. I grab *The Watchtower* and roll it up. I sneak up on the perch. I can see the flicker's tail hanging over the edge. I thrash the beam with a hard *thwack*. The flicker pops straight up and cracks its skull on the ceiling, then zigzags off in disoriented flight, perhaps headed straight into the jaws of an owl.

In the garden beds around the house, hummingbirds stuff themselves on nectar from the red poppies. Over the trumpet vine that cascades down a deck wall, the males rise and fall in the U-shaped swoops of their mating dances, whirring their tiny throats as they dive. At dusk the mad yellow blossoms of evening primrose bear crowns of sphinx moths. With their heavy, spindle-shaped bodies and rapid-fire wingbeat, sphinx moths are insects with the size and flight of hummingbirds. They hover over the primrose and feed midair.

Lately, the sphinx moths appear disoriented. They come out too early, in too much light, and several of them hit the screen door with a terrified thrash. I can see for myself the moth that is not a bird: milk-bodied and powdery, banded in thin black and white lines. Unlike the elaborate cloaks of most moths and butterflies, their wings are small and narrow with a straight, upward lift built for darting and hovering.

In his works on geology John McPhee writes of the human inclination to think of nature as a calmed rebel, an assemblage of generalized events that once wreaked havoc but now move along slow time in laconic order. In the geological sciences, he says, the tendency has been translated as the "principle of least astonishment," the idea that the earth's past tectonic forces—the violent geology—are now frozen. "To imagine that turmoil is in the past and somehow we are in a more stable time seems to be a psychological need," McPhee writes.

In biology, too, we prefer the rebel tamed. No more hippos as big as backhoes, no more giant cats with teeth like samurai swords. Many people move through their lives with a can of Raid in their hands. The elk in Yellowstone, the zebras on the eco-tour, are splendid. The vermin in the kitchen cupboards are not. We live the tension between views of the natural world as a Garden of Eden or a frenzy of killing, feeding, and copulating—Tennyson's nature, "red in tooth and claw." Between Eden and messiness we want balance, the least astonishment, creatures with predictable characteristics and behavior patterns. We don't want berserk squirrels or mutant frogs. We don't want moths bashing their heads on doors to remind us of the imminent collapse of the planet.

Among the last things to expect from animals are imagination and a sense of humor—mules, for example, with private inner lives. Yet spontaneity may be the poetry of survival. Animals respond to new features and challenges in their environment by genetically defined behavior, with few deviations. Those with complex brains, like primates and ravens, are more likely to be deviants. The opportunists invent and take risks, explore and exploit the novelty, then possibly benefit from their own agility. In our hopeless anthropomorphism we think they are being funny.

The spooked moths, the pornographic lizards, the carp breaststroking through the dust as if they suddenly forgot they were fish—I pray that these quirks signal a rise to the challenge of change rather than a portent of doom. In my animal life I hope for benign turmoil.

MY HUSBAND AND I live in a small, remote desert town where a bit of discomfort is a virtue. The distances to commercial centers are considerable, and thus far the place has avoided the fate of many overtouristed western towns that have become parodies of their own clichés. There is no numbing spectacle of consumerism. There is less than the most basic of services. But there is a river, and the river absorbs our lives and our souls. Between April and November very little time passes without a boat in the water, a float through the deep-walled wilderness of home.

One day I return from a solo trip on the river, a long string of days in a canyon lit with primordial radiance. Looking back at a logistical error involving the raft, I am convinced that I nearly died on that trip. The brush with danger so exacerbates a chronic restlessness, I unload the gear and clean up, but I cannot stay at home. The town feels as crowded as a Kurdish refugee camp with newcomers from Kosovo. On a long stretch of days off from work, Mark hangs around the house and putters, totally *pū,* a Japanese term that describes a person who is at home and unproductive, perhaps between jobs. At first I thought *pū* (pronounced "poo") translated somewhat fittingly as "wet leaves," but I was confused and mistaken.

Suddenly, I feel the urge to roar through my house and yard like a fury of locusts: Clean up this place, quit living in dust and sand and bugs and lizards, weeds and prickles and everything bone-dry and shaggy. Within a few minutes the compulsion passes. However, the brain fog that arose with the animal insurrection fails to subside. I still feel like a mental patient, wrongly discharged. It is time to seek psychiatric help.

The wild geese rise high above the house, pushing me in an easterly direction. I gas up the truck at the local inconvenience store. The bulletin board lays out a busy social calendar. A Head Start parade, tribal government chapter house meetings, the hours of worship at the Church of Jesus Christ of the Latter-day Saints, the minutes of the Mosquito Committee. "Overweight, pooped, and bored?" queries one message. Another message announces activity on the rodeo grounds. "Woping invitational," it reads. "Calf wopers' purse $200."

A tour bus overwhelms the parking lot with its sleek mass of chrome and ebony windows and the acrid exhaust of its idling. The bus is making a pit stop between official sites of scenic interest. Since we are not officially scenic, none of the tourists looks past the gas pumps to the drop-dead beauty of the town. The restroom doors at the inconvenience store face the outdoors; about a dozen bus passengers line up in front of them. A Navajo man threads his way through the crowd to his truck. In his best low-register Tonto voice he greets them as he passes. "Hello, rich people."

At the post office the velvet grandmothers—older Navajo women in long, fluted cotton skirts and velveteen blouses—give me the News of the World: lots of headaches this year, time to pick crane's bill and buffaloberry. Broken-faced sandstone cliffs embrace the river. Bright sun, no clouds. Only a hard squint can swallow the distances.

On the road to the psychiatrist the desert is everything there is of the world. Red rock and coral sand, silver rain and gilded river, the immense dome of turquoise sky—the land coalesces into flesh. Every particle of place reincarnates as fur, feather, and fin, heart, lung, leaf, and wing. Every life form carries the desert within it. Colorado pikeminnow, kit fox, desert bighorn sheep, leopard lizards, and other natives grew to this place, graceful and specific in their fit. The generalists arrive with the luggage that makes it their own: flexibility, adaptation, the ability to expand or alter, in whatever possible way, their repertoire of behaviors in order to survive. The sandhill cranes that needed the active floodplain and marshes of an undammed river diminish in numbers or go to wetter elsewheres. Eager exploiters of cultivated land, the Canada geese stay put. Without a reliable supply of dead meat and live human entertainment, surely the ravens would drop dead of boredom.

The back road slips off rocky tablelands into a gentle valley and crosses the Utah border into Colorado. Mixed stands of sweet clover, bunchgrass, and wild mustard spill from the farmlands and line the roadside fences. At several points of higher elevation the land breaks into uncultivated, ungrazed stretches. One of these stretches grows a forest of cliffrose, the desert shrub whose fragrance in spring will make you feel as if you are free-floating but tethered. Today I pass cliffrose well past bloom, but I know their power and always note their presence. No matter how often you travel home geography, the familiar roads, you cannot take the locals for granted.

A person's animal life can become high-maintenance, I think as I turn into the shrink's driveway. Nature constantly revises and rearranges itself in the face of novelty and surprises, its imperative of "order" demands a ragged, healthy turmoil, the compulsions of diverse and complex creatures trying to stay alive even as circumstances change. I would like to think that our scrubby patch of desert has opened new niches to the domestic wildlife. I hope that the whirs, chirps, quorks, peeps, rustles, and slithers are the sounds of dynamic adaptation.

For some species the pressures of humans are simply too overwhelming—the elimination of an entire food supply or habitat comes to mind—and they disappear, leaving an absence as palpable as their presence, a hollow emptiness in the human spirit. More tolerant creatures cling to verges and vacant lots, the "unofficial" ecosystems that are neither countryside nor places of wild earth but patches of real estate on what is swiftly becoming the weed planet. One of these days the starlings will have no bluebirds among them. Then, even though they are opportunistic pests, the starlings, too, might succumb to a diminished world, relegated to oblivion or the rafters of a hockey stadium. These thoughts invite images of a sludgy, sterilized planet devoid of birds and other life, a *Silent Spring* gloom so dense that arrival at the mental health clinic is fortuitous and timely.

The doctors—there is a pair of them—crop grass, twitch the skin on their muscular flanks, and amble over a rough field at the mouth of a box canyon. They are plump and happy, and they barely turn their big heads when I park the truck and walk over to their fence. They ignore the passing traffic and outpatient visitors like me, but they never ignore one another. Physically, the mules are identical, a perfectly matched set. It is their nature to form two halves into a whole, a union into intractable muleness.

The mules are nearly as husky as Clydesdales—sleek, breathing barrels of muscle and flesh and bone atop stocky legs built like pile drivers. The afternoon sun burnishes their silky coats into a deep

red-gold. Their legs and bellies are nearly white. This same paleness surrounds black nostrils and dark brown eyes. The white eye
patches make you watch their faces with mindful love, like you
would a clown's face. Most of all I adore their blond tails and the
blond, roached manes that bristle along their heavy necks. The
roaching gives them the blunt angles of punk weightlifters or
blue-collar workers with crew cuts and chests the size of a walk-in
freezer. As if they were the last two bachelor proletarians on earth,
their comfort with one another is nonchalant but needy.

For years I have passed the mules on supply runs from home to
a larger town. When I do not have the time to stop, I make sure as
I pass that both mules are still alive. Sometimes one mule stands at
the opposite end of the field from his brother or both have been
swallowed up by the pool of black shade under a cottonwood
grove, and I will panic until I spot them, nearly driving into the
ditch with the distraction.

As is usual when I park and linger for a full therapy session
rather than a reassuring glimpse of them, today the Mule Brothers
largely ignore me. Only occasionally has one or the other come over
to inspect the palm of my hand with velvet lips and a rush of warm
breath blown from the nose.

Their polite indifference does not infer poor psychiatry. The
cure they offer is simple mammalian empathy. I find contentment
in the company of these two huge strawberry blonds. Perhaps
because all three of us have hair and body heat and warm red blood,
the Mule Brothers help me feel the presence of the world.

When I am in the need of calming, when the mind fevers rage
with particular ferocity, my preferred psychiatrists are a certain
band of desert bighorn sheep that live deep in the Colorado Plateau
wilds. Putting myself in their presence requires more effort—no
vehicle access, a long, hot hike, the possibility that I will look in the
right places but will fail to find them. To be among bighorns I must
also overcome a reluctance to disturb them or in any way jeopar-
dize their precarious existence. To spend sheep time, time among

the wildest of the wild, there is distance, physical rigor, and the anguished compromise between their needs and mine, all of it rewarded by the great solace that comes when you join your own breath to the vibrant, resonating breath of living creatures.

In this light it is perhaps less strange that two old mules—common, domesticated, a couple of reproductive dead-ends—would serve as a frequent mammal-empathy substitute for wild sheep. The mules nuzzle one another. Both of them rest their standing weight on their left hind legs, then in unison lift their haunches and shift their weight to their right legs. They will not do anything without one another. They are so . . . so *spherical.* Because they are sensitive I cannot let on that I know this. I also keep the sheep secret to myself, reluctant to admit that these equine therapists are second-string guys. I don't want to hurt their feelings.

The Mule Brothers don't work. They are off duty. They are *pū.* They hold down the world when I pass this way; they offer a constant against reckless spin. Their box-canyon pasture opens to a narrow green valley and a creek lined with shady cottonwoods and Russian olive trees. Flies buzz. The mules shake them away with their punk manes. Their long, velvety ears angle to the sun, backlit with halos of molten gold. There are two of them, I remind myself. There will always be cliffrose and two mules, and they will always be here. I could not endure the heartbreak of one mule gone and the other mule looking, always looking, toward the place he last saw his brother. The sorrow of a single mule would be harder to bear than no mules at all.

SOMETIMES MY ANIMAL LIFE is pathetic, sometimes it is unpredictable, and sometimes it is downright funny, and I am grateful for this foil to aggression and harm, for the survival tactic of laughter. Most of the time, however, my animal life simply is what it is.

In the eaves of the portico, the Say's phoebes rebuild a nest of dry plants and dog fur. I kept the brushings from a friend's golden retriever and scattered them into the rabbitbrush around the house, to be collected by the birds. Dirt balls, grasses, and sticks form the nest's outside walls. The inside is lined with the dog's soft hair. Circular and thick, reddish like the sand around us, the nest looks like an Anasazi kiva. The phoebes build the nest so high, it threatens to topple off its platform. We add an extension with a short two-by-four. They are now the only phoebes in Utah with a redwood deck.

The baby peeps hatch and raise tiny plucked-chicken heads over the side of the nest. When the peeps grow into smooth-feathered hulks, they elbow each other out of the nest. I fetch a ladder and put them back in, one by one. At fledging time they are once again completely disorganized. With wings too short and undeveloped for sustained, high flights, they take low perches near the nest. I find teenage phoebes behind the grapevines, in the garden toolbox, the flower beds, the breezeway. They move away in fly-hops, only a few yards at a time. For a couple of days we cannot cross the deck without phoebes flitting about. Everyone, parent birds and offspring, fills the air with sweet, plaintive cries. The nest sits empty and forlorn.

When Mark and I built our house, we directed the drainage off the metal roof into pipes that emerge at the base of planted cottonwood seedlings. Rain, melting snow, condensation—any moisture from the roof—slips into gutters and drainpipes, then runs downhill through underground pipes to water the trees. One morning I watch a gray fox dig up the end of one of the pipes. With frantic paws he flings clouds of red dirt as if he planned to reopen the flicker route to China. Inside the pipe a baby black-tailed jackrabbit hovers. The fox is nearly as large as a coyote, feet red from digging, a sleek coat of grizzled silver, tail topped with a black mane. I stand ten feet away from the fox and it looks me straight in the eye over the utter silence of the rabbit. *Don't just stand there, help me get this bunny.*

These creatures allow us to reside alongside them, to witness their lives. As Thoreau said of his animal neighbors, "they fetch the year about me." I know this for certain when a bullsnake shows up.

Bullsnakes are harmless, creamy yellow–colored reptiles with brown markings. Behind each eye is a stroke of black, like the kohl eye makeup of an Egyptian queen. This bullsnake starts at the top of the breezeway stairs, next to the bleached white hipbone of a cow. She slips down from the bone, her long, supple body perfectly stairstepped along the contours of the descent. She drops her scarlet tongue into a pool of water left from a hose, and she drinks. I see her cheeks inflate with each sip. I go about my business, thinking about a snake that laps up water like a thirsty dog. When I return, she has assumed siesta position in a lawn chair, her tail draped over the seat like an accidental whip. This snake has a lean mischief about her. She is neither lethargic nor sinister but curious, oblivious to us but not to our possibilities.

One day her partner shows up. He is nearly five feet long, thicker, and more likely to startle you if you come around a blind corner and nearly step on him. On hot days he likes to lie against the cool, damp clay pots that hold the geranium plants. He makes yellow and brown loops under a canopy of baize-green leaves and lush umbels of crimson and coral flowers. When the phoebe peeps are very small in their high nest, the bullsnake slithers up the wall but doesn't quite reach them. Sometimes he tries to mate with the hose.

When Mark and I are gone, when neither of us are around to defend the palace, I am convinced that the creatures move in, close the door behind them, and lock us out. They gnaw chair legs and eat peanut butter out of the jar. They try on my clothes, browse the antique geography books, read Proust aloud, plan trips. Obsidian wings brush the map of Persia. Scutes and femurs traverse the page-flattened globe, the pastel world of lost places—Italian Somaliland, Colony of Niger, Côte d'Ivoire. A flicker in a head bandage noses around a daffodil-yellow Abyssinia just east of a rose-colored Sudan.

There is gossip. *These people,* the animals whisper, these overbaked bipedal rampaging Pliocenic thermal sapiens! Their existentialist delusion that life is defined by a tragicomic absence of purpose!

Outside among the stones the side-blotched lizards (*Uta stansburiana*) hatch their tiny young—the lapel pins, I call them. Someone leaves a door open and, sure enough, one of the lizards tiptoes inside to explore the Fence Posts' inner sanctum. When it sees me, it tries to race across the smooth terra-cotta tiles, going nowhere, its little lizard feet scrabbling madly in place. A cricket takes up residence in my husband's closet. At night it sings love songs to his hiking boots. The toad that lives under the mint bushes plops around the breezeway, then flings itself against a window, trying to popcorn into our bedroom window. I think it is headed for the bathtub.

The bullsnakes keep down the mice and chase off rattlesnakes. The bug-eating birds and lizards are cheaper, safer, and more fun than insecticides. Hummingbirds invite me to fill our lives with flowers. Toads reassure us that there is a lot of sex going on. We think of our domestic wildlife as useful. I do not know what they think of us, but I know that they, not we, are the hosts on this shaggy piece of desert.

One day I chase two *Utas* out of my living room. It isn't easy, herding lizards. One night, outside, a tiny bat hooks itself high in the stucco wall to rest. I stand on my head to better observe this upside-down winged mouse. When you are a guest, you adjust.

Overall, a chaotic calm has returned to Na'ashó'ii Mesa. The sphinx moths sip the primrose nectars rather than assault the screen door. Some dim bulb lights up inside a carp brain and the fish return to the river to press their noses against the wet mud. I see to it that the Jehovah's Witnesses leave an ample supply of flicker weapons, and the bird's stucco obsession appears to fade.

At my last therapy session with the Mule Brothers, brother número uno trotted up to the other brother and bit him in the ass—a hard, pinching bite with strong, square teeth. Within a few minutes, however, all was forgiven.

Red Dust

The spread of the buildings was cut off from the outside world, or from what one Indian named Quicker-Than-You called "the violent pretense of reality," by the quiet long mountains and the weird huddled mesas and the blue deep arroyos and total indifference.

WILLIAM EASTLAKE
Go in Beauty

A curving reef of slickrock held the rodeo arena in its cusp, its base afloat on a hovering stratum of red dust. The dust lasted as long as Navajo Fair—three days—and friends joked that I, an Anglo and as exotic as an alpaca in a sea of obsidian hair, would turn as red as their clan sisters. When I ran my tongue over my lips, they tasted of dust and the faint musk of cottonwood limbs freshly cut for the roofs of the dance ramadas, their leaves limp with heat.

Cowboys—Indians, that is—leaned on the rails of a holding pen, admiring several tons of Brahma bulls. The bronc riders pulled chaps over their jeans and eyed the scruffy mounts that would soon turn their spines to Slinkys. Over invisible calves the ropers twirled their lassos in practice tosses. Everything about the rodeo began late or not at all. In the stands and along the dusty track to the vendor stalls, there was a great deal of space between people.

The rodeo announcer reeled out a play-by-play of the chicken-pull event in rapid-fire Navajo, accenting his twenty-first century Athapaskan vocabulary with an impressive sportscaster's cadence. He sprinkled his commentary with terms like "Wheaties" and "chain-link fence." Some English simply does not translate. "Freckles," for instance; there is no Navajo word for "freckles."

On the reservation, chicken pulls go back many years to impromptu gatherings that brought together all that a Navajo—deeply communal within his or her own family but isolated by a home set far apart from neighbors and surrounded by a vast desert—did not have: a crowd. The larger group usually assembled near a trading post or livestock pens and used the occasion to race horses and compete in chicken pulls. A chicken was buried up to its neck in dirt. One by one, horsemen passed at a gallop, leaning over to yank the bird out of the hole. Somewhere inside *naa'ahóóhai,* the old name for the fairs, lies the word for "chicken."

Burlap sacks stuffed with prize money have replaced chickens. The chicken pull at today's fair required a slow forty-five minutes of ride-bys. No one pushed his horse to speed, no one could grab the sack. The competition dragged on. Finally, a rider from Teec Nos Pos pulled the sack out of the dirt without falling off his horse. The crowd cheered.

By reservation standards this was a small fair, drawing people from the surrounding desert to a parade, rodeo, food booths, traditional social dances, and an intertribal powwow. People met, gossiped, flirted, and joked with old friends in Navajo, a tongue at once bitten off and as dry as wind in a raven's wings. I reveled in the act of pure listening without the burden of understanding. When my group tackled what sounded like a serious subject, I asked a friend to translate. No one cracked a smile as he turned to me and said, "They're planning to get three boats and invade Spain."

Fair day began with a parade whose scale fit the town of less than three hundred people but nevertheless managed to back up a mile's worth of semis, gravel trucks, Harleys, and other vehicles on a stretch of highway along the parade route. The truckers wheezed air through their brakes and scratched their tattoos. The French tourists baked inside their rental RVs. The parade participants numbered a proud, scattered handful: a color guard, a flatbed trailer piled with Head Start kids and tribal elders, a high school band from a distant town (minus the woodwind section, who missed the bus), two floats (one supporting the initiative to legalize gambling casinos on the reservation, one against), a covey of princesses, the local fire truck, and an army recruitment official whose painted green face and jungle camouflage stood out in the parched desert like a tropical bromeliad.

One of the truckers tiptoed in on eighteen wheels behind the fire vehicle, thinking it was the last in the queue, but, wedged in between the fire truck and a late entry from the neighborhood health clinic, the trucker inadvertently joined the procession and waved to the crowd from his high cab. In the back of the clinic's pickup, kids in surgical gowns, masks, and caps sat around a CPR dummy. Occasionally someone leaned over the dummy and punched its chest.

When a friend and I showed up on horseback, the parade master asked us to escort the royalty. We rode behind Miss Many Farms, a princess from Many Farms, Arizona, on her white horse, and in front of Miss Navajo Nation, a princess on the hood of a Chevy. In long skirt, concha belt, satin blouse, pale leggings, and moccasins of soft deerskin, she sat on brightly colored Navajo and Mexican blankets draped over the Chevy, throwing candy and darts of sun from her tiara. Both young women smiled and broke hearts.

From our saddlebags we, too, threw candy to the children lined up along the parade route. My friend rationed his supply poorly, ran out far too soon, and felt terrible. I had tied a rotund, sixteen-inch-long zucchini to the back of my saddle, where the bedroll usually sits. It had appeared in my garden on the morning of the fair and, what the hell, it went with my silver belt buckle.

On the rodeo grounds the heat, red dust, and bull riding turned fierce. A makeshift marketplace drew pools of people in slower migrations. Grandmothers in full skirts and velveteen blouses, older men in black Stetsons, jeans, crisp snap shirts, satin wind-breakers, and bolo ties with slabs of turquoise so big you could eat off them. Teenagers in drooping boy-band black and sport shoes as large and white as loaves of bread, toddlers outfitted as the mirror image of their grandparents except for the tufts of pink cotton candy stuck to their hair.

At one of the food stalls a cook had arranged stacks of golden-brown frybread next to a glass jar of honey afire with oblique sun-light and a cobalt-blue bowl filled with smooth green New Mexico chiles. Her cotton tablecloth set its pale aqua against sand the color of salmon flesh. On the cooking fire behind the table a ribcage of mutton sizzled over bright embers of burning juniper, sending up smoke flushed with lilac.

In the shade of a food stall I sat near one of my neighbors. He was a medicine man, a *hataali* of the old style, a reed-thin octoge-narian with ramrod-straight posture and a face lined with sun, his silver hair pulled back into a twisted knot, or chongo, and wrapped with a band of purple cotton cloth. From silver wires on both pierced ears hung exquisite turquoise slab dangles, stones as thin and smooth as glass. This man called the Navajo Reservation—all 25,000 square miles of it—"our room." He could likely tap depths of spirit that few of us can imagine, he could tell you that there are other beings, layered in the human world and in a bottomless reser-voir of stories, who would trade rain for a gypsum tadpole or the soft breast feathers of an eagle. On this day he ate a cheeseburger across a plastic table from a shy granddaughter.

At the edge of the fairgrounds, on the tailgate of a truck, an eld-erly woman was selling medicinal herbs wrapped in clear plastic sandwich bags. She wore the dress typical of older Navajo women: teal fluted cotton skirt, purple velveteen blouse, canary-yellow cot-ton sport socks pulled straight up the calf, and a pair of immaculate lime-green Keds. Beneath a sheer, hot-pink nylon kerchief tied under her chin, a tight wrap of scarlet cotton yarn bound her thick hair knot.

The style of the matriarchs embodied their tribe's legendary ability to take ideas from other cultures, then ground them as essential Navajo traits, traits that are, in the end, composite and adaptive and therefore enduring and definitive. From their Pueblo neighbors in Arizona and New Mexico, the Navajo borrowed styles for ceramics, textiles, ceremonies, ornaments, and hairstyles. From the Spaniards they took sheep and wool, horses, tools, and silverwork and made them their own. Fashions came from the Spanish by way of the Pueblos, mixed with influences from army wives at the frontier forts of the nineteenth century.

The Navajo of that era also favored leather concha belts stamped with silver dollars and collars, lapels, and plackets studded with rows of dimes or mother-of-pearl buttons. They loaded their necks, wrists, and fingers with turquoise and coral, which was how a seminomadic pastoralist could carry all of his or her wealth that was not livestock. When someone gave a piece of turquoise to the wind, who so restlessly sought the bright pieces of blue stone, the wind would stop blowing and rain would come.

Except for special occasions—at dances and ceremonies or when you are a princess in a parade, for example—women of the baby-boom and younger age groups do not dress like their mothers and their grandmothers, the World War II generation and likely the last to be seen throughout the reservation in their skirts and their Keds, growing older and as crooked as commas over their canes, still monolingual and the sharpest livestock traders in the Southwest. These women knew how to butcher a sheep, carry a keg of water on their backs, bargain for turquoise or sugar, and sing their way home in the dark.

There are few pastels in their palette—in their dress, ornament, hand-woven textiles, household goods. Every surface draws from the high-strung, sawed-off colors in the desert around them, crimson and vermilion from the sandstone cliffs, deep amethyst from the shadows, indigo and emerald from the far mesas, all of it sparked by turquoise. In the coming decade or two, as the oldest generation passes on, the skirts and velveteen blouses will slip by as everyday attire, no longer what a woman would wear when she wove blankets, collected pinyon nuts, hitchhiked to Kmart, or tended sheep and children.

At the fair the herb seller's face looked familiar. At other times I had seen her in the county services van that once a week collected elderly Navajos from remote parts of the reservation and brought them to town for the day. The van, filled with aged men and women, stopped at the post office, where they collected their mail, veterans' benefits, and Social Security checks. When the young driver parked and opened the van door, out billowed a crashing boom of radio set at top volume: chants and powwow drums on the tape deck or Navajo-language radio from Gallup, New Mexico, or Chinle, Arizona.

On town day the women went to the senior citizens center and plotted future escapades. Over frybread and mutton stew they designed fail-safe fund-raisers to raise cash for a van, driver, and gas, perhaps overnight lodgings. Some of these trips took them to the movies, others to the mountains and pinyon-juniper forests, where they collected medicinal plants—serviceberry for indigestion, the leaves of scarlet penstemon for a horse's sore leg.

A public display of the Navajo herbarium is not typical. There are careful rituals for gathering and handling plants and rigorous apprenticeships for those who learn to do so. For traditionalists who believe that plant knowledge is sacred and secret, the herb vendor's commercialism was out of place. On the other end of the spectrum are community college classes and tribe-sponsored publications of ethnobotany, designed to stimulate young Navajos' interest in their culture and in science careers. Either way, secret and sacred or public and sacred, the Navajo have a head start of several hundred years on the Anglos' herbal health industry.

The woman at the fair was selling "everyday" medicine, wild plants gathered for household purposes. When I asked for something to cure an ailment that I could only describe as progressive lunacy, a grandson translated her response. There is no remedy, he says she says, so go ahead and stay crazy. I recognized many of her plants. They grew on my land, too, and on the high mesas to the north of us.

Inside each clear plastic Baggie lay dried desert bits and a word morphology laden with culture-based meanings. For its snowy blossoms the Navajo call a ceremonial emetic *tł'éé' íigahiits'óóz*, loosely translated as "white at night." In the European taxon this plant is *Oenothera albicaulis,* a name that exudes a whiff of social disdain. *Oinos* comes from the Greek for "wine" and a fear that the plant's roots made an otherwise abstemious person take to drink. For many others, who likely encounter the flower as scenery, it is an evening primrose.

Another example of cultural naming: Heron's bill (common name), or *Erodium cicutarium* from the Greek *erodios,* or "heron"— the seed pods look like its bill—and *cicutarium* for leaves that resemble the water hemlock family (*Cicuta* spp.). In Navajo it is *tsís'nádáá,* or "bee food." Both names add up to a plant that can be used as an antidote for bobcat or mountain lion bites.

At the herb seller's table, strokes of black marker pen on strips of masking tape identified each plastic bag. Most were labeled as "Lose Weight Medicine" (although I found one "Gain Weight" bag beneath the pile), but there were also samples marked "Arthritis," "Vomit Medicine," and the bestseller, "Basik [*sic*] Pain." For the sad ache I felt for the demise of velvet grandmothers, I bought a bag of Basik Pain.

THE RODEO WOUND DOWN in a haze of heroic dust, and the powwow drums took over. This fair had two dance arenas, both defined by shade shelters, or concentric circles of wooden posts overlaid with beams and cottonwood boughs. The brush ramadas enclosed a roofless interior. Under one disk of sky Navajo couples slow-stepped to songs with a solemn, hymnal quality. Their feet stamped a circle in the dust, a ring with a slight divot where the dance judge stood. I had seen circles like this one miles away in the Mojave Desert on the lower Colorado River—geoglyphs etched deeply into the earth by ancient people who danced at the dawn of time.

The second dance arena held a maniacal fury of drum and song and what looked like an aviary exploding in slow motion. Fancy Dancers in wild face paint, long deerskin fringe, and trembling bustles of eagle feathers. Grass Dancers in streamers of bright yarn, slim-waisted and as limber as young trees. Young women in shawls or jingle dresses, their feet so light and high off the ground they appeared to be dancing on thin air. Some of the best dancers were five years old. Tribal distinctions fell apart then reassembled under a predominantly Plains Indian influence, made organic by added flair (Oklahoma dancers are trendsetters) and personal signatures. Above his beaded headband a Ute boy wore the traditional spiky roach of badger hair. In the center of the roach sat a small plastic Bart Simpson doll. Bart wore an Indian-style headband made from a shoelace.

I admired the dancers' quiet joy and a sinuosity that was not unlike the athleticism of the rodeo's bronc riders. I drew pleasure from the Navajos' pervasive sense of a good joke and, earlier in the day, the unexplained disappearance of the giant zucchini from my saddle. I liked the drums pulsing inside my head until they seemed to drive my own blood through my veins, and the way the dance arenas opened to a sky soon to be strewn with stars like seeds cast from a gourd—some radiant combination of things so acutely visual and physical that you understand more easily what it is you love.

Fair day ended with a heartbeat of drums and a blur of feathers as the dancers whirled inside the powwow's brush ramada. Sunset drenched the slickrock cliffs in blood-red light and the air filled with juniper smoke from the cooking fires. The drummers pitched their songs to a crescent moon, their voices an eerie mix of wind, flame, wolf, and shriek.

Late into the night the Wind Singers, a women's drum group, closed the powwow with an intertribal, a kind of processional, circular social dance. Dancers and audience could participate, but since the nondancers appeared reluctant, the announcer gave them a nudge.

"The Wind Singers are sitting all alone up here, waiting for you men to dance with them," he implored. "They're all good-looking. They have lots of money and really nice cars."

The Angry Lunch Café

She was to me like yellow quartz, dulled but full of secret
veins that a skilled hand could light and make glitter.
I dreamt of smoothing her rough edges, of filing down
her rage.

LISA ST. AUBIN DE TERÁN
The Palace

The raft slid across a sleek khaki mirror. The stillness and the
dazzle of sun on the river occupied all my attention. Above
the green banks the red canyon walls rose in listless splendor. If anything moved, it was me, working the oars to make my way downstream. Without this muscle, the indolent current would barely
carry the boat. The depth of the stillness was disconcerting. If there
was a horizon, I would have scanned it. But the canyon walled off
the distance and the future. Summer held the day inside thick glass.

For this last night on the river I chose a camp for its beach and
shade, a wide band of sand lined with tamarisk and willows. The
beach was so broad I had to knot a throw-rope to double the length
of the bowline and reach a secure tie-up in the trees. A cougar had
taken a drink at the river, leaving fresh tracks in the damp sand at
water's edge. Downstream from camp the canyon framed a long
stretch of water, an unusual straightness in a serpentine river that

mostly meandered and bent and quickly hid itself in folds of sheer-faced rock.

The heat and the inertia were so fierce that I too succumbed to the stillness and sat unmoving in the shade of the trees. Several dozen cicadas lined themselves up on slender boughs as if their feet were stitched to the bark. The leaves began to tremble. The cicadas ratcheted up their buzz to a pulsating crescendo. I closed my eyes and pulled the world down to sound, only sound, as if by listening to these vibrations I was listening to the thick, sultry air itself.

What gauges their song, I wondered. Does heat throw it into a higher-pitched drone? Do cool temperatures end the opera? Cicadas are plant eaters, relatives of leafhoppers, scales, and aphids. Cicadas "sweat" through pores but don't know how to jump. When they molt, they leave behind empty carapaces of skin that crackle into pieces when you touch them. Only the males sing, and they do so by thrumming the sound organs in their abdomen. Theirs is the music of deep, deep summer.

Time passed—who knows how much time—the light shifted and something pressed the stillness, moved it aside to make room for a different weight. As if a switch had been thrown, the cicadas stopped all at once, no laggers, no random afterbuzz. I tried to note what stopped their frenzied song—the time of day, the temperature of the air, a collective exhaustion? Perhaps the cicadas shut down so the crickets could begin, a kind of accommodating bug politeness. I waited for the crickets, for the change from the elongated cicada buzz to rubbed-leg chirps and trills.

No music came, only a low rumble. A roiling mushroom of monsoon clouds had slipped in unnoticed. The color of the air changed from languid gold to an edgy metallic brass. If the thunderstorm broke, I thought, it would stay downriver. Over my head all was clear skies.

The cicadas and crickets abandoned ship, and I underestimated the speed of the storm. Far downriver a veil of rain dropped into the canyon, a thin curtain that layered the canyon walls into silhouettes of watercolor on silk, each wall fainter than the one in front of it.

In a blink the layers vanished. The downriver view turned black and blank. In a split second the wind arrived, pushing ahead of it a whirling skirt of sand and debris and turning the willows from green to silver, their leaves bared to their undersides. Caught in the canyon's straightaway, the wind accelerated upstream, like the river made into air and turned inside out. A solid mass of rain roared upstream so quickly I barely had time to grab a rain jacket and clear the camp table, flip it over, and weigh it down with stones. I dove into a small grotto under the tamarisk only seconds before the storm hit the sandbar with a hurricane of rain then hail.

The river churned into waves and whitecaps. The raft blew upriver to the taut end of its long tether. Would it slam up against a snag and puncture? Were the oars secure? Was there enough weight in the boat to keep it from flipping? Would the knots hold? Why wasn't I spending my life as a philosopher-matron, a nurse, a trucker-poet, a soap opera diva? The world's expert in metaphors of light in *The Alexandria Quartet?* The cultural attaché to the U.S. embassy in Rome? Would a career diplomat hover under spindly riparian trees with sand in her underwear, placing her faith in knots?

Heavy torrents of hail erased the upside-down table, sandbar, and boat, obliterating the view between shelter and shore. Hailstones crashed through the ferny boughs of the tamarisk, and I wished I had a helmet. In a hailstorm in Montana I had once seen a man run to his car with a cooler over his head, saving himself from a concussion. All that lay between the ice balls and my thin-boned skull was *Tamarix* spp. and a flimsy hood.

The wild weather wanted a climax, some dark, uncertain disaster, and I feared it because in all my years of summer monsoons on the river I had seen few storms of such violence. The saving grace, I told myself as I shivered under the dripping tree, is that the end will come soon, narrowing the time for destruction. These cloudbursts were extremely local, dropping buckets in one drainage while not a single drop fell a few miles away. They were not broadly cast fronts with hours of power. And as swiftly as it had moved up the canyon to my camp, the storm revealed its size. Its downstream edge paled: the light behind the angry cloud. I would not be blasted much longer.

The retreating clouds bore the color of the red sandstone on their undersides. Behind the storm came an exaltation of freshness, a sudden aromatic blooming of wet sand and musky tamarisk, the deep sweetness of roots swelling, and a river that flowed and broke its mirror of oppressive heat. Hailstones pooled in the rounded toes of the cougar tracks. The raft tether relaxed.

Down-canyon, the cliffs that embraced the river glistened with the wet. Suddenly, there was a cutting of veins, a release of desert blood: waterfalls, clay-red waterfalls cascading down lavender and crimson sandstone to the talus below. These pour-offs usually held nothing but the silky polish of the water that carved them. Now they held plunging, vertical streams, at least four waterfalls on the canyon face across the river and another behind me that I could hear but not see. The water tumbled over the high walls, filled the canyon with its rushing, then slowly subsided. The streams narrowed to trickles, then disappeared.

Uncertain if I wanted to risk another cloudburst and a night without shelter, I set up the tent as backup and spread bed and tarp beyond its door so I could sleep outside, next to cat tracks still full of ice. The cicadas buzzed again, then politely handed the night over to the crickets.

That night I had the Vine Dream, one of three similar dreams—Vine, Dirt, Moss—that were at first amusing, then began to reoccur with a peculiar frequency. In the Vine Dream my hair is hair plus vines that are so thick and heavy they make my neck sore. I spend the dream breaking them off at the scalp with an audible snap. The dream is tactile and noisy and slightly painful. The Dirt Dream gags me with a claylike soil in my mouth, tongue and lips, and I spend the dream scooping dirt out of my mouth with my finger. The Moss Dream is like the Vine Dream. I scrape and shave a kelly-green moss off my skin. Instead of a smooth tuff, the moss grows like even-bristled turf—short, tough, and hairbrush straight.

I spend a great deal of my sleeping life trying not to become a plant. It isn't funny anymore.

THE MORNING'S FLOAT to the takeout passed with the sad sweetness of leaving the river. The heat sowed its stillness again. The cicadas fired up. I thought it was Sunday, but I could not be sure. I owned a watch, but I hadn't seen it since 1999. On river trips I liked to pull into the takeout quietly, without the rush of reentry, just a methodical wrangling of gear, then the driving away, the river at my back. However, when I nosed the raft into the sloping gravel of the boat ramp, I found my truck surrounded by a posse.

A half-dozen men milled around a muddy Jeep and a couple of all-terrain vehicles—hulky, fat-tire machines that looked like the offspring of coitus between a Volkswagen bug and a *Tyrannosaurus rex*. The Jeep rack wore rifles, and more than one of the men wore a gun in a holster on his hip. None were in uniform, just T-shirts and baggy camouflage pants tucked into black lace-up boots. Except for one teenager, they were in their early forties. They held their torsos in a limp patience. They walked over to the raft and asked the first question people always ask when they see a woman alone.

"Are you alone?"

"Yes." I smiled. I folded in the oars, stepped out of the raft, and tied up the bowline.

"You break off from a group? Got someone behind you?"

"No, just me. A nice four days on the river." I saw no reason to fear them. Only their guns and their nervousness made me nervous. Concerned that someone was lost or hurt, I asked, "Are you with the sheriff's department? Search and rescue?"

"No, we have families." The man who offered this non sequitur wore a gun and a fiery pink sunburn in the line that parted his meticulously groomed hair. He appeared to be the leader by virtue of his stance just forward of the others, who stood sweating in the heat, eyeing the raft and snarl of gear with a flat, cursory interest.

Two of the men fiddled with a GPS device. One of them looked up and asked, "What's this place? Did you get coordinates?"

I told him the name of the place and how the dirt road from the boat ramp connected to the main highway. I did not have a global positioning system, a fact that reinforced their impression that they were in the company of a museum relic. Each of us had a comforting cluelessness. I was lost but knew where I was. They were not lost but did not know where they were.

All over the Southwest hand-held GPS units were the rage among seekers of points of interest. Guide books and Web sites spilled GPS map parameters and the precise coordinates of mountains, canyons, washes, and trails as if they were survival essentials. Every discordant batholith, every strike-slip fault, a great number of natural arches and bridges, prehistoric dwellings and rock art, were on a database. No one with these glorified compasses would become lost in the wilderness. They were, after all, in touch with satellites. People in touch with satellites followed their way points assiduously. Like leaving a high-tech trail of Hansel and Gretel cookie crumbs, they programmed their route so they could retrace the *exact same steps* on the return route. GPS, I thought in a great puffing up of nature girl pomposity, was a form of voluntary neutering.

In my current situation, sharing the castration theory was probably inappropriate. I wanted to be nice to these guys. I wanted them to be nice to me. And they were. After I moved the truck closer to the pile of gear and started to derig the boat, they helped me lift the boat frame to the rack on top of the truck and topper shell, a difficult task for one person.

"You lose your motor?" one of the men asked. "You camp with no guns?" he said. Gun plural? I sank deeper into an inferiority complex.

In case no one has noticed, grown men no longer simply *camp out*. A lot of people in the desert carry a great deal of armor—road machines, weapons, two-way radios, cell phones, generators, television sets, boom boxes, sides of beef, cases of beer, and contact with satellites. This is partly precaution for emergencies as well as loyalty to America's entrenched national resistance to anything the least bit inconvenient or uncomfortable. It is also insulation against fear—fear of the quiet, fear of exposure and vulnerability, fear in the face of nature's unequivocal message that there are forces far beyond our control. The desert gives an unsettling sense of the largeness of the universe in relation to the self. The desert is a scary place for a human being if you do not want to feel puny and humbled—that is, like a human being in the desert.

We talked about the storm. The brunt of it had bypassed their town, but out here they had come across several eroded washes. I told them about the waterfalls. We baked under the fiery sun. Their hot, heavy boots looked like torture, and I wondered if the prevailing western mood of borderline rage and aggressive frustration boiled down to a simple matter of cruel footwear. It would have done all of us a world of good to take off our shoes and liberate our toes in a warm wallow of river mud.

"You seen any other boaters?" Sequitur Man said. "Anyone behind you, a group, you know, kind of alternate lifestyle?"

The question was so *Dragnet*, I asked again, "Are you with law enforcement? DEA?"

"Nope."

"ATF? FBI?"

"Uh, no."

"National Guard?"

"Well, no." He paused and said, "We've come from the House of God." Everyone shifted their weight from one leg to the other.

"We're tired of indecent exposure. It's illegal, you know. All these river people think they own the place and get crazy with drugs and, uh, take off their clothes and run around like they was, you know. And in front of little kids and Boy Scouts . . ."

They had come out here from church. They carried a small arsenal. It was a hundred degrees. *They were looking for naked people.*

The river corridor was remote and obscured from the nearest town by four-hundred-foot walls and at least fifty parched, scorpion-infested miles. Unless you were traveling with the party that disrobed, you had to drive, trudge, and crawl on your belly to the lip of the canyon and use high-powered binoculars to offend yourself with someone's bare butt. I noted several pairs of binoculars around several necks. I packed the last of my gear and sprinted toward the truck, mumbling something about an appointment with my hairdresser.

Sequitur Man followed me. He was working himself into heatstroke. He pointed to the teenager. "That's my son. He's only seventeen. He can't be seeing breasts. Women's breasts."

If he is seventeen and feels he must carry a weapon against bare breasts, I thought, I would be a worried parent. The kid was probably aching to go out and get his left nostril pierced. However, this was not the time to compare pedagogical philosophies. I was caught dead center in the love-it-to-death wars, the struggle among recreation cultures over what each felt was its entitlement to the western wildlands and its prerogative to demand how one behaved there.

These days westerners live in a land full of love, hate, and indifference. There are people who have no engaged conversation with the land whatsoever, no sense of its beauty or extremes or limits and therefore no reason to question their actions in a place that is merely backdrop. There are those who would decry the Naked Other and impose a moral order on the untamed lands and anyone who uses them. And there are people who like the desert but hate one another. They snarl and yap and spar over the other's means of expressing affection. Some have cartooned the controversy into a class conflict—youthful, pampered, overeducated, gorp-propelled urban androgynes on foot versus petro-propelled, overweight, manly men who cry that taking away access for snowmobiles, Jet Skis, ATVs, and other motorized toys is taking away their freedom.

I confess up front that I am on the side of freedom. Freedom to have sanctuary, some peace and quiet in the paltry 6 percent of the nation's public lands that remain roadless. Freedom to close a few wild places to our infernal motors and machines so that we might open the land to *us*, to human beings. Freedom to have places where one can feel and know the skin of the earth through something besides a wheel. Some people do not know how to bond with machines. When I use machines, I tend to get my hands caught in them.

As the West fills up with people and their rabid appetite for playgrounds, time is running out for the "wild preservatives" who remember solitude instead of crowds, ranch fences respected rather than cut by trespassers, backcountry without tire tracks every forty steps, friendliness instead of paranoia. When the eco-Luddites scorn technology's sensory deprivation, they echo a previous generation, which saw the outdoors as a place to build character and self-reliance. When my father reminded my soft-life brothers and me how as a boy he trudged seven miles to school through snowdrifts in a subzero blizzard, we marveled at the arcane fortitude even though we knew he grew up in Los Angeles.

Now it is our turn to drone eulogies for a less cluttered life. I worry about the evaporation of the last sanctuaries from the slings and arrows of advertising. I wonder why a country like ours spends billions of dollars to build roads anywhere and everywhere only to want to drive *off* them. I wonder why rich people need mountaintop mansions with bathrooms large enough for their Lear jets—atrophy homes, a friend of mine calls them, because the owners use them hardly once a year. I am too dim-witted to fathom the need to pack a cell phone and call up my personal investment banker from a canyon spring when I could be conversing with monkey flowers and tiny damp toads. To want to be lost or alone, to want to shed, for a moment, the devices that engineer every facet of our lives—to want to be aware—is to be a whining anachronism.

Scarier than the lack of sensory intimacy with nature, or perhaps a direct result of this estrangement, is a dark side, an undercurrent of escalating hostility verging on violence. It is as if disagreement—over lifestyles and land use, politics and technology—is no longer enough. The argument must also become personal to the point where resentment is so concentrated against *someone,* usually the wrong someone or someone amorphous and "different," it becomes dangerous and obsessive.

The rural communities of the intermountain West are isolated and insular, conservative to a fault. Here a surprising number of people believe that environmentalists are the instruments of Satan. Local governments have passed ordinances that require every head of household to own a gun. They have been pressured to ban xeriscaping and refuse licenses to New Age "crystal shops," calling both businesses the peddlers of heresy. There are social programs to make gay people ungay, to bring them into the heterosexual fold with counseling. The only enemy missing from the list is the federal government, but only because the government is considered to be the sum of the parts—that is, composed entirely of tree huggers, gays, and the crystal people.

The regional identity crisis, of course, involves deeper layers of complexity than guns, lawns, and an anti-ATV Antichrist. The West's rampaging pace of change, its long history of humans shaped by the land and spaces around them, its politics, passions, and pathologies, have made a compelling stage for historians, philosophers, and barstool metaphysicians, who deftly place the current episodes of discord into context. These broader perspectives—libraries were the only arsenal I knew—were of little use in the face of the take-no-prisoners evangelism here by the river, served up by six GPS-powered churchgoers whose feet were killing them. Here things were getting local.

The khaki river ran gently between banks overflowing with summer's heavy biomass. Coyote willows collected the day's heat between their parrot-green leaves; the air moved only along the trajectories of saffron-colored dragonflies. I secured the boat frame to the truck's roof rack, then laid the big yellow oars along the frame and strapped them in. All of my gear was loaded.

Of course, I wanted to go for a final swim in the river before the hot drive home and of course I figured that if I bared my navel the posse would riddle me with bullets and I would float off facedown in a bloody pool of water toward the Grand Canyon, pummeled into soggy bits of flesh by rapids and gravel bars, and some poor boater or hiker would find a Teva sandal attached to a milky-white foot with bones sticking out of it and I would never again see my husband, who would gaze sadly from the cliffs above the river with the wind in his hair, maybe hear an eagle's cry, then move back to Montana to find consolation in the arms of a ski bunny.

The man with the sunburned scalp stood eleven inches from my ear, quoting Scripture. His righteousness seemed rooted in panic or fright—of what, I wondered, the human body? An inquisitive or a questioning mind? His ire was not directed at me, but it frightened me nonetheless. His lecture made all of us stand hard and sharp-angled, awkward in the soft and lovely summer morning. To me a fully clothed, armed zealot was more dangerous than a naked person. I told them I was grateful for their help and drove my satanic butt out of there.

The struggle over western recreation lands is reaching a vitriolic fervor that sends me diving under the blankets. The quarreling factions cause me untold strife. I lose sleep, I lose hair, I lose years off my life with the worry of it all. I need so much therapy I feel like packing up and moving into the full-time care of the Mule Brothers, making their pasture a sanitarium for the politically wimpy. I weave my worry into a ludicrous conclusion: I am responsible for the world's anger and unhappiness. I merely have to try to *fix* it. In the hallowed tradition of squishy doughball liberals, I believe that science, reason, kindness, and understanding—maybe a little food—can set the world right.

BUDDHA'S LAST WORDS: "Tell the cook, thanks for the meal." Kit Carson's last words: "Wish I had time for just one more bowl of chili."

Sometimes the desert exhilarates me to the point of soaring. Other times I am so heartsick I cannot bear up against the despair, a palpable, aching longing. Longing for this wild beauty to last and for me never to die and no longer be able to feel, see, hear, taste, and breathe it. A yearning to die before the desert's wild heart is lost so I do not have to witness it. A longing to be a better person, for the world to be a better place, for us to truly measure up to this land, for this land to not be a battlefield of anger and greed. When these two opposing conditions, elation and despair, follow one another too quickly, the universe seems careless and precipitate. I soar, I crash, a squall of heat let loose in the ethos.

Or else I get hungry.

I left the river and the vice squad behind and drove to a town midway between the boat takeout and home. The distant mesas quivered in the sweltering light. I scanned the highway for hunter-gatherer potential—berries, a yucca pod, some roadkill Doritos. I was starving.

In town I went shopping for a nifty GPS device so I could be in touch with satellites. Then I found a pay phone, one of those prole-tarian antiques with soundproof Plexiglas wings that don't let everyone else hear your conversation so that they, on their cell phones, can share their conversations with you. I phoned my hus-band to give him my precise latitude and tell him about the storm and the posse.

"Keep your pants on until this blows over," I warned him. "Can't *find* your pants, honey? Well, let me just ping up some coor-dinates . . ."

I phoned an acquaintance to confirm an upcoming meeting. A recorded voice, designed for security screening rather than messages, instructed me to state my name after the tone, then asked me to stay on the line while my call was cleared. "Please hold," the recording droned, followed by this morsel of AT&T-style metaphysics: "You will now hear silence."

When I telephoned a friend who owned a local inn and restaurant, he invited me to dinner. At his place I cleaned up and put on a skirt and teal silk blouse that could have used an iron, something I owned but hadn't seen since 1998. My only pair of sandals was a mess from the mud of river and storm so, since he owned the place, my friend let me into the restaurant barefoot. Even though I tucked my feet under the linen-covered table, all civilized behavior evaporated. I suddenly felt an involuntary turn to the primitive, to things in the hidden realms of instinct and intuition, maybe sex. Candlelight flickered against crystal wineglasses. The other diners looked refreshed and earnest. On trays the wait staff carried towers of pastries as if they were heart transplants.

Another traveler joined my friend and me at the table, an elegant septuagenarian with upswept silver hair and a dress the color of garnets. She was on vacation from her job as a concierge at a historic hotel in a national park, one of those log-cabin-Baroque inns built with half a mountain's worth of pine, a view into majestic eternity, and, to the dismay of the proprietors, a pair of ring-tailed cats that would not stop running up and down the rafters in the giant dining room.

The woman ordered what looked like a roasted flicker, toes-up on a white china plate, surrounded by a skirt of kelp. I inhaled twenty Brie-drenched *aperitivos,* stormed my way through an awkward gazpacho and several glasses of cabernet. My friend, who knew me well, and knew a woman's tendency to once in a while rise up and self-combust, actually raised an eyebrow but became mischievously encouraging, curious to see where all this might lead. When he wasn't looking, I used my fork to stab and eat his *aperitivo.*

The dining room filled. I tried to live up to an upbringing of family dinners with multiple pieces of silverware on either side of one's plate and a mother who always said, "Please come to the table," never "Get your asses over here," although my brothers and I wanted her to, *just once,* and tried our best to push her to the brink.

From other tables scraps of conversation drifted our way.

"She actually found a masseuse who fluffed auras."

"He wasn't your average mass murderer."

"The kids are bored. They don't want to see another Indian dwelling. They want to go to Sea World."

At our table the conversation roamed from mad-cow disease to national parks. Suddenly, my soup seemed to hold deep wells of pathos and dread. Why worry about the end of the wild, I thought, when it had not yet ended? A person could go crazy with longing.

The concierge told us about gridlock in national parks and the push for buses, trams, and monorails. Many of the parks were reexamining their history, she said. "The older hotels in Grand Canyon and Glacier—mine was built in 1904—were built by the great railroad companies. Rails brought people to the western wilderness."

I recalled the last train I had seen, a string of freight cars parked on a side rail somewhere on the Arizona-California border. Graffiti covered the lower halves of the boxcars. The swaying, fluid letters were gangish and illegible but ornately artistic. Across one boxcar someone had painted a name in old-fashioned stick letters: VLADIMIR KABINGKABONG.

"I heard about one of those idiot savants who are geniuses with numbers," our host said. "This man stood beside the tracks when a train passed, moving at a fast clip, and memorized the ID numbers on the sides of each railroad car. After the train passed he could recite them in nearly perfect order." I envisioned a Ukrainian sort of fellow in overalls too small for him, his head going back and forth like a woodpecker's but sideways.

The silver-haired concierge and our host talked. They were

about the same age. I felt like some brown mammal they had brought with them. My appetite was monstrous. I did not want kelp. The waiter brought me a plate of artfully singed meat. I felt as if my teeth had been sharpened to points.

Over our entrées the other two kept up a flood of cheerful dinner topics. New nuclear waste dumps in the neighborhood, the international market in animal parts, whirling disease among trout, scream fights among recreationists, the prospect of coal mining in one of the region's most spectacular national monuments. Lead poisoning and the lower IQs of second-graders, skyrocketing Viagra sales in polygamist colonies. Biotech crops and herbicides that poison the food of butterflies, a genetically modified food supply that dooms future generations to fish sticks with monkey genes and who knows what other horrors. Shredded genes, shredded ozone, mutant frogs, legless ducks, eviscerated elephants.

I felt a prick of laughter. Not socialite laughter but creepy laughter, some inept way to alleviate the hard sadness of all this earth damage, the strains and strivings of the "hopeful monsters" known as the human race. I was unwilling to assume that hostility was the basic language among people. Humor, a biologist once posited, may be a deterrent to aggression. At the river should I have stripped, then challenged the posse to a duel in the buff? If you were not merely laughing but full-tilt, harebrained hysterical, did the lion eat you anyway?

My table partners put their heads and wineglasses together and began to plot: They would rent an off-road vehicle and ride it through a cemetery. My friend gave me one of his best Chester the Molester grins and said, "When they arrest us, we'll ask them why it's wrong to desecrate a religious sanctuary but okay to desecrate the land."

Somewhat taken aback, I pictured two fermenting radicals in silver hairdos and leather, carving doughnuts on the turf-covered breast of a deceased Republican. I saw them at their arraignment giving the "defiling of sacred places" argument to a mind-set that would order a physician's review of their heart medicine, then try them for the heresy of secular humanism. The crowding of the West was making warriors of us all, even these sweet little grandparents.

There was saffron on the risotto and no time for responsible behavior. For once in my self-righteous life I did not care one bit that I was eating the warmed-up gynoecium of purple, perfumed flowers, that 14,000 teeny-weeny golden stigmas of *Crocus sativus* had given their lives to make one teeny-weeny ounce of saffron.

Nishapur, the heartland of turquoise in northeastern Iran, is also the habitat of saffron. Behind the houses of Nishapur, the ancient Persians grew small garden paradises—*pairi-daēzas* (from *pairi*, "around," and *daēza*, a wall or enclosure). In these gardens they mixed iris and saffron, a plant that prefers the sunniest locations and driest soils. Iran still grows much of the world's saffron. When the saffron crocus is harvested in the fall, each stigma is extracted by hand.

Over food the world is examined, plots hatch, cheeses are passed, life's joys and regrets slosh around with the cognac. Aphrodite may slip in with the oysters. To end the wars over western lands, perhaps all of us should sit down at the dining room table like a family, minding our manners. Do not allow anyone to make personal attacks or smirk at the tofu. Have everyone hand-extract their own stigmas. Hire a few mothers to glare down outbursts of self-centered myopia or rampant greed. Serve pie. Who on earth could be mean over pie?

According to a seventeenth-century Persian herbal, "The use of saffron ought to be moderate and reasonable, for when the dose is too large, it produces a heaviness of the head and sleepiness. Some have fallen into an immoderate convulsive laughter which ended in death." My roaring hunger persisted; fullness did not come. I felt the rise of some not very immoderate laughter. I desperately sought remorse for eating insane beef, not to mention several thousand sex organs from *Crocus sativus*. All I found was an agonizing hopelessness, a little pea on a string, hanging inside an empty cranium.

I held my fork at bay and stared at my plate. Suddenly, I wanted to lick each golden-yellow, eyelash-sized stigma off every single rice grain, one by one.

IF YOU CAN EVER lay your hands on a few antique Freudians and dust them off, you will hear that finding villains is a common diversion from fear and self-reproach. Freud called it *projection*, a psychological stratagem in which people expel unacceptable thoughts from their own minds and ascribe them to others. To label others as selfish, lustful, greedy, or mean-spirited may be a subconscious way to transpose such qualities from oneself to someone else, preferably to a stranger or those beyond one's like-minded group.

When projection takes the leap from a normal human impulse to a pathology, it demonizes the Other. In its extremes it reduces a group or race to stereotype, even subhuman stature, thereby providing an excuse for oppressing them. The enslavement or extermination of a "lesser species," the argument goes, arouses no guilt. Claims of superiority over a humanity-deprived Other run deep in history. According to a papal bull, for instance, the Indians found by Europeans in the New World were not human beings until 1537, when the bull decreed them to be so.

The American West has always been adept at "otherizing." These days people who see a familiar world disrupted—and no place creaks and groans and lurches with change quite like this region—want to blame someone for the erosion of rural simplicity, for the cracks in the old ways, be they mythical or real. Without a bunch of Communists to kick around any longer, the current scapegoats of social upheaval, lumped into a nebulous category of faceless brutes, make easy targets of blame for hangnails, nasty divorces, broken transmissions, and the entire worldwide collapse of faith, morality, and the beef industry. Wariness of outsiders, fear of change and a sense of powerlessness in the face of it—fear, in fact, of the rest of the world—have bred a convenient duplicity of perpetrator and victim and an unwholesome battery of revenge politics.

Many will argue that the fundamental social tissue that binds the human race is not love but power. The West's undeveloped lands are the spoils of this power struggle, yet too often end up its victim. Too many wants compete for too few remnants of wild places, and the fury of it all blinds us to the sublime and humane. In *The World as Will and Idea,* Schopenhauer wrote that "in the mind of a man who is filled with his own aims, the world appears as a beautiful landscape appears on a battlefield." I wanted to round up all of the tired and angry warriors and go for a walk in the battlefield, to sit together on some godforsaken lip of wide-open eternity with a picnic hamper and turkey vultures circling our auras. This was my fatal naïveté: to believe that if you simply look at this wild desert, use all your senses to respond to it, you would reflexively love it, save it, care for it, behave yourself in it.

The stripped-down desert, the desolate, hostile, "empty" terrain, brings a person closer to dust and mystery, to something buried deep in the blood and nerves. "How can we know God unless we are radically alone in the purity of His creation?" said a friend of mine who is a Jesuit priest, the Jesuits being quite good at wilderness asceticism, the holiness and humbleness, faith and revelation, that come in spare, arid environments. "To feel that we belong to the world, we must be deserted."

After dinner I waddled to an edge of my friend's ranch property and set out my sleeping bag under a juniper tree and a sky dense with stars. The night's darkness had robbed the tree's green and given it muted, achromatopic grays. I could not shake the free-range anxiety that followed my most recent public appearance as Piglet. In my worry over the land wars I had nearly eaten the tablecloth. I longed to bury my face in the warm flank of a Mule Brother and figure it all out. But I could not. My gourmet adventure had not set the world right. I lay down for the night. My stomach growled. Unbelievable hunger!

Perhaps the West is in a state of mass, pathological projection, I thought. Blaming the Other avoids self-reproach for honing America's wildlife and wilderness heritage down to a contentious and limited supply, for carving it up for profits or loving it to death with an inexhaustible appetite for recreation. Finding an enemy disguises a failure to stand outside our own self-interest and remember a deeper, dependent, and common love for the natural assets of this land, the way that wild places, if you truly look, persuade you into their grandeur. If we are to hunger, let it be a hunger of the senses, not material desire. Let it be a surrender to the instinctive pull of remoteness and the intimacy of beauty. How can we rage and quarrel when there are summer storms that bring sky-borne balls of ice and two-hundred-foot waterfalls to the waterless desert?

Oh how brilliant, I said to myself, I have just added aesthetic sensitivity to potlucks and mothers as ways to save the world.

Above the juniper tree the starry night sky sort of looked like a cake I once made, a cake with midnight-blue icing and tiny dots of silver candy. When I decorated the cake, I tried to lay out the Pleiades but got carried away and made a galaxy. The night-sky cake made me think of my mother and the exquisite layer cakes she made from scratch, the silken, ivory-colored batter poured carefully into two round aluminum pans, then baked and cooled, and how her cake frostings were never buttercreams or glazy fondants or Safeway-bakery plasters but sugar and whipped egg whites, billowy and sweet and spread in a sea of satiny peaks with tips that fell over and curled, and soon I was in my starlit bed thinking about my mother and desserts and how as a young adult I made the most pathetic fruit pies known to man until my late brother taught me how to make pie crust, and to this day I did not know where he, an artist and U.S. Navy pilot whose airplane carried devices used to spy on Russian submarines in the Pacific, learned how to make pies.

If I did not fall asleep soon, I fretted, I would start to think about my best friend the stuffed teddy bear and the bite marks on its face and dead pets and all the years I spent in the Sierra by a clear mountain river, about war and little kids with lead in their brains and a world without monarch butterflies and about the disheveled Indian fellow I once saw by the side of a road in the middle of nowhere, slumped next to a broken suitcase, weeping as if his heart would break, and I could do nothing to help him so I sat down beside him and wept, too.

Daylight was a long way off. I lay awake and listened to the mysterious captivity that is memory. I wondered what time the café on the road home opened for breakfast in the morning.

"Silence all greed in yourself," says a Hindu teaching about entering meditation. The stars spread overhead, firing up their cast of thousands for the Perseid meteor shower. My body calmed into a meltdown of reminiscence, hunger, sorrow, and the aimless float of sleep. The night desert held me in a fluid quiet.

You will now hear silence.

THE RISING SUN KNIFED into Utah from Colorado, bathing the redrock desert in an immediately brutal heat. The crickets carried the morning, but in the trees along the washes, they would hand over the peak of the day to the cicadas. Arizona would hand over afternoon thunderstorms from the southwest, and the highway would hand me over to my next meal, then on to the salsa farm beside the river.

My scalp was sore from another Vine Dream and, if I thought long and hard about it, my appetite was actually waning—swinging, in fact, in a full, fast arc toward seriously ascetic fasting. I was no longer hungry but terribly thirsty. I pulled into a café short of home. The parking lot was full. On the side of one vehicle was the commercial name DROP DEAD PEST CONTROL. Not a good sign.

The café was ramshackle and forlorn, a rare fifties roadside kind of place that had yet to succumb, thank the river gods, to some hyperactive marketer's belief that people actually *like* to eat while sitting on orange and purple Naugahyde furniture. The walls held several vintage Coca-Cola posters, their colors faded to an unthreatening, Bible-school-art palette. Off the single dining room, behind a heavily locked iron gate, lay a room full of dead pawn—Navajo wedding baskets, Ute beadwork, rugs, jewelry, and other piles of goods that had been traded for gas or cash or food and never reclaimed. In big letters a handwritten sign near the gate said NO MORE, then listed items no longer accepted for pawn. COLAR PINS. STEREOS. CHEAP CAMRAS. TIRES OR RIMS. The last item on the list was NO BOGARDS.

The counter framed a cluttered kitchen with a sizzling grill. I ordered a large iced tea from the proprietor, a sixtyish woman with stand-by-your-man hair that was too bouffed for her hard, pale face. She wore a brown-and-yellow-plaid poplin cowgirl shirt with fringe on the yoke and piping on the pockets. Rows of faux Mercury dimes outlined the pockets on her skintight Wranglers. She was very sour as she took orders. She watched everyone in the room with a look that said we were thieves. She glared at a table of kids and at the tired, limping Navajo grandmother in a long jade-green skirt and pink Keds who pulled up a chair to rest.

A teenager carried a newborn in a thin flannel blanket, waiting her turn at the counter. An old Anglo man in thick glasses, a straw Stetson, and a faded blue chambray shirt walked up to her with the warm smile of greeting someone he knew.

"You remember me, don't you?" he said.

The Navajo girl drew a blank but remained polite, holding her baby with a shy smile. Her look said, No, she had never seen this man before.

He grinned at her. "I was here in 1938."

Twenty minutes passed after I ordered my drink. In the kitchen an elderly woman hovered over a counter with her back to the customers. The crabbed motion of her shoulders made it look as if she were wringing the necks of small animals. Then she stood at the hot grill, tending meat. She wore a floral Mother Hubbard apron and a terribly pained expression on a face weathered by work, worry, and sun. It occurred to me that she was the mother of the woman in the cowgirl shirt.

The café was experiencing the somewhat awkward state of being busy, as if this were the first crowd to come since the Coke posters were first hung. The old cowboy left, maybe planning to return in another sixty-some years. The mother-daughter team appeared unable to bear up, a permanent rather than a reactionary condition. One glared at the thieves. The other collapsed, certain to weep into the cheeseburgers at any moment. NO MORE and the black iron gate looked downright mean. I wondered why "bogards"—bow guards, the leather and turquoise bands that protected the wrists of archers—were no longer desirable pawn.

The café filled with grill smoke. The Navajo kids remained oblivious to all but their french fries. Resting her weary feet, the grandmother in the pink Keds sat quietly. Suddenly, the café proprietor turned to her mother and yelled, "I'm mad at you. I am so mad at you!"

The mother went rigid, eyes shut and arms clenched to her sides like a child who expected to receive blows. She began to cry. I desperately wanted to find a way to repair this awful unhappiness, but I was merely one of the thieves, standing there like a paralyzed ground squirrel facing an oncoming semi.

The cook did not seem to be cooking, so the daughter took over the grill, flipping meat with a spatula. I decided that she would never pour my iced tea, not because she was too busy but because she never intended to fill the order in the first place. Amid the backed-up cheeseburgers and family strife, iced tea was about as important as a shortage of mushroom-scrubbing brushes in a world war. I left the café.

◆　◆　◆

A MONTH LATER the cicadas disappeared, the monsoons and brutal heat passed, naked people migrated to the warmer Sonoran Desert, and the land wars still raged, stoked by a continuing epidemic of national bitterness and incivility. We put away the boat gear for the season but kept the river in our lives, on walks and visits to gravel bars to watch the Canada geese and the coyotes that sneaked up on them as they fed. My appetite remained normal, and the plant dreams were mercifully thwarted by a sequence of flying dreams. The wings on my scapulas felt much better than moss-green Astroturf body hair or vines growing out of my head.

One fine autumn day, when the cottonwoods were turning bright gold, I made a pie. I mixed the dough and rolled it out as my brother had taught me. I made a filling of apricots, honey, and cloves. After it baked and cooled, I carefully wrapped the pie, put it into the truck, and drove to the highway café. I would give it to the old woman and her daughter. I thought we might sit outside at a table under the cottonwoods with warm sun on our shoulders and apricot pie on our plates. We would have a conversation. We would find contentment in the simple refuge of the day and the desert around us. Perhaps we would talk about picnics, the only nature experience that everyone in the tattered, turbulent West could agree about. This would be a start.

It was unlikely that the mother-daughter discord had ended. It seemed a relationship rooted in a lifetime symbiosis of being completely stuck. Nevertheless, I gave the gesture some hope. As Brazilian novelist Jorge Amado wrote, "Every living person, no matter how miserable and dispossessed, how sad and lonely, has the right to a quota of joy; there's no destiny made entirely of bitterness."

The café was quiet and empty of all customers. Only the daughter tended shop, and she wore a grim look even as I presented my gift. No, she snapped, she did not want to go outside, she had too much work to do. But we sat for a while with two cups of terrible coffee between us, she in a pink cotton snap shirt and jeans with knife pleats, a bright pink bow holding back a balloon of carefully waved hair.

In a lengthy monologue she explained how difficult it was to run a business when Starbucks was already in Denver, several hundred miles away but edging closer and closer, ready to force her to close. Life moved too quickly, we agreed; one longed for a slowness that revealed the value of things. Perhaps we should run the world, time, and love with the patience and pace of saffron.

On the café walls the Coca-Cola posters had faded to greater paleness. The locks on the iron gate kept their steely bite of security on the pawn room. There was nothing to show that the room had been opened or that there had been any customers in the café since the time I had been there weeks earlier.

Only the subject of work interested this desert woman. She wanted to remodel the place, she said, but building materials cost too much. When I mentioned stucco, she lit up for the first time. Stucco required sand and both of us knew sand. Sand was Home. Sand was picnics. Sand made our monsoon waterfalls red. Sand was everywhere, in all colors from the pale ecru of river sand to the distinct coral and terra-cotta of the blow sand that piled into our pants and shoes and houses and every crevice of the three states around us. In the grope for a language to speak beyond anger, sand was mutual territory, a familiar geography.

The woman tore off a sheet from a tablet, a green-and-white kitchen order check printed on pulpy comic book paper. On the back, in a hand of loops and flourishes, she wrote a stucco recipe.

Parts:
Screend sand 4
White for cement 2
Maisonary cement 4
1 tide soap

"Mix it to the consistency of paint," she instructed. "Use a cal-cimine brush."

I thanked her and put the stucco recipe in my pocket. The Tide soap part sounded quite practical. I asked, "Why don't you retire?"

"Retire and do what? I'd be too bored," she replied.

I thought of the gray-haired woman, blubbering over the hot grill. "Is your mother off work today?"

Her pale face clouded with fury. "I'm so mad at her."

I turned to the pie and stared at it like a pervert. I wanted it back. "You're still upset with her?"

She looked more lost than resentful. "Whatever," she shrugged. Then she scowled. "My mother died."

Her expression was so falsely indifferent, so cynical with hurt, I was terrified that she would follow this pronouncement with, "And you know, you just can't get good help these days." Instead, she poured me another cup of terrible coffee.

"Always mad at her, mad since the day I was born."

Brides of Place

Steep thyself in a bowl of summertime.

VIRGIL
Minor Poems

SOLSTICE DAYBOOK, JUNE 21

Four descriptions of nature writing: The literature of loss, an elegy, a lamentation. An "antidote to despair." The antibodies to doom, words and experiences that remind us of our vital connections to the natural world so that we might repair and revere them. My favorite: Writers write because they can't shut up.

THE RISING SUN bathes me in a slow, languid blush. My fleece blanket heaps up around my ankles in a sorry puff of rejection. Even at this early hour the red sandstone walls are a magnet for heat; I can feel them pull the sunlight across my skin. Beyond my bed a small stream shimmers its spirit over a ledge of slickrock. A *Uta stansburiana* passes my sleep-gnarled hair in such a prim strut that I swear it is wearing two tiny pairs of spike heels on its four tiny lizard feet. From somewhere nearby come the chewing noises of a large herbivore. The home terrain of Colorado Plateau canyon country is familiar but my sleeping place uncertain. (I arrived in the dark, in a thicket of cricket sound, and went to sleep.) I know the day—summer solstice, my birthday—but not the time. Things rock-solid change places with thoughts tenuous, then change back again.

To be this old seems a terrible thing. At least I think I should feel terrible.

Here is what I am thinking: A body is never final. Mine still functions despite a lingering backache, which may be a boulder under my pad or an injury suffered in the past winter when a white horse reared up in a Lone Ranger maneuver and, unlike the masked man, I left the saddle and hit frozen ground flat on my back, *fwump,* like a raw chuck roast slapped down on a stainless steel table.

I am thinking that some of my women friends talk less of happiness or of Whitman's metaphysical exuberance or clear-cut forestry and more about their gynecological histories. Others are running out and having their ankles tattooed. Their memories turned to porous sludge, graying men and women obey daily schedules embedded in compact electric notebooks, they swig gringo balboa or whatever they call the smart herb that obviously cannot help me because I have entered old age without ever living the New Age, too dim-witted to know what to ask for from the bright young vegan with the pierced tongue at my local health food store, assuming I can *find* my local health food store and can communicate with someone who has driven a gold spike through her taste buds. My contemporaries mature into wisdom, reflection, and abject panic. They are attending church in droves because they realize they are going to die.

I lie on the ground in a sweet, wild canyon and think that it is somewhat pleasant, actually quite a relief, not to be smart anymore, to let a few flies orbit my cranium in an indolent buzz. On the solstice, the dawn of long summer light, I roll over onto a dense cluster of dried-up, blackish pellets and this is what I think: I am having a midlife crisis on top of a pile of sheep dung.

◆ ◆ ◆

THE CHEWING HERBIVORE is a mature desert bighorn ewe. She browses a blackbrush and watches me. I sit on the forehead of a cow's skull and watch back. At a greater distance three more ewes feed on a talus, superbly balanced and agile on the steep slope. Some of them have black tongues, others have pink tongues. Only one of the ewes has a lamb. All of the sheep have gentle faces and the legs of a troop of weightlifting ballerinas.

If you look for desert bighorns, you will not find them easily. Even hard-rock patience can end in their absence from where you think they are. Writer Peter Steinhart believes that these elusive creatures live in "seams of time," that "their thoughts run to realms so remote that they lift bighorns right out of the material world." I am inside the seam with five of them. I am getting old. The sheep have become rare enough to raise the specter of their vanishing.

Of Eurasian origin, North America's Ovinae subfamily crossed the Bering land bridge during the Pleistocene and, south of Alaska, evolved into the distinct species *Ovis canadensis*. The species reached its southern limits in the provinces of northern Mexico. Desert bighorn distinguishes the sheep that live in Mexico and the arid Southwest from the more abundant, adaptable mountain bighorn, denizen of the intermountain West and northern Rockies. Biologists group four races, or subspecies, under the term "desert bighorn." One of these races adapted to local environments in the Great Basin and Utah's canyon country: *Ovis canadensis nelsoni*, the hosts of my birthday party.

Maps that speculate on the desert bighorn's historic range a century ago show broad puddle shapes that cover plateaus, badlands, and low, rocky hills. Today's remnant herds reside in habitat the size of water droplets—reduced in number, sparsely distributed in isolated mountain ranges and broken canyon country, the most remote reaches of their once expansive territory. The causes invoke a familiar mantra: habitat loss, human encroachment, fire suppression, diseases from domestic livestock. Then the story grows sadder still.

The ewes and lamb around me exercise a remarkable and dangerous fidelity to place. They feed in defined territory and frequent water sources used by generations. From the older ewes the young learn where to forage, quench their thirst, bed down, mate, give birth, seek escape, and die, all of it usually within range of an ancestral water supply. The bighorn became a *desert* bighorn by forming a relationship with its environment—dry, austere, unpredictable— and encoding *home* into its genes. It ended up smaller and shorter in leg than its hulky mountain cousin, with bigger horns that help regulate body temperatures in desert extremes and a metabolism that accommodates drought. With influence from geographic separations, such adaptations evolved into hereditary differences and diversified the species.

The press of modern culture tends to homogenize biological diversity. Those life forms best suited to a changing world, the most aggressive and adaptable species, some would say the least poetic, survive: poison ivy, catfish, the mummichog, a topminnow that can live in the dirtiest water imaginable. The quirky ones, the brides of particular habitat, the place-faithful, may find their biological lineage at a dead end. In favor of the generalists we have chipped off nature's specialists, the latecomers and the homebodies. Environment-specific variations on a main genetic theme, a subspecies is a young evolutionary, so to speak, and among the most recent to differentiate. They can be very local. Commonly, they are the first to become extinct. In small numbers, confined to a single patch of landscape and reliant on a precarious niche, the risks escalate. Infections, usurpation of water, or other misfortunes could result in catastrophe.

My locals, among them the solstice ewes, comprise a population of about forty sheep. Laws and biologists protect them and other bands in the Southwest. For now their numbers hold steady. Perils surround them in a land they can no longer safely inhabit, a demarcation that amounts to an asylum. The sheep remain loyal to their beautiful and fateful desert. It is their entire universe.

THE EWES JERK their busy jaws over scraggly shrubs and chew. They remain wary of me but not alarmed. They strolled into my bedroom, aware that I am some sort of prolapsing prefossil and ought to be permitted to stay that way. Nevertheless, I must walk away soon and let them browse in peace. They know their escape route and will use it. Escape usually means an uphill scramble to a higher vantage point and the casting of a farewell look over their shoulders. Or they might vanish into thin air, as I have seen wild sheep do, leaving me alone with blue sky and their likenesses, pecked a thousand years ago on the varnished sandstone cliffs around me by aboriginal hunters, people who surely loved the shape, the power, the meat of this magnificent creature. In this region the frequency of bighorns in rock art is second only to the prints of human hands.

I have purged the suffocating mope, the incipient snap of aging brain cells, and given myself over to the sheep. The ewes lose themselves in their own sensations, perhaps the succulent flavor of a fourwing saltbush leaf on their thick tongues or an itch behind the ear, relieved with a stroke of a hind foot and a head shake. I pull a leaf from a saltbush and taste it: salty with a pungency that feels like porcupine quills up the nose.

IF ANYTHING COMPELS ME to write about the natural world, it is that many wilderness worshipers are so busy choking on awe or so depressed by the triumph of greed over preservation that they forget nature can be absurdly funny. I thrive on the quirks and puzzles and mazes, the raw material for paradox and pleasure. Around wild ungulates I behave in a nonsensical manner. I invite pathological color experiences. Sand amuses me. I am addicted to cotton-wood sex, to the S&M of a hedgehog cactus with a maniacal sheath of spikes topped by a velvet bloom of delirious scarlet, to the lone-liness of someone who steps out of a crushingly social world to seek, where there are few humans, the riddles of what it means to be human, knowing well that the riddles end up unanswerable, know-ing that sealed into a solitary world, my only companions might be a band of wild sheep. And when I laugh, I begin to feel the dreaded creep of hysteria, lyricism edged with pain. Have I noticed that I might be laughing my head off *at a funeral?*

A great deal of nature writing sounds like a cross between a chloroform stupor and a high mass, in Latin, on a hot day, sur-rounded by bleeding plaster icons. Words penned to the "wild" chronicle a failing purity, where no land or seascape is untouched and all that is truly wild is lost. In the real world, I think, more and more the profane inhabits the sacred. Even I use words like "clear-cutting" and "gynecology" in the same breath. I write a book about a river and cannot tell if it is a love story or an obituary or both. On another desert river, miles and miles from any town, I find a barrel of toxic herbicide, discarded with a facile and illegal carelessness into a resplendent dance of sunlight on water. As I bury my face in the voluptuous innards of cliffrose petals on a remote mesa, a low-flying, kelp-colored military jet passes over with a roar so thunder-ous it nearly makes my ears bleed. Today is my birthday, and during its twenty-four hours nineteen species will become extinct.

Look into the eyes of a domestic sheep and you will see the back of its head. Look into the eyes of this bighorn, the black, curiously horizontal irises set in amber orbs, and you will see a lost map to place, a depth that we may extinguish before it touches us. The bighorns' tenacity to this paltry remnant of wildland inspires as well as frightens me, for like them I cannot abandon the geography that feeds my every breath. The creative process, too, can be noth-ing less than an indestructible fidelity.

Between the sheep and me, our prospects diverge radically: my mortality, their extinction. If the sheep fall below the numbers needed to replace themselves, biologists would bring in desert bighorns from game farms or different stock. Nevertheless, there would be an extinction, though not of the desert bighorn. This band's ancestral fiber of desert woven into living tissue—hundreds of years of wild faith to *this* wild place beneath their hooves— would shred, unraveling the seams of time.

THE SHEEP BROWSE no longer but stand quietly with eyes that seem to look inside themselves. The little *Uta,* the side-blotched lizard in the high heels, parks her four-inch body on a warm rock, her eyelids at half-mast and a rather queasy look on her face. She has caught and eaten three fat black flies. She feels how I would feel if I had swallowed three turkeys. A swallowtail alights on my knee, then on my hand. I cup the butterfly in both palms and open them as if they were wings. A soft breeze makes the butterfly tremble. In the breeze: wings closed. In the stillness: wings open. We are a joined pulse. The butterfly stays with me all morning, flitting about as if it were my birthday gift.

Diminished by the intensifying heat, the stream has narrowed to a thin ribbon across the red slickrock. I press my forehead into its cool sheen. I shall try to age with grace rather than sorrow. I shall inquire about that smart tea, gecko bermuda, ginglo biboola. I shall never ride white horses. The solstice light stretches before me, and I know I shall fill it. In the words of poet Mary Oliver, "I would like to do whatever it is that presses the essence from the hour."

It pleases me that the sheep do not move, for I could not bear that farewell look over their shoulders if they scrambled away. The lead ewe remains close by. She and I are a couple of old ladies in an asylum, our heads stuck stubbornly in a precarious niche, clinging to an instinct to inhabit this far-flung, prickly place as if it were to be forever. It is our entire universe. As Steinhart said of the bighorn, I would like someone to say of me, *Her thoughts run to realms so remote they lift her right out of the material world.* Among my species this is not an asset but a liability, and I have paid dearly for a reckless devotion to roofless places of mind and body. At last I have reached an age where I know it is useless to resist.

Passing Through Green to Reach It

> Back there in the scrublands beyond the river this lack of objects for the eye to focus on seemed like deprivation of the spirit, and I spent my whole time longing for something to break the skyline, one of the slim dark cypresses of my home country, or a chestnut with the sun pouring through it, making every big leaf transparent, a luminous green. Here the immensity, the emptiness, feeds the spirit, and leaves it with no hunger for anything but more space, more light—as if one had suddenly glimpsed the largeness, the emptiness of one's own soul, and come to terms with it, glorying at last in its open freedom.
>
> DAVID MALOUF
> *An Imaginary Life*

It would have been best to take the necklace outside in the morning light, carry it as if it were made of ash, lay it gently on a curve of slickrock. Against red sandstone the color of the "beads" would deepen, taking on the blue-black darkness that lies in the thinnest cracks of the wildest canyons or in the luminous sheen of desert varnish across the face of a vermilion cliff. On rock or in sand, in a pouch of animal skin or woven plant fibers—this is where the necklace likely rested for several hundred years, away from the warm throat of its wearer.

Now the necklace cannot leave the protection of the museum. The museum houses a collection of artifacts from the Anasazi, a culture well known for its exquisite pottery, enigmatic rock art, and elaborate masonry architecture, which peaked in cliff dwellings scattered in the Four Corners region and in the great pueblos of Chaco Canyon in New Mexico. The Anasazi left behind objects that were utilitarian, decorative, ceremonial, and wholly mysterious.

The museum held artifacts from local Anasazi groups. Antler and bone tools, blankets of rabbit fur and twine, sandals with toe rings and their heels worn through. Axes, hammerstones, atlatls, arrows, and strands of olivella shells or discoid stone beads. A woman's menstrual apron made as a waist cord hung with cedar or yucca fibers and soft down. Baskets woven with willow and sumac. Pots, bowls, cups, and other ceramic vessels. The handle of one red clay *olla* was molded into the shape of a dog or fox, its legs attached to the jar's curve. Your fingers would curve around the fox's belly, you would lift the jar to your lips and see the eyes of the fox, two round inlays of turquoise.

One of the museum's storage rooms held a collection of small, complexly crafted objects. There was a rattle made from a desiccated beaver tail attached to a stick, with a lineup of holes in the tail to refine the sound, and a bone joint (deer? bighorn sheep?) from which hung a fiber string. The stone at the end of the string tether fit into the cusp of the knobby bone joint—the patellar surface—as if the challenge was to hold the bone in your fist and flip the stone into that notch, like a Chinese toy.

The most intriguing artifacts, to me, were sticks, bones, and flat stones wrapped with pieces of twine or string-thin braids of jet-black human hair. These were the extras, the knotted, coiled, or twisted fibers and cordage kept intact until they were needed—unintentional works of art, intimate examples of how humans wrap, tie, and save things. One stone held a skein of three-ply yucca cordage, thin plant fibers woven in an S-twist that looked sturdy and taut.

I wanted to spend an hour, a day, a week with each artifact, but I had come to see the dark blue thing. It, too, was kept in a locked room, a cool and clean chamber with a tomblike quiet that made me slip the necklace into my cupped hands, lunge out of the room, knocking over security guards like bowling pins, and race outdoors to the desert light—but only in my imagination.

One hand at a time, like a surgeon, a friend who worked at the museum donned white cotton gloves. He slowly pulled out the drawer that held the necklace. A bed of soft, clean foam material lined the steel tray. Against this lining—a field as white as snow—the "beads" were the color of azurite, the color of the ocean when you fly over it at night, unsure if its depths evoke solace or menace.

The necklace was as delicate as air. It coiled in several strands, perhaps long enough for two or three courses around a slender neck, centered on the dip of flesh at the collar bone, where tendons anchor themselves and you notice a woman's throat when she turns her head.

In the center of the necklace lay a single disk of abalone, a pendant about the size of a dime. The shell, likely traded from the Gulf of California to the interior Southwest, was the only ornament besides the flat, azurite-colored ellipses, strung end to end on the necklace. Not beads, not shells, but the thighs of beetles. The necklace was made with a hundred or more beetle thighs, some of them still with a faint hint of fluorescence, like the back of a scarab.

The necklace came to the museum from a private source with the implication of a past crime of looting and no record of its provenance, only a nebulous allusion to its collection from an unnamed site in this area. A similar necklace, the only other one found, was discovered by archaeologists on my winter ridge, the ridge of crayons and toads in ice, the bold rib of sandstone that knifes through this homeland.

Pieces of what kind of beetle? A dogbane? A darkling, the lumbering insect with a smooth black carapace that I see in the desert nearly everyday? The beetles that burst forth in an excited herd when you kicked a tree stump and suddenly shrieked, *"Necklace!"*? The order Coleoptera, the beetles, is the largest order of insects. The species that gave its legs to this ornament had relatively stout appendages, gorgeous enough to collect and string into beads. Who dreamed it? Who made it? Who wore it?

The museum's ceiling lamps failed its color. Again I envisioned chips of darkness in a sharp desert light. Perhaps the necklace, so odd and meticulous, was a burial item too fragile for an earthly life. Perhaps it was made for someone laid to rest under a tumble of stone on a canyon talus, where she (or he) began a spirit journey. With the necklace stored in the drawer of the museum, what did she wear to the place it was meant for?

ON THE DRIVE BACK from the museum I took the long way home, which is what you end up doing when the distant buttes and mesas distract and lure you over rises and around cliffs until you begin to understand that you will never understand this land. I turned off the highway onto a rough dirt road that led to a trailhead for a future hike. Someday, when the season cooled, I would explore this piece of canyonlands. The way the earth was put together here explained a great deal about Someday Country, the places that lie a few intentions beyond the thickets of daily life. I often thought about this place but never quite went there. This time I had a map that would make me think harder about going there. I parked, then walked to a slickrock ledge to study the map and take in the view.

On the topo map the country was too wild for the usual grid of section lines, too dry for an overlay of green that notes vegetation. The contour lines ran so close together they nearly merged in edgy black waves and scallops, representing the deep clefts and sheer canyon walls that followed not a linear course but the sinuous absence of water. A boxed graphic on the map warned me about "deviant quads." Most contour intervals on U.S. Geological Survey maps code intervals at a standard eighty feet. On this map some of the intervals deviated from the standard. The concept of deviant quads reassured me; the hardscrabble, unruly land yet defied its own reproduction.

The ledge lay under a full blue sky and a horizon marked with seductions in every direction—serrated hogbacks, jagged mesas, labyrinthine canyons, an island mountain range with an intriguing tailbone of low peaks too steep to hold a pinyon pine upright, peaks that formed some of the most rugged, impenetrable country in the region. In another direction rose the twin buttes that guard the land with the certainty of instinct. Whenever I look at them, only one word comes: home. Beyond them I am in places devoid of form. Beyond them the earth drops off into empty space. This landmark figures keenly in the lives of my Navajo neighbors, who say that prayers given over to it should come with *shashchiin,* miniature bears made from turquoise or jet.

Between the ledge and the horizon flowed a sea of petrified sand dunes. There was little that was flat or straight, that did not break up into rolling swells of beige and terra-cotta rock. In the wells between the dunes the sand was deep coral, dotted with silver and green blackbrush, occasional stands of ephedra, and the snow-white petals of sweet-faced evening primrose. In the lee side of a tuft of broom snakeweed, protected from a sweeping wind, the sand still bore divots of rain that fell a week—a month?—before, miniature craters stitched together by the drag marks of a whiptail lizard's rather pompously long tail.

At this moment I wanted to see a map of my brain as it enfolded this tremor of beauty into my body. The sun sent down a stream of photons, tiny particles of light that hit the earth's surface, there to be absorbed or stopped in their tracks. The densely packed cells in my retina captured the photons with pigments and translated them into nerve impulses. The cells sorted out the spectrum of visible light, its wavelengths of color, even though my tongue would then render them into words that cannot explain them.

This three-pound blob of meat between my ears, with its river deltas and ghostly lobes, its fervent nodes and fearless gyri that make me read or lonely or crave avocados or bolt from a place where the light is "wrong" and the horizon is obscured—all of these pieces of my head, these deviant quads, shaped the distant mesas into familiarity and solace, re-created the silken feel of primrose petals without touching them, fired taut aches to the heart so that a certain rose or blue or green could exalt or break it.

Sometime early in a child's life, neurobiologists speculate, light flavors the senses toward yellow, then, as we mature, sends us on to blue. Along this path I was to pass through green to reach blue, there to feel not the press of its "enchanting nothingness," as Goethe wrote, but blue pulling me after it. But I am stuck. Stuck in between. Stuck in turquoise, the color of yearning, the color that borrows the concentric tension of green and holds blue's enchanting calm.

Despite the obliteration of the natural world by environments entirely of human invention, despite the preponderance of lives now spent in artificial light, the human eye evolved in daylight. Our "sunless box of bone" still carries around its silent brain, that three-pound mass of neurons wired for an organic, sensory relationship to place. Our bodies are still profoundly timed to the heavens. Our perceptions remain our only internally generated map of the world. We are blood-tied to landscape by the language of cells. Although we may be hell-bent for metaphysical starvation, trying with all our might to surrender our sensory intelligence to technology and massive artifice, it will take time for these million-years-old senses to atrophy, to go the way of our tail, devolved to a bony nub. In the meantime here we are staggering about the diminishing wilds, greedy to feed those ossifying lobes with light.

The map's deviant quads offered up place names like prayers. I could match some of them to the broken ridges and dusty-rose escarpments beyond the ledge but most lay hidden and I would not live long enough to walk all of them.

Thin contour lines of rust, coral, mustard, and sandy white etched the cross-bedded sandstone around me, the imprint of Triassic winds. In this intricate play of lines, scattered patches of lichen in pale celadon took purchase. A half-teaspoon of loose sand grains was enough "soil" for a dome of moss about the size of a cowry shell, as soft as velvet and dark pine-green with tip hairs of silver. It looked like someone's pet.

The moss and lichen stayed put with the faith that holds mountains. The horizon insisted on motion, and I wanted to take off toward that tailbone of rock, as if it were two, not forty, miles distant. But the dusk came down swiftly, layering sky bands on the western horizon—lemon yellow, turquoise, cerulean—light separated by the lucid, prismatic desert air. With these most transient of colors, dusk in this arid land nourishes a kind of fathomless reverie. There is sorrow in the light at this hour, a sorrow that can be comforting when you are alone and let it come right into you.

In this bumpy, eccentric geography that is a life, light has carried an abundance of small riches that make a place seem like destiny. A ribbon of jade river. Moths with amethyst veins. A crescent of white sand shelving into a turquoise sea, a reef with a language spoken entirely in colors. Chocolate-brown stones arrayed on a pale pediment above a murdered river. Petals that drive spears of passion through the heart, blossoms so satiny they are best felt with the tongue even though it is a cactus that presents them.

And this place, this slickrock ledge above seventy square miles of unknown familiar territory. Something about it was defiant of life but cut to its quick, soothing and fearful, distant yet intimate, heart and nerves, empty and full, and this is the metaphor of the desert itself.

I felt the chips of blue-green stone in my ears. I wondered how much turquoise I would have to trade for a necklace made from abalone and beetle thighs. The midnight-blue of the Anasazi necklace was only two shades of darkness away from the blue of solemn grief.

No, I would keep my turquoise, not trade it for anything. It is the stone that strengthens the eyes, said the Persians, the desert dweller's equivalent of a bulletproof vest against pain or demonic influences. It is water, say the Zuni. For the Aztecs this is the color that supplies the heart. For me it is simply instinct, and perhaps this is all that a person can try to put into each of her days: attention to the radiance, a rise to the full chase of beauty.

Acknowledgments

Over many years spent in a wild river canyon called Desolation, I marked the absence of ravens where, by all conditions, there should have been ravens. Of course, as soon as I declared this raven "void," they flew right back into it. The ravens taught me to observe not only what is present but also what is absent and that this, too, can change. Nature's cycles are indeed far longer and more organic than my own tenure or notice.

In a writer's life, too, there are invisible guides and few occasions to mark their gifts. To friends, family, and other animals, I am indebted. On river trips and canyon hikes, the fine poetic company of Ann Weiler Walka always inspires me. My cousin Cynthia Gorman and her late husband, John, performed dauntless labors of family research. Don Snow, Deb Clow, and Michael Collier saw some of the stories come to first light. Flip Brophy remains my skilled agent and loyal friend. For her faith, patience, and editor's wisdom, I owe much gratitude to Jane Garrett.

For Mark my love is as deep and certain as a summer day's last sunlight, red-gold on the high slickrock rims beyond Oljeto, walking back together to the San Juan.

ABOUT THE AUTHOR

Ellen Meloy has spent most of her life in the remote, wild places of her native West. She is the author of *Raven's Exile: A Season on the Green River* and *The Last Cheater's Waltz,* which was recognized with a Utah Book Award for nonfiction. She is also the recipient of a Whiting Writer's Award. Meloy lives with her husband in southern Utah.